The Mind in Creation: Essays on English Romantic Literature in Honour of Ross G. Woodman

The Mind in Creation: Essays on English Romantic Literature in Honour of Ross G. Woodman celebrates the career of one of Canada's finest teachers and critics, whose more than forty-one years in the Department of English at the University of Western Ontario have profoundly influenced scores of undergraduate and graduate students. From his important early study *The Apocalyptic Vision in the Poetry of Shelley* (Toronto: University of Toronto Press 1964) through dozens of scholarly essays and papers (in addition to his well-known work on James Reaney and Jack Chambers), Ross Woodman has illuminated the English Romantics in ways that engage both the poetic and the critical imagination in the process of what Shelley calls "the mind in creation."

The seven contributors, all of them professors of literature at Canadian universities, from Dalhousie to Simon Fraser, offer a representative view of the diversity of Romantic studies in Canada today. Both senior scholars and younger critics, some of them colleagues and former students of Professor Woodman's, bring different critical perspectives, including historical, textual, and deconstructive methodologies, to bear on a variety of Romantic authors: Blake, Wordsworth, Byron, Shelley, Keats. This collection of essays, the first of its kind in Canada, both contributes to contemporary Romantic scholarship and criticism – from Byron's use of history to Blake's theory of illustration – and makes that contribution from within a uniquely Canadian context. A retrospective essay by Ross Woodman himself surveys the past and future of Romantic studies in the twentieth century.

This volume is to honour a man whose lifelong commitment to teaching literature and whose prolific criticism have indeed been acts of the mind in creation – inspirational, exemplary, and lasting.

J. DOUGLAS KNEALE is an associate professor in the Department of English, University of Western Ontario.

Ross G. Woodman
Courtesy of Dr Martin L. Robinson

The Mind in Creation

Essays on English Romantic Literature in Honour of Ross G. Woodman

EDITED BY J. DOUGLAS KNEALE

With my very best wishes,

R. Ross Woodman

© McGill-Queen's University Press 1992
ISBN 0-7735-0898-8

Legal deposit second quarter 1992
Bibliothèque nationale du Québec

Printed in Canada on acid-free paper

Canadian Cataloguing in Publication Data
Main entry under title:
The Mind in creation

ISBN 0-7735-0898-8

1. English literature – 18th century – History and criticism.   2. English
literature – 19th century – History and criticism.   3. Romanticism – England.
I. Kneale, John Douglas, 1955-   . II. Woodman, Ross Greig

PR457.M46 1992   820.9'145   C92-090096-8

Typeset in 10/12 Palatino by Nancy Poirier Typesetting Ltd., Ottawa.

Contents

List of Illustrations

For the Students

Acknowledgments

There are many people I wish to thank for their help in preparing this volume. First, I express my appreciation to those colleagues who assisted in different ways with the "Romanticism in Canada" conference held in October 1988 to mark Professor Woodman's official retirement from the University of Western Ontario: the other members of the organizing committee, Professors David Bentley, James Good, and Richard Shroyer; the moderators, Professors James Good, D.H. Hensley, Richard Shroyer, and Thomas Tausky; the Office of University Relations; the Chair of the Department of English, Dr J. Alan B. Somerset; the Dean of the Faculty of Arts, Dr Thomas M. Lennon; and the Vice-President (Academic) and Provost of the University of Western Ontario, Dr Thomas J. Collins. I also thank Professors John Graham, Balachandra Rajan, and James Reaney for their part in the after-dinner ceremonies at the conference banquet. For their financial support of the conference I am grateful to the Department of English and the Faculty of Arts at the University of Western Ontario, and the Social Sciences and Humanities Research Council of Canada.

Publication of this volume has been made possible by the generous funding of the Social Sciences and Humanities Research Council of Canada, the Faculty of Arts at the University of Western Ontario (Thomas M. Lennon, Dean), and the Good Foundation Inc. To all I express my great appreciation for their generosity and timely support, without which this project would not have been realized. My thanks also go to Philip J. Cercone, Executive Director of McGill-Queen's University Press (who today still remembers the influence of Ross Woodman's Romanticism), for his helpful advice.

I am grateful to the following for permission to reproduce four Blake illustrations: The Tate Gallery, London, for *Pity*; The Pierpont Morgan Library, New York, 1949.4:4, for *A Sunshine Holiday*; Trustees of the British Museum, London, for *As if an Angel Dropped down from the Clouds*; The Collection of Mr and Mrs Paul Mellon, for *Ode on a Distant Prospect of Eton College*: "Yet see how all around them wait / The vultures of the Mind." I also thank Dr Martin L. Robinson of London, Ontario, for permission to reproduce the photograph of Ross Woodman as the frontispiece.

The following essays have appeared previously in substantially similar form and are reprinted here with permission of the editor or publisher: J. Douglas Kneale, "Romantic Aversions: Apostrophe Reconsidered," *ELH* 58 (1991): 141–65, copyright (c) 1991 by The Johns Hopkins University Press; W.J.B. Owen, "Such Structures as the Mind Builds," *The Wordsworth Circle* 20 (Winter 1989): 29–37; Tilottama Rajan, "En-Gendering the System: *The Book of Thel* and *Visions of the Daughters of Albion*," from *The Supplement of Reading: Figures of Understanding in Romantic Theory and Practice*, 197–220 (abridged) and 238–52, copyright (c) 1990 by Cornell University. I thank the above for permission to reprint. My one regret is that I have been unable to include Vincent A. De Luca's fine essay "Blake as a Theorist of the Sublime," which was read at the 1988 conference; an expanded version of that paper now appears in Professor De Luca's recent book *Words of Eternity: Blake and the Poetics of the Sublime* (Princeton: Princeton University Press 1991).

The Mind in Creation

Introduction

J. DOUGLAS KNEALE

Approximately halfway through book 2 of his autobiographical poem *The Prelude*, Wordsworth pauses to ask a series of questions about origins, personal, poetic, and intellectual. "Who shall parcel out / His intellect," he writes,

> by geometric rules,
> Split like a province into round and square?
> Who knows the individual hour in which
> His habits first were sown, even as a seed?
> Who that shall point as with a wand and say
> "This portion of the river of my mind
> Came from yon fountain"?   (2.203–10)

It is a moment characteristic of Wordsworth, a multiplying of interrogatives whose rhetorical structure both seeks and puts in question an "individual hour," in this case a history or an archaeology of imagination. The "river of [the] mind" described here turns out in the end to be the "stream" of imagination (14.194), "the feeding source," Wordsworth calls it, "of our long labour" (14.193–4).

I begin with this autobiographical moment for a reason. It was some eighteen years ago, in the very room in which the 1988 conference marking his retirement was held, that I first encountered Dr Ross Woodman, in a very different kind of "individual hour." He was standing up there on the stage lecturing and I was sitting down below in a Canadian literature class. While I am considerably less adept at parcelling out my mind than

Wordsworth was his, I nevertheless recall on that occasion that it was a lecture on Emily Carr's *Klee Wyck*. Though other courses taught by Dr Woodman would follow, especially those in Romanticism, in many ways that first encounter stands in my mind as a paradigm of Ross Woodman's style as both a teacher and a critic: I think of the oratory of his lecturing; the presence, even the prophecy, of that voice; the Promethean intensity of focus and commitment; the inspired free associations; the spontaneous crossover between literature and art; totems; dreams; the death of the gods; the immense background of archetypal psychology and psychoanalysis; Jung and Freud, more Jung than Freud; the personal myth; Marion as intertext; the mind in creation. I speak not just for myself, but for those countless undergraduate and graduate students over the last forty-one years at the University of Western Ontario who have had the privilege of learning from Professor Ross Woodman. I know I can say, in no uncertain sense, that a portion of the river of my mind came from yon fountain!

These essays are presented, therefore, in recognition of Ross Woodman's lasting achievement in the classroom and in criticism – in celebration of, in particular, his enormous contribution to Romantic scholarship and criticism over the past four decades, a contribution that includes his 1964 book *The Apocalyptic Vision in the Poetry of Shelley* (Toronto: University of Toronto Press), and numerous essays and reviews in *Studies in Romanticism, Journal of the History of Ideas, English Studies in Canada, The Wordsworth Circle, The Keats-Shelley Review, artscanada, Queen's Quarterly, Art International, Business Quarterly, Journal of Analytical Psychology, Spring, Alphabet, Dalhousie Review*, and the *University of Toronto Quarterly*.

The seven contributors represent a selection of some of the best-known Canadian scholars and critics of English Romanticism. Both senior scholars and younger critics, more than one of them former students of Ross Woodman's, address a range of Romantic authors and texts from a variety of methodological perspectives. The essays thus provide one picture of the state of Romantic studies in Canada today: historical, theoretical, hermeneutic, bibliographical, deconstructive. The first essay, by Milton Wilson, reads Byron's *Childe Harold's Pilgrimage* as "a pilgrimage through historical myths" as much as "a pilgrimage through genres." Beginning with a discussion of Byron's historical mythmaking in the Waterloo stanzas, Wilson shows how a transformation of genres moves the poem, overall, "from mythic place to private elegy." W.J.B. Owen leads us to Wordsworth, to a close analysis of a passage on London in *The Prelude*, book 7, which Owen demonstrates to be important (but difficult) for an understanding of the distinction between imagination and sensibility in Wordsworth. Owen's essay concludes by relating these faculties and the description of London to the idea of the sublime in Wordsworth. Jared

Curtis examines Victorian editions of Wordsworth, chiefly Arnold's *Poems of Wordsworth* (1879). Using his recent research into Arnold's letters, Curtis surveys Arnold's revisioning of Wordsworth – his editorial principles as well as his motivations – to uncover how Arnold attempted to recreate Wordsworth in his own image. Ronald Tetreault's essay on Keats shifts from historical and textual modes of reading to a consideration of "those most characteristically Keatsian activities, reading, loving, and writing." Relying on both Keats's letters and poems, Tetreault explores Keats's relationships with women, and how those "most characteristically Keatsian activities" are crystallized in *La Belle Dame sans Merci*. The last three essays openly announce themselves as theoretical in approach, though not uniformly so. Tilottama Rajan's study of radical indeterminacy in two texts by Blake reveals both typological and hermeneutic modes of reading, while J. Douglas Kneale's reconsideration of the figure of apostrophe applies historical and rhetorical approaches to a close reading of Wordsworth's Boy of Winander. David L. Clark, another former student of Ross Woodman's (though considerably removed from his teacher's psychological and phenomenological methods of reading), sheds light on Blake's "hermeneutics of illustration" through a deconstructive spectatorship.

What is valuable and stimulating about such a collection by Canadian scholars – the first such collection on the Romantic poets – is its critical diversity: while there are inevitable congruences in the essays, both theoretical and interpretive, there is no denying the fundamental critical differences among them. This cross-sectional view thus contains within itself both a history of recent Romantic criticism and a sense of current possibilities. The retrospective essay by Professor Woodman, followed by his bibliography, concludes the volume with a reassessment (vintage Woodman) of the history of Romantic criticism and theory over the latter half of this century.

I return not to Wordsworth, but turn rather to Shelley, whose phrase "the mind in creation" serves as the title for this volume. If any teacher and critic has embodied this creative process, if anyone has personified in the classroom and in print Shelley's imaginative ideal, it has been Ross Woodman. He has *lived* Romanticism as he has taught it, and those who have heard or read him know well what it means to have seen the coal awaken to transitory brightness, in him as well as in themselves.

1 Byron and the Battle of Waterloo

MILTON WILSON

"Stop! – for thy tread is on an Empire's dust!"[1] Thus Byron addresses the reader at his side, forcefully, suddenly, without preparation (3.17). We have no idea where we are. "Self-exiled Harold" (3.16) has re-embarked on his pilgrimage during the canto's previous, preliminary stanzas, but which part of the world he has now travelled to is still to be revealed. Where is the dust and whose is the empire? Priam's or Cyrus's? Caesar's or Alexander's? Some Christian monarch's of yore? None of the above. Byron's phrase may echo the moment in Lucan's *Pharsalia* (McGann thinks it does)[2] when Julius Caesar visits the plains of Troy and is commanded not to tread on the remains of long-dead Hector,[3] but the dust of Byron's opening line turns out in fact to be less than one year old. It lies under our feet, indeed Byron writes the very stanza, on 4 June 1816, and it was shed on 18 June 1815. This is a very recent, and also a very brief, empire whose end is being signalled with such a sweeping historical flourish. But readers who encountered that line hot off the press in 1816, and who for a moment wondered whether maybe they were in (say) the Roman Coliseum meditating on the decline and fall of the Roman Empire, would be reacting in an entirely appropriate way. The places and events of *Childe Harold's Pilgrimage* (even the Byronic hero himself) are all equally historical, indeed somehow all equally distanced (or equally present) in time. One of the most memorable sentences about Byron's Waterloo is by Arthur Symons; students of Byron are likely to have first encountered it in Samuel Chew's much used edition of the poem. Byron "add[ed] history to Waterloo," says Symons, "when the history of that field had only just written itself."[4]

One way of discussing these nineteen stanzas is to examine how Byron transforms an event that has just happened (the final defeat of a Napoleonic empire) into a historical myth of more than yesteryear.

If the first Waterloo stanza suggests one approach, the last stanza (I'm not including the epilogue on Napoleon) suggests a quite different one. Instead of the history beneath our feet, there are all those dead human beings. In this stanza the English future looks back at "fatal Waterloo" (3.35) and sees not a historical turning point so much as all the particular Britons who fought there, cut off before the Psalmist's optimistic threescore and ten. The future's last words are simply "our countrymen were warring on that day" (3.35). In other words, "Kilroy was here," the ultimate military elegiac consolation. My second approach, then, will be generic. What Byron does, not to history, but to elegiac conventions will be my theme. Some of these conventions are familiar in many kinds of funeral elegies. Some, however, belong especially to the tradition of the pastoral elegy. Not that Byron transforms soldiers into sheep and their officers into shepherds; the pastoral world of Byron's battlefield is notably agricultural. But a reader who remembers the formal pastoral elegies of Moschus, Spenser, Milton, and Shelley, not to mention their less formal relatives from the *Vigil of Venus* to *The Waste Land*, will certainly feel at home in the various ways by which Byron interrelates the natural cycle with the very different human pattern of life and death.

I propose, then, to discuss the Waterloo episode in two distinctive, although often complementary and overlapping, ways: on the one hand through Byron's historical mythmaking and the spirit of place and event created by it, and on the other through the generic traditions of elegy that he employs.

I choose these two approaches, however, not just because they work well with the Waterloo stanzas, but because they can be usefully applied to *Childe Harold's Pilgrimage* as a whole. The road along which the poem travels passes one cultural landmark after another. Waterloo's temporal immediacy makes it an extreme case, a test case if you like, but it belongs with all the others, from the castles on the maternal Rhine that we next encounter to all the Roman places on which Byron exercises his imagination in the climactic stanzas of canto 4. It doesn't stretch a thesis very far to call the poem a pilgrimage through historical myths. Even the Alpine sublime or Rousseau-haunted Clarens could be thus categorized well before Byron's time. It may inspire more scepticism if I apply my second approach just as broadly. Nonetheless, let me also call the poem a pilgrimage through genres (mostly lyrical ones), indeed a kind of generic anthology. Stuart Curran has recently considered the whole work in relation to what happened to the genre of romance during the period.[5] I prefer a more piecemeal consideration, focusing on its component elegies, prospect poems, odes, prayers, portraits, epitaphs, complaints and benedictions – to mention some of only the most obvious genres and subgenres.

Before I scrutinize Byron's Waterloo at length through my dual perspective, I want (as a context) to demonstrate – in some detail – how that perspective works with a few striking episodes elsewhere in the poem, two as examples of historical mythmaking and two of generic transformation. As mythmaking material I choose the Coliseum and St Peter's; as generic frameworks I choose two distinctive subspecies: the odal address to an unidentified art object and what (with a bow to Wordsworth) I shall call the spot-of-time meditation.

The Coliseum of canto 4 offers the most complexly layered piece of mythmaking in the whole poem. Byron anticipates it tentatively in *Manfred*. Before that drama's hero dies, he utters three soliloquies, one centring on the beautiful, one on the sublime, and one (to Manfred's own surprise) on the Coliseum by moonlight. Two lines summarize what he sees in it: "The gladiators' bloody Circus stands, / A noble wreck in ruinous perfection" (*Manfred*, 3.4.27–8). In the *Pilgrimage*'s Coliseum, that perfect ruin and bloody circus are certainly two layers in Byron's composite myth, although there are others as well. His Italy as a whole is, of course, full of decay transcending itself: he calls its "wreck a glory" and its "ruin" both "graced" and "immaculate" (4.26). But it all comes together in the vegetation and the moonlight of the Coliseum. The prolific vegetation has been cleaned off in the twentieth century, but when Byron was there, Time, he tells us, "hath leant / His hand, but broke his scythe" (4.129). Ministered to by this "adorner of the ruin" (4.130), which turns, we are told, a "wreck" into a "temple" (4.131), the Coliseum decays and grows simultaneously. Deforming and perfecting become two sides of the same coin. And the moonlight and starlight take over where the vegetation leaves off:

> when the rising moon begins to climb
> Its topmost arch, and gently pauses there;
> When the stars twinkle through the loops of time,   (4.144)

the "ruined battlement" (4.129) turns into a "magic circle" (4.144). The scene painted by eighteenth-century artists and visited by Madame de Stael's Corinne in a memorable episode achieves mythic finality in *Childe Harold's Pilgrimage*.

Then there's the bloody circus. Byron sees what happens to the Coliseum as emblematic of the fall of the Roman Empire. He also sees that fall as somehow a punishment for what Rome did, inside the Coliseum and outside it. As the stanzas on the so-called dying gladiator make clear, the "ruined circus" pays for all the imperial victims "butcher'd to make a

Roman holiday" (4.141). But he adds his own personal myth to this historical one: the Coliseum is a marked place being visited by a marked man. Signs of ruin are no less apparent on the Byronic hero; so he offers them, "though few, yet full of fate" (4.131), to his counterpart. Byron can identify, however, not just with the guilt-laden place, but with the victim too. He is Coliseum and dying gladiator in one. So he adds a further, non-Roman, Aeschylean layer to his multiple myth. After his separation from Lady Byron, she had a role in his own, intimate version of the *Oresteia*. His letters keep calling her "my moral Clytemnestra," and thus he is Agamemnon, victim of that crowning injustice, being destroyed by one's wife. Byron deserves punishment, he insists in these stanzas, but not from such an unjust weapon. So, like the Gothic gladiator, he turns from victim to avenger, from Agamemnon to Orestes, calling on Nemesis as the Furies "howl and hiss" around him in the Coliseum, eager to pay back one "unnatural retribution" with another (4.132). But, of course, the Furies that surround Orestes in the third play of the Aeschylean trilogy are not urging revenge *by* him but *on* him. So the allusion moves in two directions. Through this second one, the Byronic avenger seems, for a moment, to turn into the Byronic victim again.[6]

The ultimate layer arrives with the recall-of-the-curse motif. Somehow, while the Coliseum must include Lady Byron and her associates among its victims, Byron himself must be left without responsibility for their fate. Although he cries "shall *they* not mourn?" (4.131) and prophesies a future that will "pile on human heads the mountain of my curse" (4.134), he then insists, "that curse shall be Forgiveness" (4.135). Nemesis must somehow punish Byron's enemies, even as Byron curses them only with forgiving coals of fire. This curse-layer of Byron's myth disturbed his friends, not to mention his publisher. When Hobhouse tried to persuade Byron to expurgate it, he replied, "I can't give up Nemesis ..., I can't, I can't."[7] No doubt he thought that by cursing and uncursing at the same time he had spiked objections. Shelley certainly thought otherwise when Byron read him canto 4 in Venice. As G. Wilson Knight was perhaps the first to emphasize, Shelley's recall of the curse in *Prometheus Unbound* is intended (among other things) to show up the limitations of Byron's.[8] Shelley then went on to write an unfinished short story called *The Coliseum* as a kind of countermyth: its roots Sophoclean not Aeschylean, its blind father led and consoled by an unavenging child, its resident deity not Nemesis but Love, its ruins not moonlit but sunlit, our only reminder of Byron's enchanted night being "the noonday waning moon ... hanging ... out of the solid sky."[9] But Byron was unmoved. Two years later when Lady Byron's lawyer committed suicide, he could not resist saying in a letter: "it was not in vain that I invoked Nemesis in the Midnight of Rome from the awfullest of her Ruins."[10]

If Byron's Coliseum shows his mythmaking at its most richly layered (and with a very personal icing on the cake), his very impersonal St Peter's creates its myth out of a single historical strand – a strand which is related, moreover, not to any aspect of imperial or papal power, but to the perceiving eye of the tourist during the previous couple of centuries. Its historical myth is aesthetic. In recent years Byron's central four stanzas (4.155–8) have provoked some fine comments on their importance,[11] but what lies behind them has been missed. According to a Restoration visitor to the basilica, Gilbert Burnet,

its length, heighth and breadth, are all so exactly proportioned, and the eye is so equally possessed by all these, that the whole, upon the first view, doth not appear so vast as it is found to be upon a more particular attention.[12]

In other words, the eye is deceived by the proportions into underestimating the size. According to Tobias Smollett, nearly a century later, "the church seems considerably smaller than it really is."[13] But if St Peter's is the big building that looks small, its opposite number would seem to be the Pantheon, the small building that looks big. According to Addison in *Spectator* 415, the Pantheon's "Greatness of Manner" in "small Building" causes the "Imagination" to be "filled."[14] Addison had already contrasted the Pantheon with St Peter's in *Remarks on Several Parts of Italy*, although primarily to set the rotund against the cross form.[15] The comparison in terms of size-perspective is stated with striking clarity about ten years before Byron's Roman spring when Madame de Stael has her Corinne juxtapose the two buildings for Lord Nelvil's benefit. After telling him that "the Pantheon is so built as to make it look much larger than it really is," she adds, "the church of St. Peter will produce quite a different effect upon you; you will think it, at first, much less than it is in reality."[16]

But the optical illusion exists not just from the outside but from within as well. Smollett's perspective, in the sentence already quoted, is, in fact, internal. The visitor who, like Byron, enters may find his moving eye perpetually reorienting itself. Smollett describes the effect vividly:

the figures of the doves ... which are represented on the wall, appear to be within your reach; but as you approach them they recede to a considerable height, as if they had flown upwards to avoid being taken.[17]

Guides seem to have liked testing the perspective of visitors. "It is usual," we are told, "to desire strangers, on their first entering this church, to guess at the size of the objects."[18] There is, however, a further aspect to be considered. From Addison on, the aesthetics of scale had to cope with the Longinean revival. The paradox of St Peter's may be incompatible with the sublime that visitors liked to invoke. At the end of the century, John Moore (much of whose work Byron was acquainted with) states the problem clearly:

It has been frequently remarked, that the proportions of this church are so fine, and the symmetry of its different parts so exquisite, that the whole seems considerably smaller than it really is. It was, however, certainly intended to appear a great and sublime object, and to produce admiration by the vastness of its dimensions. I cannot, therefore, be of opinion, that anything which has a tendency to defeat this effect, can with propriety be called an excellence ... In edifices of vast dimensions, capable of sublimity from their bulk, the vice of diminishing is not to be compensated by harmony. The sublime has no equivalent.[19]

One might add that the mind-expanding or identity-dissolving effect of the sublime could be especially thwarted by such harmony.

Byron's central stanzas on St Peter's are about this aesthetic myth of tourists, but handle it in a series of different ways.[20] The first stanza opens provocatively:

Enter: its grandeur overwhelms thee not;
And why? it is not lessened; but thy mind,
Expanded by the genius of the spot,
Has grown colossal ...   (4.155)

Byron here absorbs in his own special way the components of the tradition I have been outlining. Yes, the basilica's vastness *is* somehow shorn of its overwhelming effect; but no, despite John Moore, it is somehow not lessened thereby; and why? because the "colossal" stretching of the mind under the influence of the sublime makes it unnecessary to suppose any but a comparative lessening of the object. The expanded mind contains an undiminished St Peter's. The next stanza begins very differently:

Thou movest – but increasing with the advance,
Like climbing some great Alp, which still doth rise,
Deceived by its gigantic elegance;
Vastness which grows – but grows to harmonize –
All musical in its immensities ...   (4.156)

The paradoxes are striking, but they are also traditional; Byron just sharpens them. Moore, you will recall, insisted that the harmony of St Peter's cannot make up for the loss of the sublime. Byron forces together Moore's incompatibles: gigantic elegance, harmonized vastness, musical immensities. But he also combines the test case of the natural sublime with its architectural equivalent. Entering St Peter's is like crossing the Alps. In the back of Byron's mind is the image which Samuel Johnson in his life of Pope called "the best that English poetry can show": Pope's comparison in *An Essay on Criticism* between how a student learns and how a traveller crosses the Alps. For Pope the genuine student's "little learning," like the genuine traveller's "short views," ultimately turns into an infinitely extendable prospect. Pope's verbs, his advancing, rising, growing, and increasing, become Byron's verbs too, as does the conception of a journey whose length continually deceives; and surely to no reader of Byron can it seem a coincidence that in the *Essay* Pope's Alpine image is followed in the next paragraph by a St Peter's one, where bold size is somehow united with proportion and regularity:

> Thus when we view some well-proportion'd Dome,
> (The *World*'s just Wonder, and even *thine* O *Rome*) ...
> No monstrous Height, or Breadth, or Length appear;
> The *Whole* at once is *Bold*, and *Regular*.[21]

Byron's next two stanzas start with his least traditional approach to the paradox of small in large: "Thou seest not all; but piecemeal thou must break, / To separate contemplation the great whole" (4.157). The eye which cannot manage all of St Peter's must break it up into small manageable segments. Indeed, he goes on to say, the soul must "condense" itself by attending to "more immediate objects" (4.157). Then, having taken the building apart and interrelated its fragments in the memory, we can "unroll / Its mighty graduations, part by part" (4.157). So, from piecemeal perception suited to our "Nature's littleness" (4.158), we gradually come to terms with this "greatest of the great" and "growing with its growth, we thus dilate / Our spirits to the size of that they contemplate" (4.158). We have now returned to the psychological expansion of the sublime. But whereas these four stanzas begin with the mind expanded (as it enters) by the genius of the spot, we reach this last dilation only as a result of a previous shrinking.

In now moving from historical mythmaking to generic transformation, I shall, for the sake of variety, not stick to the Coliseum and St Peter's, but start with another Roman art object: the tomb of Cecilia Metella. Byron's seven stanzas belong to a species of which the two most famous Romantic instances are *Ode on a Grecian Urn* and *The Solitary Reaper*. Considered just from this specialized generic point of view, Keats's ode is about what to do when an art object refuses to answer all the questions you somehow feel impelled to ask it, or how to get from an interrogative to an assertive, even definitive, mode. Keats is forced by a contextless, unidentifiable, self-sufficient urn to see the poised objects on one of its panels as also sufficient unto themselves and therefore definable. But he is somehow unable to maintain this stance, not fully at any rate. So he looks at another panel on the urn and produces another set of questions or speculations, very different, but equally impossible to answer or confirm. The process from interrogation to definition then repeats itself. But this time it is neither the objects on the urn nor even the poet that makes the assertions, but the speechless, self-sufficient object itself, in lines too familiar to quote. You will, I trust, excuse my reducing a rich and complex poem, for my limited purpose, to such a formulaic pattern. *The Solitary Reaper* follows a similar process in its second half, although not twice over. "Will no one tell me what she sings?" asks Wordsworth, and goes on to suggest alternative answers, one from the past and one from the present, between which he cannot choose. He then makes it clear that the questions are irrelevant to where his poem is going. "Whate'er the theme," he tells us, the apparent endlessness of the song remains, as does its continuing presence in the mind of the hearer. Questioning the song has finally turned into those simple assertions of survival.

In Byron's version of the genre his questions are the most persistent of all. He knows, or thinks he does, the name of the husband of the woman whose body is locked in the tomb before him, that fortress-like, ivy-covered "stern round tower of other days" (4.99). But he knows nothing else. The art object is bombarded with questions and speculations. Who was she really? Every conceivable and unsettleable issue about her family, her character, and her fate that can be crammed into four Spenserian stanzas is raised. "But whither would Conjecture stray?" he finally asks. "Thus much alone we know – Metella died, / The wealthiest Roman's wife; Behold his love or pride!" (4.103). Indeed, in that last phrase the grandiose tomb offers nothing of her as a person at all, just her husband's uncertain motives for erecting it. The next two stanzas produce the resolution that the genre needs. To begin with, Byron turns the buried corpse that the tomb cannot identify into a person he himself must have known, indeed (it seems) into someone charged with "recollected" but "dying" "music" from Byron's personal past (4.104), almost as if she were the true bride he never had. In the lines that follow, however, he returns from what the tomb contains to the ruined monument itself, which, in an extraordinary passage, becomes an emblem, not just of Byron's ruin or of his lost bride, but of aesthetic ruin, and of the creation that can come out of it. "Yet could I," he wonders conditionally,

> seat me by this ivied stone
> Till I had bodied forth the heated mind
> Forms from the floating wreck which Ruin leaves behind.   (4.104)

Then, almost before we know it, that ruin described as "floating" turns into a wrecked ship from whose "shattered planks" we may build a new vessel "once more / To battle with the ocean" (4.105). Among other things, Byron is here giving us yet one more example of his aesthetic of ruins – how different from the totally self-contained "Beauty is Truth" epigram which Keats's questioning finally seems to evoke from his silent urn. The Coliseum's ruining is necessary for its perfection by moonlight; "the great whole" of St Peter's must be broken into pieces in order to be reintegrated; and here "the heated mind" that contemplates the tomb of Cecilia Metella rebuilds a wreck into new forms. But the new forms of what Byron in the end calls his "rude boat" have no port they can steer to, "no home," he tells us, "save what is here" (4.105). And with that phrase suddenly the tomb is gone, the brief lyric is over, and in the next stanza Byron confronts another Roman challenge to his mythmaking and sense of genre: the Palatine hill.

I won't follow him. Instead, as a last preliminary before returning to Waterloo, I give you a spot-of-time meditation that has nothing to do with any spot in Rome. A few sweeping generalizations will serve to set the stage. Traditionally there are two basic attitudes toward the spots that stick in your memory: one positive and one negative. There is the aging Wife of Bath's attitude: Christ, it tickles me to remember all the wonderful things that happened to me when I was young. Then there is the one which Boethius has stamped with his name. I paraphrase Chaucer's paraphrase in his *Troilus*: the worst misfortune is to remember happy times when they are past. Wordsworth is normally on the side of the Wife of Bath, and, being fostered by both beauty and fear, the memories that renovate his growing mind do not have to be pleasant, indeed often are not. He does, however, have one powerful Boethian moment, expressed through the person of Matthew in *The Fountain*. This old man of mirth, with his happy days long gone by, resists being forced to remember images from the past. Senile forgetfulness is preferable. "The wiser mind," he tells us, "Mourns less for what age takes away / Than what it leaves behind." He then paints a grim picture of people, "glad no more," who "wear a face of joy, because / [they] have been glad of yore,"[22] unlike the birds, who keep living in the present. In *Childe Harold's Pilgrimage* Byron is a lot closer to Matthew than to the Wordsworth of *The Prelude*. We are confronted with the curse of memory, not its consolation. His response to images that nothing can remove from the mind may sometimes resemble a Wordsworthian cry of gratitude, but is more likely to suggest "Out, damned spot!"

I am tempted to choose as my generic instance the passage in canto 3 about the Rhine as failed Lethe, but the epilogue to the Venetian stanzas that open canto 4 develops its argument more elaborately, and I think of it as Byron's version of meditations like the one beginning "dust as we are" in *The Prelude* or, more obviously, the one beginning "there are in our existence spots of time" – passages which, of course, Byron had never read. This epilogue (stanzas 19 to 24) reaches its climax in his most vivid and original image for the mind stained with ineffaceable memories. What precedes it, the Venetian stanzas themselves, is a prospect poem in which the poet stands and seems to gaze at a whole embalmed city, historically dead since 1797. They end with a stanza on the Venice he remembers from his boyhood, before he had ever seen it, an image purely literary:

> I lov'd her from my boyhood – she to me
> Was as a fairy city of the heart,
> Rising like water columns from the sea, ...
> And Otway, Radcliffe, Schiller, Shakespeare's art,
> Had stamp'd her image in me. (4.18)

At the beginning of the epilogue itself, memories of Venice are emblematic of happy moments "wrought / Within the web of my existence," "feelings Time can not benumb" (4.19). But for Byron existence is not renovated by them. The images of existence which he goes on to present, the tree rooted in barrenness, the animal enduring in desolate silence, suffering coming to an end in its various futile ways, are incompatible with any Wordsworth-like renovation by images "stamp'd" in memory. Then, in the concluding stanza, after something of a false start, with that image of the scorpion's sting already given its full treatment in *The Giaour*, Byron presents the memory not as the home of those unbenumbed Venetian feelings but as a conductor of electricity burned black by charges that keep repeating themselves. The phrasing is anticipated in the Rhine meditation of canto 3, where he speaks of "the blackened memory's blighting dream" (3.51), but only here do we get the image of that "electric chain wherewith we are darkly bound," and the way in which the most commonplace natural images ("a tone of music, – ... a flower – the wind," for example) strike it with the "lightning of the mind" (4.23–4). What ultimate cloud produces that lightning cannot be traced; we simply (according to Byron)

> feel the shock renew'd, nor can efface
> The blight and blackening which it leaves behind,
> Which out of things familiar, undesign'd,
> When least we deem of such, calls up to view
> The spectres whom no exorcism can bind. (4.24)

In the final lines of this epilogue, perhaps the weakest in their phrasing, those spectres are not just the natural images but also the human figures that Byron cannot separate from them.

Having established a context from the rest of *Childe Harold's Pilgrimage*, I return to Byron's Waterloo: first his myth and then his genre. I began this essay with his abrupt opening line (3.17), in which he tells us to stop and consider the empire's dust beneath our feet. That, however, isn't the stanza's only significant one-liner. Think of "How that red rain hath made the harvest grow!" It is significant in a variety of ways. But for the moment I want to neglect the line's overall, year-later meaning and concentrate simply on what it meant to the battle as actually fought and remembered. After all, Waterloo (along with its inseparable prelude Quatre Bras) is the agricultural battle *par excellence*. It is as inseparable from wheat as the Flanders of the First World War is inseparable from mud.

The various species of grain and field grass which covered much of these two battlefields had grown to a striking height by mid-June 1815, when the battle was fought. And if the poem makes something out of harvests growing, so do the soldiers who took part. I start with the comments of three of them: Sergeant Morris speaks about "rye ... of an extraordinary height, some of it measuring seven feet"; Sergeant Alton says, "the stalks ... like the reeds that grow on the margin of some swamp, opposed our advance; the tops were up to our bonnets"; according to Colonel Llewellyn, "the rye in the field was so high, that to see anything beyond our own ranks was almost impossible." These comments are about the Quatre Bras prelude, but Waterloo inspires similar responses. Sergeant Cotton includes the whole agricultural gamut of that field: it is, he says, "covered with splendid crops of rye, wheat, barley, oats, beans, peas, potatoes, tares and clover; some of them were of great height." When the French artillery opens the battle, Ensign Leeke is astonished to see (as one modern writer rephrases him), cannon-balls "swishing through the corn." The battle's final turning point occurs when Colborne's 52nd regiment springs out of "a screen of high-standing corn" and panics the French Imperial Guard.[23] Non-combatants could also be impressed. Sir Walter Scott, two months after the battle, speaks in *Paul's Letters* of the "gigantic" grain of Flanders and reminds us how the valley between the opponents "on that memorable day bore a tall and strong crop of corn." But he also describes the surface now before the visitor, with the "tall crops of maize and rye ... trampled into a thick black paste."[24] The noses of soldiers like Ensign Leeke remembered "the mingling of the wheat trodden flat down with the smell of gunpowder."[25] But the "black paste" mingles more than wheat and gunpowder. There is also Byron's "red rain" (3.17). The soldiers and tourists of 1815 encounter more than enough to justify Hardy's phrase about the field of Waterloo in *The Dynasts*: "a muddy stew of crushed crops and gore."[26] Byron's poem had emphasized that crush long before. His word is "pent" and he rhymes it with "blent." The word had plenty of justification. As Southey says in a footnote to his own Waterloo poem, "so important a battle perhaps was never before fought within so small an extent of ground."[27] A modern historian (David Chandler) speaks of forty-seven thousand dead or wounded lying, when the fighting was over, on a field of only three square miles. But human bodies weren't all. The repeated French cavalry charges compounded the space problem. The same historian speaks of ten thousand horses attacking a front that could justify no more than one thousand at a time – a front that Fuller describes as about five hundred yards across.[28] The memoirs and letters convey an extraordinary sense of "men and horses piled on each other like cards" (to quote one soldier) or "promiscuously entwined" (to quote another).[29] In stanzas 27 and 28 Byron tries to communicate this coming together of men and animals and grain and soil ("clay" and "grass" being his ultimate containing terms). But he gives us not only the grass beneath, but also the future grass above – that growing harvest[30] that the visiting Byron now sees fed by the red rain. The imagery of above and below are joined – for clay as well as for grass. Here are the lines that do it all: first the ones about how those soldiers are "Ere evening to be trodden like the grass / Which now beneath them, but above shall grow" and then the succeeding ones about how

> The earth is covered thick with other clay,
>   Which her own clay shall cover, heaped and pent,
> Rider and horse, – friend, foe, – in one red burial blent! (3.28)

As an anticlimactic epilogue to my account of Byron's battle as agricultural, I quote a passage from the *Autobiography* of Elizabeth Butler, that most remarkable of English battle-painters. She is preparing to put the Quatre Bras prelude on canvas. Here is part of her diary entry for 16 July 1874, as she and her mother search Henley-on-Thames for the right field. "We had great difficulty," she says,

in finding any rye at Henley, it all having been cut, except a little patch which we at length discovered by the direction of a farmer. I bought a piece of it, and then immediately trampled it down with the aid of a lot of children.

She starts drawing forms with a pencil while her mother copies the right "tints with two slimy water-colour brushes." The entry ends: "we laughed a good deal and worked on into the darkness, two regular 'Pre-Raphaelite Brethren,' to all appearances, bending over a patch of trampled rye."[31]

What Byron avoids in his treatment of the battle, however, is, in its way, as interesting as what he includes. Other writers (journalists and poets) in the immediate aftermath of Waterloo are likely to give some close attention to the field's chief buildings: the chateau of Hougoumont and the farm of La Haye Sainte, around and in which important parts of the fighting raged. Certainly Scott and Southey do. Byron avoids them completely, and not certainly from ignorance (he visited Hougoumont). What he adds to the grain is a second natural aspect of the scene: the forest of Soignies at the rear. In the opening lines of stanza 27, before turning to the red burial that ends the battle, Byron depicts the trees of that forest waving in grief above the doomed soldiers as they approach the field, mourning in advance "the unreturning brave" (3.27). His earliest surviving manuscript of the stanza uses the name "Soignies" but he finally revised it to what we have now, "Ardennes." In a note Byron justifies this name, claiming that the Soignies forest "is supposed to be a remnant of the forest of Ardennes." Commentators have made merry with this suggestion that a forest just south of Brussels was once part of a bigger one about a hundred miles south, though a link in the distant past is not *that* hard to imagine. In any case, as the rest of Byron's note makes clear, his intention is to mythologize the place by the literary associations of the name "Ardennes" in Tacitus, Boiardo, and, most notably for the English reader, Shakespeare.[32] He wants the soldiers to march out of a pastoral forest of Arden into the pent-up pastoral death-trap of Waterloo.

But leaving out the central landmarks of Hougoumont and La Haye Sainte for that peripheral forest is not Byron's most striking omission. The readers who encountered canto 3 in 1816 must have found it almost impossible to imagine a battle of Waterloo without the Duke of Wellington. If they had read some of the English flood of celebratory poetry that poured off the press between the battle and the appearance of Byron's stanzas, they would have found those stanzas especially shocking. Waterloo poems could no more avoid thanking Wellington than they could avoid thanking God, indeed found it easy to thank both at the same time.

> Oh, Wellesley! on thy conquering sword
>   Their tears the rescued nations shed;
> And thanks of thousand hearts are poured
>   Around thy many-laurelled head:
> Thou art a boon to mortals given,
>   A minister of God on high;
> And by thy will the Lord of heaven
>   Speaks to his children Liberty!

Thus writes William Sidney Walker in November, 1815.[33] Anything of the sort would be too much to expect from the Byron whose first verbal reaction to news of the victory was "I am damned sorry for it"[34] and whose first poems in its aftermath were a series of laments by imagined Frenchmen. We get no God and no Duke, even (like Napoleon) in an epilogue. We don't even get the grudging mention that Hazlitt provides, who in his pages on Waterloo presents Wellington's victory as a triumph of mediocrity in which "the greatest reputation in modern times" becomes "a prey to the most shallow and worthless." Hazlitt, like Byron in his Notes, quotes from *Macbeth*: "An eagle in his pride of place / Was by a mousing owl hawked at and killed," but he at least identifies his owl, whereas Byron's remains nameless.[35] Indeed, after Waterloo Byron never uses the Duke's name in a poem, whether Wellington or Wellesley (except for one allusion to street names), until 1822. He saves it for canto 9 of *Don Juan* and even Frenchifies it as "Villainton." "Fame / Sounds the heroic syllables both ways," he tells us (9.1), and goes on to wonder "who, / Save you and yours, have gained by Waterloo" (9.4), that "crowning carnage" which in *The Vision of Judgment* causes Satan to hold "both generals in reversion" (5–6). In a special sense Byron's only recognizable allusion to Wellington in the *Childe Harold* stanzas is his use of the name Waterloo, qualified in the second stanza as "deadly Waterloo" and in the final one as "fatal Waterloo" (3.18, 35). This is the name that Wellington insisted on for the battle, taken from the behind-the-scenes village which housed his headquarters. Marshal Blucher had other ideas, like La Belle Alliance, the name of the inn near which the two leaders met at 9 p.m. when their joint victory was assured. But Wellington resisted. Maybe he thought that Waterloo was the one name in the vicinity that could be pronounced (unmistakably) by the average Englishman. When Southey visited the scene his guide couldn't understand why anyone would want to name the battle Waterloo.[36] A passage where Byron decides *not* to call it Waterloo occurs in canto 11 of *Don Juan*. He is identifying his own chequered poetic career with Napoleon's military one. What poem, we may wonder, is he going to choose as *his* Waterloo? "My Mont Saint Jean seems *Cain*," he writes and then in the next line calls his rival poets *"La Belle Alliance* of dunces" (11.56). Waterloo is here replaced by two names that Wellington rejected.

But I'm straying too far from the stanzas in *Childe Harold*; and I haven't yet mentioned their most famous line, which is neither "Stop! – for thy tread is on an Empire's dust!" nor "How that red rain hath made the harvest grow!" but, four stanzas later, "There was a sound of revelry by night" (3.21). What is memorable, however, is not simply that the battle is preceded by the Duchess of Richmond's ball, but the way ball and battle are juxtaposed, even at moments fused. Although Napoleon's artillery was well beyond earshot that night on the dance floor, Byron's "voluptuous swell" of music and his "merry" image of the "marriage-bell" are interrupted by the "deadlier" sound of "the cannon's opening roar":

Did ye not hear it? – No; 'twas but the wind,
Or the car rattling o'er the stony street;
On with the dance! let joy be unconfined! ...
But, hark! – that heavy sound breaks in once more ...   (3.21–2)

The "flying feet" of "Youth and Pleasure" become the "hurrying to and fro" of separating lovers, the "mutual eyes" that once "look'd love" may

never "meet" again, the "cheeks" that "blush'd" turn "all pale" as "partings
... press the life from out young hearts," and the "sound of revelry" is
replaced by the sound of "choking sighs." No sooner has "awful morn"
succeeded "sweet nights" than suddenly "the ranks of war" are on their
way to the battlefield (3.21–4):

> And there was mounting in hot haste: the steed,
> The mustering squadron, and the clattering car,
> Went pouring forward in impetuous speed,
> And swiftly forming in the ranks of war.   (3.25)

The two stanzas from which a moment ago I quoted the centre of Byron's
pastoral myth summarize the pattern of this one too:

> Last noon beheld them full of lusty life,
> Last eve in Beauty's circle proudly gay,
> The midnight brought the signal-sound of strife,
> The morn the marshalling in arms, – the day
> Battle's magnificently stern array!   (3.28)

Now, no one is going to claim that Byron invented the idea of such a jux-
taposition. The stanzas retain their power to shock, but not because of their
originality. They have the commonplace but striking inevitability of myth.
They also correspond very closely to the way the Duchess of Richmond's
ball broke up that night. Byron was always fascinated by the interrelations
of myth and fact. When he visited the legendary places of Greece, "all the
Muse's tales seem[ed] truly told" (2.88); when he visited the supposed
plains of Troy the only thing that made his pleasure less was the way the
myth-scholar Jacob Bryant had cast doubt on the authenticity of the Trojan
war.[37] The separating and combining of the fabulous and the factual
becomes almost a kind of verbal tic in *Don Juan*. An allusion to the trans-
formation of lovers into beasts by Circe and her kind in one half of a line is
promptly followed by "but that's a fact" (3.34) in the other. The student of
Byron's Waterloo should not be surprised that what seem like his most
striking mythical inventions are confirmed in what the letters and memoirs
tell us about the coming together of ball and battle. Captain Verner relates
how he arrived at the ball late (between 2 and 3 a.m., I would estimate)
when Wellington himself was about to leave. He writes,

the room was in the greatest confusion and had the appearance of anything but a
ball-room. The officers were hurrying away as fast as possible, in order that noth-
ing might prevent their joining their regiments. At this moment Lord Uxbridge came
to the door and said, "You gentlemen who have engaged partners had better finish
your dance ..."

More than half a century later, the daughter of the Duchess of Richmond writes, "while some of the officers hurried away [after the first news], others remained at the ball, and actually had not time to change their clothes, but fought in evening costume." After helping her brother pack, she returns to the ballroom and finds "some energetic and heartless young ladies still dancing." Fighting in evening dress may seem like a fanciful invention long after the event, but Captain Mercer, on the road to Quatre Bras, actually sees an aide-de-camp "posting away as fast as his poor tired beast could get along, and dressed in his embroidered suit, white pantaloons, etc. etc., having evidently mounted as he left the ball-room."[38]

I don't claim to know what actually produced the factual substratum of Byron's myth. He talked at length with Sir Walter Scott after the latter returned from visiting the field, he may have talked with actual participants, he undoubtedly read accounts like (say) the remarkable one by the journalist John Scott, and of course he had his own tour of the field with his cousin Pryse Lockhart Gordon in June 1816, starting out inevitably from the Brussels where all those officers danced before fighting. But no verbal or imagistic sources can be tied down, other than what Byron and his cousin claim to have said to one another – not much – during that tour. Still, as one looks back at all the words that Englishmen have accumulated around Waterloo over the years since it was fought, it is the inseparability of Byron's myth and his very selective facts (whatever their actual source) that strikes one about these famous stanzas. That ball-to-battle myth, however, keeps becoming more and more mythical as the century proceeds, until at the beginning of the twentieth century Hardy could claim in a footnote to *The Dynasts* that the factual site of the ball had been completely lost. He had tried to find it thirty years before (on his honeymoon) without success. "The event happened less than a century ago," he writes, "but the spot is almost as phantasmal in its elusive mystery as towered Camelot, the palace of Priam, or the hill of Calvary."[39] But Hardy hadn't read the correspondence of the Richmond family (published before he wrote *The Dynasts*), which explains where the ballroom was set up and what happened to it later. When Hardy visited Brussels and Waterloo the site of the ball may have seemed as elusive as towered Camelot, but it was there all right, under an asphalt road.[40]

My final point about the historical mythmaking concerns the relation between Quatre Bras and Waterloo. A reader who relies on Byron's stanzas alone assumes the day's battle that immediately followed the night's dancing to be Waterloo. But of course it wasn't. Two battles followed the ball, with a rainy day in between. Byron's Duke of Brunswick, full of ominous prophecies when he hears in the ballroom that distant peal of a cannon, "rush'd into the field and foremost fighting, fell" (3.23). He fell, historians will tell us, on the field of Quatre Bras. But "the wide field" (3.30) on which Byron mourns "young gallant Howard" (3.29) seven stanzas later belongs to the Waterloo in which Howard died. Earlier in this essay I have called Quatre Bras the prelude to Waterloo, but Byron doesn't relate them as a prelude might be related to the whole thing. He unites them without differentiation. The dancers don't merely leap from floor to field, they land on two fields at once. But I've never read anyone's complaint about this foreshortening. Byron was simply pushing to an extreme the commonplace feeling of any of those who fought. As John Naylor wrote, a few years ago, without any thought of Byron's stanzas, "to the soldiers who took part in the campaign there seemed to be little distinction between Waterloo and the battles which they fought two days before."[41]

As I move from mythmaking to generic transformation, much of the poetic material will be the same, but its function will be different. Immediately after the line about the harvest fertilized by the "red rain," Byron finishes his first stanza by asking, "And is this all the world has gained by thee, / Thou first and last of fields! king-making victory?" (3.17) and then goes on at the beginning of the next to call his Alpha and Omega of fields "this place of skulls," that is, this Golgotha (3.18). I keep thinking of a story that Byron certainly never heard, but would have appreciated. Sergeant Thomas Morris describes how his young comrade with a speech defect kept crying out, as wave after wave of French horses charged the British line, "Tom, Tom, here comes the calvary."[42] But if there has been a crucifixion, for Byron there has surely been no resurrection. Apart from some new grain, there is nothing to show for Waterloo other than a lot of new or restored kings. This Golgotha has just led to counterrevolution. As Byron phrases it, we have "struck the Lion down ... [to] pay the Wolf homage" (3.19). He underlines that "in vain" theme (3.20) so familiar to the present century from some of the literature that followed the First World War.

At this point one can start to see Byron's agricultural myth meeting his elegiac conventions. Among recurrent patterns in the tradition of the pastoral elegy, one of the most interesting contrasts the cyclical pattern of nature with the linear pattern of human existence. Nature revives its plants but not its people. Considered in a purely naturalistic sense, we are, as Earl Wasserman explains in another connection, annuals in a world of perennials.[43] In the pastoral elegies of Milton and Shelley (following Moschus) the funeral flowers offer only "vain surmise" and "mockery" to the corpse below. "April is the cruellest month" or, as I have heard Jay Macpherson put it, quoting *The Mikado*, "the flowers that bloom in the spring tra la / Have nothing to do with the case."

Byron works out the traditional motif, not with flowers, but with foliage and fruit and grain. But his agricultural imagery offers an almost irresistible temptation to invoke something that could easily thwart that pastoral-elegiac pattern. I'm thinking of a myth that nobody forgets: the grim reaper. Both Southey and Scott, eager to make their poem exploit Waterloo's field of grain, succumb to it. "Insatiate death," cries Southey, "Devourer whom no harvest e'er can fill." "No vulgar crop was theirs to reap," Scott tells us. Before nightfall "lay / The ghastly harvest of the fray, / The corpses of the slain."[44] The danger is that by metaphorically uniting the natural and human harvest the elegiac contrast will be diminished. Byron escapes this danger strikingly. He blends the crops and the corpses, but he also keeps them apart. Even in the first instance, where he has the forest leaves shed the dew of "nature's tear-drops," he introduces such pastoral empathy only to question it in a parenthesis: "if aught inanimate e'er grieves" (3.27). And the surprising adjective "inanimate," used in that special sense which excludes the vegetative soul from life, pushes the normal pastoral-elegiac contrast to an inverted extreme: compared to the still living soldiers walking beneath them, even the "green leaves" seem lifeless. What follows in the same stanza walks a similar tightrope between identification and differentiation. The dead soldiers are "like the grass," but unlike the field grass, which will move from "below" to "above" in the "next verdure," this human grass will still "moulder cold and low" (3.27). Even in the following stanza, the earth's "own clay" and man's "other clay" come together almost, yet not quite (3.28). But Byron's most skilfully written and moving treatment of this pastoral-elegiac motif occurs in stanza 30, in response to the death of Major Howard:

> But when I stood beneath the fresh green tree
> Which living waves where thou didst cease to live,
> And saw around me the wide field revive
> With fruits and fertile promise, and the Spring
> Come forth her work of gladness to contrive,
> With all her reckless birds upon the wing,
> I turn'd from all she brought to those she could not bring.   (3.30)

These strong and simple lines, with their world of revival (all Spring brought) set against the unreviving dead ("those she could not bring") need no praise or explication. But I can't resist noting two details. First, there is that finely chosen adjective when Byron finally moves from vegetable to animal life: "all her reckless birds upon the wing." It is his very different equivalent to Keats's "Thou wast not born for death, immortal bird!" "Reckless" has its basic sense, "fearless of consequences," including that ultimate one. My second detail is the unexpected rhyme-word in "her work of gladness to contrive." Readers of *Don Juan* know how the search for rhymes stimulates Byron's invention. It does here too. "Contrive" means "to plot ingeniously, to fabricate." Just for a moment spring somehow seems like a wonderful fake, at least compared to the real thing human beings call death, their death.

The final elegiac theme I want to discuss is the most basic to the genre, that profit-and-loss equation which elegies try to work out so that in some way the plus column wins, both for those who died and for those who mourn. To be sure, elegies don't always swallow up death in victory – the communion of saints or the burning fountain – but something is likely to survive: in nature, in the bodies and minds of those who follow, in human achievement, that prevents death from being the end and leaves the poet and other mourners willing to move on to pastures new, or come to terms with their own prospect of death. Even Wordsworth's Matthew poems offer some minimal consolation, and of course the question of how much consolation there is, or how little (if any), is crucial to critical debates about Wordsworth's *A Slumber Did My Spirit Seal* or about the elegiac end of Shelley's *Alastor*. In this sliding scale of elegiac consolation where do Byron's stanzas stand? Certainly near the bottom, for both the corpses and the mourners. In the first place, a single, minor participant is made the focus of the final stanzas, not General Picton, who died with his top hat on in a famous incident which Byron knew all about, but instead someone who died near the same place, "young, gallant Howard" (3.29), Byron's cousin, whose father he had wronged in *English Bards and Scotch Reviewers* and for whom he here makes a personal act of reparation: the poetry itself as consolation. In Byron's prose account of his visit to the field and also in that of his companion, he does two main things: first he looks around and compares it with such places as Marathon and Troy and then he locates the spot where Howard was supposed to have died.[45] The movement, like the poem's, is from mythic place to private elegy. Stanza 31 begins, "I turn'd to thee, to thousands." Howard becomes an emblem for the thousands of individual, unnamed Englishmen who died at Waterloo. And what consolation does the poet now offer? "The Archangel's trump" will wake them, we are told, but Byron tells us only in order to emphasize the fact that glory won't. And the honour and fame of the dead are certainly no spur for the mourners, just the source of "a stronger, bitterer claim" (3.31). As I said at the beginning of this essay, the final consolation is simply that bare minimum, which nothing, certainly not death, can take away: Kilroy was here. But Byron's last line suddenly insists that what seems so minimal is in some ultimate way not just all we can expect but also a consolation of some magnitude. The line hovers between a kind of elegiac irony and a genuine commitment to the mere historical fact as eternity: "And this is much, and all which will not pass away" (3.35).[46]

What dominates the final stanzas, however, is not the historical destiny of the dead soldiers, but the condition of the mourners themselves, indeed mourning as a state of mind. It is conveyed at first by a host of images: dead but unfallen tree, ship with torn sails and mast, building with a caved-in roof, sunless day dragging to its close – each an image for the surviving but broken heart. I've left the most surprising one out: "the bars survive the captive they enthrall" (3.32). Here, unlike the others, it is the destructive agent that survives: bars remaining, captive gone. But the surrounding images force this one into a meaning like theirs. The mourner survives, a released prisoner who is a prisoner still, as at the end of *The Prisoner of Chillon*. The next stanza works quite differently: a single multiple image. I doubt that Byron had been reading Donne's *The Broken Heart*, as McGann suggests,[47] but they share an image. Byron calls the mourning heart

> a broken mirror, which the glass
> In every fragment multiplies; and makes
> A thousand images of one that was,
> The same, and still the more, the more it breaks.   (3.33)

In the second half of the stanza the phrasing fades out rather ineffectively; yet it includes a strange half-presented paradox, as that brilliantly visible scattering of glass images inside is finally described as "showing no visible sign" outside. The thousand-fragment mirror in the breast is ultimately without light. In the last of these three stanzas we return to Byron's favourite blasted tree, complemented by Dead-Sea fruit. But the stanza's main function is to pull together the elegiac conception of Waterloo's mourners that Byron wants to leave us with. The sequence began with a picture of the mourners smiling and mourning at the same time, as if the two states will now forever remain inseparable. It ends by calling their existence "life in ... despair," "vitality of poison" (3.34). If the mourners' suffering is in some way positive, even some sort of elegiac consolation, it is because, for Byron, only from a root of suffering can we realize the fact that we exist. I think of one of his strongest lines in the *Epistle to Augusta*: "not in vain / Even for its own sake do we purchase pain" (39–40).

So, with these two consolations, "Kilroy was here" for the corpses and "vitality of poison" for the mourners, Byron's Waterloo stanzas are over and give place to the Napoleonic epilogue. In retrospect it is easy to apply their last phrase, "all which will not pass away," to Byron's Waterloo itself as well as to the soldiers who fought there. Its readers haven't forgotten it, and Byron's great successors, like Thackeray in *Vanity Fair* and Hardy in *The Dynasts*, never seem to be superseding, just continuing it. Of course, if you are a student of French literature, you will see a different pattern, centring perhaps on *Les Miserables*, where not only is the genre very different, so also are the crucial images of the historical myth: the weather

– that tropical rainfall on 17 June – and the supposed hollow – a kind of underworld – out of which the English arise to doom the French cavalry near the end of the battle. A French reader might even want to fuse the Waterloo of Hugo with that of Stendhal in *La Chartreuse de Parme*. But for students of English Romanticism what won't pass away is this Waterloo of Byron's, and the question we need to answer was first raised by Francis Jeffrey in his 1816 review of canto 3. "All our bards," he writes, "great and small, and of all sexes, ages and professions, from Scott and Southey down to hundreds without names or additions, have adventured upon this theme – and failed in the management of it." He goes on: "scarcely a line to be remembered had been produced." The implied question is: why would Byron "venture on a theme ... deformed with the wrecks of so many former adventurers" and how in the world did he manage to succeed where they failed?[48] This essay is simply one attempt to answer that question.

2 Such Structures as the Mind Builds

W.J.B. OWEN

Near the end of book 7 of *The Prelude* are two episodes from Wordsworth's experience of London, which are presented in parallel fashion and with parallel purpose: the city by night (623–44) and Bartholomew Fair (644–740).[1] They are presented in parallel, in that each descriptive passage is preceded by introductory lines which propose that the scenes about to be recorded differ from those given earlier in the book, such as that of the blind beggar; the difference lies in that "These ... are such structures as the mind / Builds for itself" (624–5), whereas the scenes about to be presented are "Full-form'd [and] take, with small internal [i.e., intellectual] help, / Possession of the faculties" (626–7); an instance is the night scenes that follow. A parallel instance is Bartholomew Fair, which is "A work that's finish'd to our hands, that lays, / If any spectacle on earth can do, / The whole creative powers of man asleep!" (652–4). The treatments of both passages are again parallel in that, in both cases, the proposition that mind, or the "creative powers," are absent, or virtually absent, from the observer's reading of the scenes is denied at the end of each sequence:

> these ...
> Are falsely catalogu'd, things that are, are not,
> Even as we give them welcome, or assist,
> Are prompt, or are remiss. (641–4)

Bartholomew Fair, which was offered as an instance of the working on the citizens of "one passion," in this case, presumably, the desire for amusement, parallel to "vengeance, rage, or fear," or the excitement of an execution or a fire or a riot (646–8), is finally presented as "blank confusion," upon which "even highest minds" impose order and significance only with difficulty (695–706). We might define the layout of each sequence as the proposition, followed by the description, followed by the recantation (of the opening proposition). I deal with the two sequences in order.

There is, however, an initial difficulty: to define, in Wordsworthian terms, the faculties involved in these episodes. The proposition which opens the earlier one dismisses any suggestion that the night scenes are "Full-form'd" (that is, aesthetically complete) "structures" by virtue of the mind "Build[ing] for itself," unless to the extent of "small internal help" (623–6); the night scenes are, then, formed by "Nature," or what the Preface of 1815, dropping the personification, calls "external accidents."[2] The recantation denies this; or, rather, it denies that the mind is uninvolved in the perception: such things

> are, are not,
> Even as we given them welcome, or assist,
> Are prompt, or are remiss.   (642–4)

In commonplace terms which avoid philosophical technicalities, we might say that the observer sees or notices, or fails to see or notice, according as he gives or does not give attention to the environment. Walking through London on a moonlit or a rainy night, the observer might be giving his attention only to reaching his destination quickly, or to avoiding puddles. In such circumstances he might not notice the absence of people, or the general quiet, or the hailing of the prostitute; or he might, as Wordsworth says, according to his frame of mind, to the activity and focus of his attention. Wordsworth uses the word *attention* in various rather vague contexts; I shall propose a statement in more clearly defined Wordsworthian terms shortly.

The proposition distinguishes such episodes as those of the people in the streets seen as "A second-sight procession" on Cumbrian mountains or of the blind beggar (600–22) (such structures "as the mind / Builds for itself") from "Scenes different" and "Full-form'd" (624–6), such as the night scenes that follow. The mind building for itself is defined by Wordsworth in various places and in various senses; in the simplest sense, in the mode of the imagination of the infant babe of book 2, whose mind is

> eager to combine
> In one appearance, all the elements
> And parts of the same object, else detach'd
> And loth to coalesce.   (2.247–50)

This (I have suggested elsewhere)[3] is the mode of Coleridge's primary imagination, without which we could not make sense of our environment; at this simple level – "that first poetic Faculty / Of plain imagination and severe, / ... a mute influence of the soul, / An Element of the nature's inner self" (8.511–14) – it results merely in the perception of a meaningful environment. I say "merely" because our use of this faculty is so common as to appear commonplace; yet it is of the utmost importance to our survival. Those in whom this faculty fails are usually unfit for survival in society; if they survive, it is because society takes special care to ensure that they do. But if the faculty is to succeed in its operations, it is necessary that the mind should be "*eager* to combine ... all the elements / And parts of the same object"; or, in the commonplace terms I used earlier, it is necessary that the mind be able to give its *attention* to the environment.

This faculty is obviously involved in any significant act of perception; to that extent it is active in the perception of, say, the night scenes in our passage; it is indeed the faculty which permits "outward things" to be perceived as "outward *things*" rather than as mere sense-data, shapes and colours which have no significance beyond themselves. Its activity implies that the mind is indeed involved, at a comparatively basic (or "primary," in Coleridge's word) level, in this as in any other act of perception. But it is not the faculty that builds upon the base of outward things – rather, it is the faculty, as we have just seen, that supplies outward things to the mind – nor is it the faculty that perceives outward things organized, by whatever agency, into a scene "Full-form'd." It is the latter of these faculties that I am at present seeking to define.

If you had pressed Wordsworth for the name of such a faculty, he would probably have answered: Imagination. Imagination tends to be a catch-all word in his aesthetics for any sort of praiseworthy activity of the mind. But he did provide a transitory hint and a more permanent definition for the faculty I have in mind. I have elsewhere discussed lines in the last book of *The Prelude*, where it is stated that "higher minds ... can send abroad / ... transformations" like that achieved by Nature over Snowdon in changing cloud to seacoast: such minds

for themselves create
A like existence, and, whene'er it is
Created for them, catch it by an instinct ...
Willing to work and to be wrought upon.   (13.90–100)

And in particular I have discussed Wordsworth's seeming failure to distinguish, here and elsewhere, between creating a new existence and observing a created one; between working and being wrought upon.[4] In book 13 and its forbears, the clouds over Snowdon seen as seacoast, the

three-legged horse seen as a statue; in our passage in book 7, the night
scenes and the sights of Bartholomew Fair; these are the products of
"external accidents" (*Prose*, 3:35, textual note), whether in nature or in the
humanity of the fair. Since Wordsworth in his recantation insists that,
after all, the mind is involved, we have to ask: What faculty, apart from the
primary imagination involved in mere perception, is involved in the
appreciation of these events? To say, as Wordsworth might well have
said, *Imagination*, is merely to repeat the confusion of the lines quoted from
book 13, a confusion of activity and passivity which seem to appear under
the same name.

Wordsworth's revision of MSS. A and B of *The Prelude* adds, in the passage
last cited, after "catch it by an instinct," two lines which did not survive
beyond these manuscripts: "Say rather by an intellectual sense / Or
attribute, inevitably fine" (*Prel.*, p. 485). We might suppose from the
phrase "Say rather" that Wordsworth is here recognizing and attempting
to define a faculty different from that which creates a new existence,
different from the faculty that "works," different from what is clearly
Wordsworth's version of the Coleridgean secondary imagination.
Elsewhere I have proposed as a name for this faculty, transitory in the text
of *The Prelude*, the better established faculty defined in the Preface of 1815
and hinted at in the Preface to *Lyrical Ballads*, namely sensibility:[5]

which, the more exquisite it is, the wider will be the range of a poet's perceptions;
and the more will he be incited to observe objects, both as they exist in themselves
and as re-acted upon by his own mind.   (*Prose*, 3:26)

I now propose that the night scenes of book 7 and the scenes of Bartho-
lomew Fair are perceived by this faculty. Certainly they are seen "as they
exist in themselves"; how they are "re-acted upon by [the poet's] own
mind" will occupy us shortly.

Another mode in which the mind builds for itself is defined by
Wordsworth in his letter to Lady Beaumont of May 1807, where he under-
takes to defend the sonnet "With ships the sea was sprinkled": "who is
there," he asks,

that has not felt that the mind can have no rest among a multitude of objects, of
which it either cannot make one whole, or from which it cannot single out one indi-
vidual, whereupon may be concentrated the attention divided or distracted by a
multitude?[6]

The point made in our passage, given by "Full-form'd," corresponds to the
first of these alternatives, making one whole out of a multitude of objects;
but with the qualification that sometimes the unification of multitude

has been, or appears to have been, made by "Nature" or "external accidents" before (logically before) the observer's mind is called to action (625–7): a qualification the latter part of which (the absence of mind) is denied in the recantation (641–4). It is not denied, however, that the agency of unification is Nature or external accidents; but it is affirmed that the perception of the unification indicates the presence of an appropriate recipient faculty such as Wordsworth calls (I am proposing) sensibility.

A third way in which the mind builds for itself, and the mode with which we are most familiar in contexts of aesthetics, is the mode of Coleridge's secondary imagination, which works upon the products of the primary imagination, the "outward things" which have already been recognized and defined by the primary imagination. Wordsworth is saying, in our passage, that sometimes Nature or natural accidents will perform an analogous process, seeming to build a "structure" (624) such as is built by the secondary imagination in other circumstances. Such a structure is necessarily a unity: the secondary imagination, says Coleridge, "struggles ... to unify";[7] it "draws all things to one," says Lamb on Hogarth, quoted by Wordsworth in the Preface of 1815 (*Prose*, 3:34). Such a structure is the vision from Snowdon, where Nature has transformed and unified clouds into a seascape; or the other scenes in MS. W of *The Prelude*, the storm over Coniston, the statuesque horse standing on three legs (Prel., pp. 623–4); or the city in the clouds seen by the Solitary in *The Excursion*, 2.830–81, or by the Wordsworth family on the Hambleton Hills.[8]

In such instances the "external accidents" of Nature have produced a unity to which the mind contributes nothing (or so *The Prelude* now says): a unity demonstrating "The Power ... which Nature thus / Thrusts forth upon the senses" (13.84–6); "appearances which Nature thrusts / Upon our notice, her own naked work / Self-wrought, unaided by the human mind" (*Prel.*, p. 624), says MS. W. But we observe that there *is* a recipient: " the senses," "our notice"; later, "an instinct"; "an intellectual sense / Or attribute, inevitably fine" in the revision of MSS. A and B; or sensibility, in the Preface of 1815. Such an activity on the part of Nature "is the express / Resemblance ... a genuine Counterpart / And Brother of the glorious faculty / Which higher minds bear with them as their own" (13.86–90); obviously the imagination. Such scenes, that is to say, provide analogues for the working of the imagination, and in particular of what Coleridge called the secondary imagination. Cloud is "re-created" (Coleridge's word) as sea and coast or as gorgeous city; living horse is recreated as statue.

The characteristic of such passages is that the normal has been altered by natural processes; Wordsworth's words are "abrupt and unhabitual influence" and "transformations" (13.80, 94). The Snowdon vision alters mist or cloud to sea and coast; the horse is altered from living animal to lifeless statue ("lifeless" is Wordsworth's word, *Prel.*, p. 624); the Solitary's clouds are altered to a city. The object concerned has been given, in the words of the Preface of 1815, "a new existence" (*Prose*, 3.32). In order that the transformation may be perceived, the normal must be present or latent in the mind ("remembered," we might say), so that the change from the normal to the abnormal, from the regular to the new existence, may be recognized. It is the deviance from the norm, and the recognition of the deviance, that makes the event remarkable; there is nothing remarkable about cloud or about seacoast, but the transformation of the one to the other by "abrupt and unhabitual influence" is remarkable. It is an instance of the aesthetic principle canvassed in the Preface to *Lyrical Ballads* (*Prose*, 1.149): "the pleasure which the mind derives from the perception of similitude in dissimilitude." What is new may be a unity capable of definition: the Snowdon scene is a coastline; the horse is a statue; the Solitary's vision is a city. But in some instances no such unified definition is immediately obvious: only the transformation of the normal is observed. The normality of London is daylight, noise, many people in the streets: here we have darkness or moonlight, quiet, few people or none. There is a similar transformation in the unpublished poem *St Paul's*, where, again, the noisy, populous, dirty city is altered to a quiet, deserted, clean street by the natural accidents that it is Sunday morning and that there is a snowfall. Again, the normal is transformed to the unusual; as the poem puts it, Wordsworth "saw at a glance in that *familiar* spot / A *visionary* scene" (14–15). But it is difficult to give names or definitions to the new existences which emerge from these episodes, except, sometimes, in terms of Wordsworth's abstractions: in book 7, "hours of rest ... human life stands still ... calmness ... stillness"; or, in *St Paul's*, "quietness," and a whole string of adjectives (I count nineteen describing Fleet Street, Ludgate Hill, and the cathedral). We have a new existence only in so far as what is now perceived differs from – often, is the opposite of – what is known or remembered as the normal. This is stated plainly in the lines introducing the episode of the Discharged Soldier: Wordsworth liked "to walk alone / Along the public Way, when, for the night / Deserted, in its silence it assumes / A character of deeper quietness / Than pathless solitudes" (4.364–8). Here are two norms and a deviant: the noisy public way in daylight, and pathless solitudes, are the norms; the deviant is the deserted public way at night, the opposite of the primary norm; and differing from the secondary norm, pathless solitudes, in degree if not in kind.

An intermediate case, perhaps, is "I wandered lonely," in which the multeity of the daffodils is transformed into the unity of "a crowd, / A host of golden daffodils ... Continuous ... never-ending line ... a jocund company." The collectives stress the unity of the "Ten thousand" so that they may be taken in "at a glance"; as Dorothy Wordsworth commented in her Journal: "There was here and there a little knot, and a few stragglers a few yards higher up; but they were so few as not to disturb the simplicity, unity, and life of that one busy highway."[9] Here the norm is multeity, the novel is unity; but we cannot proceed beyond these abstractions to such a concrete novelty as a coastline or a statue. Our passage in book 7, and *St Paul's*, make no such transformation, either into a new concrete such as coastline or statue or cloud-city, or into the newly unified multeity of the daffodils, except in so far as they offer a unified *mood*: of peace and calm and desertion which is felt as such, primarily because it differs from the normal, which is noise and busyness and frequentation.

I distinguish between such scenes, so interpreted, and others where another step has been taken: where, in fact, the poet's secondary imagination has worked on "outward things" so as to give them a new, and often a new and abstract, significance. I think of the Snowdon vision, not as the natural transformation of cloud into coastline, but as "The perfect image of a mighty mind" (13.69), to which the transformation into coastline is irrelevant.[10] That transformation is analogous to an act of the secondary imagination, but not to this particular act; the only point of contact is that both are transformations, and transformations of the same "outward things"; but the agents and the products are different: the agents are the poet on the one hand and nature on the other, the products are a quasi-solid coastline and the abstraction of a mighty mind. The perception of the image of the mighty mind by the poet is an act of secondary imagination; the transformation of cloud to seacoast is a natural accident, analogous to an act of secondary imagination; its perception is an act of primary imagination acting upon the sensibility. Likewise in the episode of the Simplon Pass in book 6, the secondary imagination, seeing various physical phenomena as continuously expending and renewing energy, finds in them and in this process "The types and symbols of eternity" (6.556–72). In the dimension of time, energy runs down; this energy, seemingly endless, must therefore be in the dimension of eternity. In these instances there is no transformation by "external accidents" or by "Nature"; what is actually present – darkness below, light above the clouds, and noise becoming silence, on Snowdon; various manifestations of natural energy in the Simplon – is read as it now exists, without a transformation to a new quasi-physical existence; it is read as an image of mind or a symbol of eternity.

We thus have various levels of the natural or urban scene: 1) the normal, the "familiar spot," as *St Paul's* has it: the noisy populous street in the city by day, clouds as mere clouds, and a horse standing or moving on four legs; 2) the deviant, brought about by natural process: the quiet, unfrequented street in the city by night or on a public holiday; 3) the deviant which transforms the normal to "a new existence": the clouds to seascape, the horse to statue, the cuckoo (Wordsworth's example in the Preface of

1815, *Prose*, 3:32) into a disembodied "wandering voice"; all definable, concrete, or quasi-concrete novelties. A variation of this deviant is the recognition of the one in the many, unity in multeity, as in "I wandered lonely"; we can give the deviant a name and say that it is new, but it is not what I have just called a concrete or quasi-concrete novelty; 4) the deviant which is imposed by the secondary imagination of the poet, and which is commonly an abstraction, as the image of the human mind on Snowdon, or the types and symbols of eternity in the Simplon Pass. Here there will not usually be a quasi-imaginative transformation by Nature; the data remain data, such as anyone might observe; the novelty lies in the poet's reading of the untransformed data in a symbolic sense.

I revert to the passage in book 7 from which these observations began; it falls into the second of the categories just defined. The scheme of the passage, as we saw earlier, is the statement that some scenes appear to be "Full-form'd, [and] take, with small internal help, / Possession of the faculties" (625–7); that is, they have their own particular quality by virtue of "external accidents," and not, or not much, by the intervention of the mind. At the end of the passage this characterization is rejected, and it is proposed that this quality depends on an act of attention: "things are, are not, / Even as we give them welcome, or assist, / Are prompt, or are remiss" (642–4); that is, according to my proposal, things are, or are not, according as they do, or do not, impinge on the observer's sensibility. This scheme is repeated in the following passage, where Bartholemew Fair is first presented as, seemingly, an unchallengeable instance of things shaping themselves or shaped by natural accident: "A work that's finish'd to our hands, that lays, / If any spectacle on earth can do, / The whole creative powers of man asleep!" (652–4). Since the fair is "A work that's finish'd," laying "The whole creative powers of man asleep," we are presumably intended to see it as a unified whole; the observer's mind cannot add or subtract or modify anything by way of completing or unifying. There is some trace of this in the pointed use of some singulars: "A work" (652), "spectacle" (653), "a hell" (658), "a dream" (660), "Parliament" (691), "one vast Mill" (692); and overall we are aware, as we saw earlier, that here is a gathering of people who have a single aim, amusement; the people are to that extent "Full of *one* passion" (646–8). Yet the passage as it proceeds is full of plurals and, especially, random, unordered lists. And after the description of the fair, the characterization of it as a whole thing is rejected: it is "blank [= ?meaningless] confusion," like the city itself; it is "An undistinguishable [= unidentifiable, indefinable] world" to ordinary men. Faced with this confusion, of fair or city, the mind submits to "Oppression under which even highest minds / Must labour, whence the strongest are not free; ... the picture wear[ies] out the eye, / By nature an unmanageable sight" (695–708). Wordsworth is anticipating the question in his letter of 1807: "who is there who has not felt that the mind can have no rest among a multitude of objects, of which it ... cannot make one whole" (MY, 1:148). In this instance, the favoured few, especially those subject to the influence of the natural sublime in Cumbria, can attempt to order the chaos (709–29). The implication of the proposition was that the mind did not need to be active to understand the fair and, by implication, the city; the implication of the recantation is that the mind is indeed needed, but is usually frustrated.

How then, in these two instances, the night scenes and the fair, does the mind operate, as Wordsworth eventually concedes it must? How, in terms of the definition of sensibility in the Preface of 1815, are the "objects" "re-acted upon by [the poet's] own mind"? In the night scenes, perhaps, by establishing the norm from which they deviate. The scenes belong to "nature's intermediate hours of rest," and "intermediate" is glossed by the next three lines; "When the great tide of human life stands still, / The business of the day to come unborn, / Of that gone by, lock'd up as in the grave" (629–32). This is the time intermediate between two normalities, today and tomorrow, identical as normalities must be, when the tide of human life has flowed and will flow, a border state (in Jonathan Wordsworth's phrase)[11] imaged in terms of the inevitable in humanity, of life today ending in death tonight followed by life tomorrow. Here, surely, is an intervention of the mind, a reaction from the mind upon the objects of a London street, remembering that a normal today has been and that a normal tomorrow will ensue, and that both have been/will be concerned with "business," the concern of the normal day but not of the "intermediate hours of rest." The intervention of mind continues, less conspicuously and sometimes inconspicuously: "calmness" and "stillness" are significant only against the background of the "business" of the normal day; "beauty" and "Sky" are quite neutral; but "empty streets, and sounds / Unfrequent as in desarts" compel the reader to remember scenes earlier in the book: "The endless stream of men, and moving things" (158), "The Comers and the Goers face to face, / Face after face" (172–3), "the roar" (184), "the thickening hubbub" (227), "the overflowing Streets" (594), and the like; whether readers remember Wordsworth's phrases or merely their own experiences of the city, the normal is always present in the mind, and the mind therefore is always adding to the merely visual and auditory, saying, in effect, "It is not normally like this"; not only giving welcome, being prompt (643–4), but assisting with the memory. Readers say this in effect as they read, prompted by the poet, who must have said the same thing as he meditated at the time of the experience, or recollected in tranquillity, or wrote the lines concerned.

The mind enters in other ways: as in a poem like *Airey-Force Valley*, minimal sounds and movements emphasize the stillness: "the brook itself ...

Doth rather deepen than disturb the calm / Where all things else are still and motionless" (4–6). So here, lesser deviants from the norm emphasize the deviation which is sometimes total opposition to the norm. Rain falls hard (and therefore noisily), people are "yet astir," and the prostitute solicits feebly; so that the streets are not quite as empty as we were told just before. But we are still remote from the "hubbub" and "the overflowing Streets"; here "the great tide of human life" does not quite stand still, but it is drawing to a halt; the people yet astir will go home out of the rain, the prostitute will move off with a client or will abandon her efforts, and the streets will be, abnormally for the city, finally empty.

Deviation from the norm is the obvious and major topic of the description of Bartholomew Fair (658–94). It is a "hell," involving "anarchy and din"; a "dream / Monstrous in colour, motion, shape, sight, sound." It involves "prodigies"; "chattering monkeys" parody the people. The showmen exert themselves abnormally: "those that stretch the neck, and strain the eyes, / And crack the voice in rivalship." The music is abnormal in its unorganized crudity: the hurdy-gurdy, fiddle, salt-box, kettle-drum, trumpet. Clothing is outrageous: "Girls, and Boys, / Blue-breech'd, pink-vested, and with towering plumes." Abnormal humanity is on display: "Albinos, painted Indians, Dwarfs"; more animals that parody people: "The Horse of Knowledge, and the learned Pig," and machines for the same purpose: "The Bust that speaks, and moves its goggling eyes." All this is summed up with an adaptation of Milton describing hell, thereby recalling the "hell" of "anarchy" in earlier lines: "All out-o'-th'-way, far-fetch'd, perverted things, / All freaks of Nature, all Promethean thoughts / Of Man ... All jumbled up together to make up / This Parliament of Monsters."

In what sense is this outrageous miscellany "A work that's finish'd to our hands, that lays ... / The whole creative powers of man asleep"? In two senses: the one we have already seen, referring to the audience of the fair, devoted, like those who flock to "executions, to a Street on fire, / Mobs, riots, or rejoicings" – devoted to "one passion," the desire for amusement. The other sense is the more important: here the abnormal has become, for the time being, the normal, or, rather, the universal. This is, of course, true for the night scenes also; but there is a difference, in that the normal, which in the night scenes is constantly recalled, is here almost entirely latent. The positives of the description, the operative words, are the vocabulary of the abnormal: "hell," "dream," "Monstrous," "prodigies," "moveables of wonder," "marvellous craft / Of modern Merlins," "out-o'-th'-way, far-fetch'd, perverted ... freaks," "madness," "Monsters." All, by contrast, imply the normal, but little or nothing of the normal is stated. This is, perhaps, why Wordsworth introduces the description with such a flourish of confidence in his example: after the rejection of the proposition of the night scenes, his question, "What say you then ... ?" implies that an unchallengeable instance of the occurrence of "one passion," of a "work that's finish'd to our hands," is about to be produced. The confidence is justified, but not in the sense proposed, of the citizenry under the influence of "one passion," for amusement, which scarcely appears in the description (there are perhaps two instances: "children whirling in their roundabouts" and "the crowd / Inviting" to encourage the noisy showmen [668, 670–1]). The example is indisputable in the sense that it provides an instance of a conscious and successful production of chaos, to which all elements contribute. And the success of the example is wryly or ironically acknowledged in the summarizing phrases "blank confusion" (of the fair) and "undistinguishable world" (of the city of which the fair is the type).

How does the mind operate in such a context? According to the recantation which follows the description, not at all, except in specially equipped minds like William Wordsworth's, benefiting from early contact with the natural sublime in Cumbria. And this is true, in that the mind's recognition of the deviance from the normal is here only latent, not from time to time expressed or implied as in the night scenes. The mind in the context of the fair does not say, as I suggested it does in the night scenes, "It is not normally like this." The mind does not say this in the context of the fair because the "it" of "It is not normally like this" does not exist or cannot be defined. There is no general norm against which the monstrosities of the fair can be seen, as there is a general norm – the "business" of a weekday in London – against which we see the night scenes. There are, indeed, individual norms: most Londoners are not, for instance, "Albinos, painted Indians, Dwarfs," but persons of general Caucasian complexion and stature; most of those who solve problems are educated human beings, not horses or pigs; normal diets do not include stones or fire. It is because the deviants are deviants from these norms that they are here on show at the fair; but the norms are too many, and too remote one from another, for the mind to grasp them. In its effort to do so, the mind meets only "blank confusion," and is thereby baffled; "the mind can have no rest among a multitude of objects, of which it ... cannot make one whole ... whereupon may be concentrated the attention divided or distracted by a multitude," Wordsworth wrote in 1807 (MY, 1:148). Here the "multitude," whether of monsters or the implied norms by virtue of which the monsters are monsters, is so numerous that "the attention is divided or distracted," has therefore "no rest," and is therefore frustrated by "blank confusion."

Is it not, ironically, the frustration of the mind that "lays ... the whole creative powers of man asleep"? Is it not the baffling multitude of disjointed elements in the fair, or in London, rather than the completeness of the scene ("a work that's finish'd to our hands"), as originally proposed, that induces the mind to give up the hopeless task of finding significance? The work is "finish'd to our hands" because, to most minds, ordering it into significance is an impossible task; the city is "An undistinguishable world to [ordinary] men," and is "By nature an unmanageable sight" (699, 708); the "creative powers" are asleep because it is realized that their frustration is, for most minds, inevitable and permanent. Yet, ironically again, there is a unity for such minds in the city, for the "men, / The slaves unrespited of low pursuits" (699–700), for they live "amid the same perpetual flow / Of trivial objects, melted and reduced / To one identity" (699–703). Paradoxically, the objects are reduced to one identity "by differences / That have no law, no meaning, and no end" (703–4). I say "paradoxically," since it is difficult to see how objects can be reduced to identity by differences, the absence of which is implicit in identity. We can skirt the paradox if we read the sentence as meaning: "reduced to one identity *because* any differences between the objects have no law, no meaning, and no end [= ? aim, purpose]." Such an interpretation is perhaps confirmed by the earlier description of Wordsworth's reaction to the ordinary London streets:

Thus have I look'd, nor ceas'd to look, oppress'd
By thoughts of what, and whither, when and how,
Until the shapes before my eyes became
A second-sight procession, such as glides
Over still mountains, or appears in dreams;
And all the ballast of familiar life,
The present and the past; hope, fear; all stays,
And laws of acting, thinking, speaking man
Went from me, neither knowing me, nor known.   (598–606)

Here the "laws of acting, thinking, speaking man" are perhaps the laws which are absent from the differences, or the non-differences, which reduce London to one identity: an identity of dullness, a unity of insignificance. The lonely city-dweller in *Home at Grasmere* is "He of the multitude, whose eyes are doomed / To hold a vacant commerce day by day / With objects wanting life" (594–6).

This is a difficulty which affects everyone, it seems: "Oppression under which even highest minds / Must labour, whence the strongest are not free" (705–6). "Oppression" here echoes "oppress'd / By thoughts of what, and whither, when and how" (598–9); "highest minds" anticipates the "higher minds" of 13.90, to whom is attributed "the glorious faculty" of imagination. Parenthetically, one might doubt the credibility of that "even"; would not "only" or "especially" be more appropriate? Do the "Men, Women, three-years' Children, Babes in arms" who are swallowed or vomited by the fair, who are "The slaves unrespited of low pursuits" (such as attending, and enjoying, the fair) – do these really care about the unity or the disunity, the "blank confusion," of the fair or the city? If you are "doomed / To hold a vacant commerce day by day / With objects wanting life"; if you are concerned, as rejected lines from MS. W put it (*Prel.*, p. 629), with

> petty duties and degrading cares –
> Labour and penury, disease and grief,
> Which to one object chain the impoverished mind
> Enfeebled, and devouring vexing strife
> At home, and want of pleasure and repose
> And all that eats away the genial spirits

– if this is your condition in London, what does unity or confusion matter? Perhaps the exciting confusion of the fair is a relief from the dullness, from the "vacant commerce day by day / With objects wanting life."

Not so "highest minds"; or at any rate not so

> to him who looks
> In steadiness, who hath among least things
> An under-sense of greatest; sees the parts
> As parts, but with a feeling of the whole.   (709–12)

The "feeling" may be acquired from, or encouraged by, "sundry and most widely different modes / Of education," and especially from the Wordsworthian mode (714–16). The other modes are not specified; perhaps Wordsworth was thinking of the Coleridgean mode, based "in the depths / Of the huge city," from which Coleridge acquired "learning, gorgeous eloquence ... subtle speculations," even though these produced

> wild ideal pageantry, shap'd out
> From things well-match'd, or ill, and words for things,
> The self-created sustenance of a mind
> Debarr'd from Nature's living images.   (6.275–6, 306–13)

To Wordsworth, blessed with a "widely different mode," "Nature's living images" were freely available:

> By influence habitual to the mind
> The mountain's outline and its steady form
> Gives a pure grandeur, and its presence shapes
> The measure and the prospect of the soul
> To majesty; such virtue have the forms
> Perennial of the ancient hills; nor less

The changeful language of their countenances
Gives movement to the thoughts, and multitude,
With order and relation. (7.721–9)

"Multitude," the baffling characteristic of the fair and the city, here has
"order and relation," not "differences / That have no law, no meaning, and
no end." The drift of the whole passage, of course, is the influence of the
natural sublime on the mind of the observer, a notion canvassed in many
places in the canon: in the description of the youth of the Wanderer in
The Excursion, book 1, and its textual predecessors; in Wordsworth's letter
of 1802 to John Wilson (*EY*, pp. 353–4); and in drafts of the description of
the depressing "one identity" of the city and of the passage now before us
(*Prel.*, pp. 566–7).

And how is the "unmanageable sight" of the city seen by

him who looks
In steadiness, who hath among least things
An under-sense of greatest; sees the parts
As parts, but with a feeling of the whole   (709–12)?

How does he apply "Attention ... comprehensiveness and memory"
(716–17) to define "An undistinguishable world ... an unmanageable
sight" such as London presents to his sensibility? How does his mind
"re-act" to the "objects," the "outward things" which primary imagination
reports? The answer is not here, for the imaginative man's perception of
London is modified away from "blank confusion" according as he has
"among least things / An under-sense of greatest; sees the part / As
parts, but with a feeling of the whole" (710–12).

The whole is the London of book 8, which was seen in three stages,
imaged by the famous simile of the cave (8.711–41): the first stage, the swell
of feeling, corresponds to Wordsworth's first entry into the city, described
in the paragraph preceding the simile (8.689–710); the second stage, the
scene as it really is, "in perfect view, / Exposed and lifeless, as a written
book," corresponds to the generally detached and satiric view which
obtains through most of book 7. The third stage, corresponding to the cave
seen as the home of visionary figures, shows London, not exposed and life-
less, but as the cultured imagination sees it, building "upon the base of
outward things." The application of the simile is made briefly:

No otherwise had I at first been moved
With such a swell of feeling, follow'd soon
By a blank sense of greatness pass'd away
And afterwards continu'd to be mov'd
In presence of that vast Metropolis. (8.742–6)

The "swell of feeling," occurring as Wordsworth first entered London, is given thus:

> A weight of Ages did at once descend
> Upon my heart; no thought embodied, no
> Distinct remembrances; but weight and power,
> Power growing with the weight.   (8.703–6)

And the concept of power dominates the vision of London for the remainder of the book: in a crude political sense, London is a seat of power: "The Fountain of my Country's destiny / And of the destiny of Earth itself" (8.747–8); a more subtle sense emerges as the book proceeds.

The concept of power is a major element in what Wordsworth and the eighteenth century called the sublime; and it is clear that the unifying factor, that "whole" which the cultured observer of book 7 sees, through and in spite of the seeming chaos which is the "parts," is London as the sublime city. I have urged this view elsewhere;[12] I recall briefly the evidence.

Power is one of three elements in what Wordsworth, in his fragmentary essay on the Sublime and Beautiful, calls "a sensation of sublimity": "a sense of individual form or forms; a sense of duration; and a sense of power" (*Prose*, 2:351). In the case of the "works of Man," only form and duration are needed, according to the essay; the case of London, if my reading is correct, differs from this theorizing, in that form is generally neglected, and power and duration are stressed. Indeed, the only form specifically mentioned is the opposite of the sublime: "vulgar forms / Of houses, pavement, streets, of men and things, / Mean shapes on every side" (8.695–7). But duration, and especially power, appear regularly: "weight and power, / Power growing with the weight," as Wordsworth entered the city; and the weight was "A weight of ages," that is, a sense of the duration of the city and its history (8.703–6). And later:

> With strong Sensations, teeming as it did
> Of past and present, such a place must needs
> Have pleas'd me, in those times; I sought not then
> Knowledge; but craved for power; and power I found
> In all things; nothing had a circumscrib'd
> And narrow influence; but all objects, being
> Themselves capacious, also found in me
> Capaciousness and amplitude of mind.   (8.752–9)

The antithesis of knowledge and power is a Wordsworthian commonplace which does not concern us here; we need to notice rather that London teems with "Sensations ... Of past and present," that is, with a sense of duration, of the past surviving into the present; and we need to notice also the expansion of the mind in the context of, and in response to, the external sublime. This is a commonplace in eighteenth-century discussions of the topic, in Wordsworth's essay (*Prose*, 2:354) as in many other discussions. The argument of the poem goes on to say that Wordsworth was not much attracted by British history or by "extrinsic accidents" in "records or traditions" connected with "place or thing" (8.779–81); nevertheless

> a sense
> Of what had been done here, and suffer'd here
> Through ages, and was doing, suffering, still
> Weigh'd with me. (8.781–4)

That is, a sense of the tradition of London's humanity weighed with him, as the "weight of Ages" induced a sense of power in him when he entered the city. Moreover, this sense of tradition

> Was like the enduring majesty and power
> Of independent nature ...
> And out of what had been, what was, the place
> Was thronged with impregnations, like those wilds
> In which my early feelings had been nurs'd. (8.785–92)

The city with its duration and power is equated with the sublime landscape of Cumbria; as, in that other vision of London, as beautiful rather than sublime, we are told that "Never did sun more beautifully steep / In his first splendour, valley, rock, or hill" (*PW*, 3:38). Moreover, a characteristic of the sublime is unity:

whatever suspends the comparing power of the mind & possesses it with a feeling or image of intense unity, without a conscious contemplation of parts, has produced that state of mind which is the consummation of the sublime. (*Prose*, 2:353–4)

The vocabulary of this is close to that of the poem, though the sense is not identical: though London is

> By nature an unmanageable sight,
> It is not wholly so to him who ...
>   hath among least things
> An under-sense of greatest; sees the parts
> As parts, but with a feeling of the whole.

It is not clear that unity recognized "without a conscious contemplation of parts" is precisely equivalent to "see[ing] the parts / As parts, but with a feeling of the whole," but at any rate both passages stress the subordination of "parts" to the recognition of a unified whole.

The sublime landscape of Cumbria, we recall from book 7, is one of those regions "where appear / Most obviously simplicity and power":

> By influence habitual to the mind
> The mountain's outline and its steady form
> Gives a pure grandeur, and its presence shapes
> The measure and the prospect of the soul
> To majesty. (7.719–25)

The Cumbrian landscape trains the mind to recognize grandeur, to take into its sensibility the sublime, whether in nature or in the "works of Man" in London. For this vision of the city is purely of the mind; like the Simplon Pass as "The types and symbols of eternity," or the vision from Snowdon as "The perfect image of a mighty Mind," the London of this vision is not changed into "a new existence" by "external accidents," but by the mind's reading of the scene as it is, by the mind's building upon the "outward things" presented to the sensibility by primary imagination. The novelty is added, in all these instances, not by any quasi-imaginative activity on the part of Nature, but by the poet's imagination, which out of the blank confusion of the city builds on its outward things the "Composure and ennobling harmony" of the sublime.

3 Matthew Arnold's Wordsworth: The Tinker Tinkered

JARED CURTIS

Wordsworth very nearly published a poem called *The Tinker* in the collection of 1807, but he vigorously crossed it out before sending copy to the printer, and never printed it thereafter.[1] Had he published the poem, then or later, it might have tempered somewhat his Victorian reputation as a sombre poet of ideas. Sprinkled with cheerful *non sequiturs* and local slang, the fifty-line poem is an amusing portrait of an itinerant pot-mender with a penchant for humming loudly at his work. No one has ever taken the poem seriously enough to suggest that it is a mock-heroic picture of the poet, but the notion seems apt.

> Through the meadows, over stiles,
> Where there are no measured miles,
> Day by day he finds his way
> Among the lonely houses:
> Right before the Farmer's door
> Down he sits; his brows he knits;
> Then his hammer he rouzes;
> Batter! batter! batter!
> He begins to clatter.   (5–13)

Like the poet, his home is everywhere, "Through the valley, up the hill," and like him, "He sings the sun to bed" (19, 27). Unlike the poet, he hasn't a care in the world. But oddly enough, the Tinker's refrain, "bumming, bumming, bumming" (37), as he terrorizes boys and startles "market Maidens" with his singing, produces the same sound Wordsworth was alleged to have made, many years later, while composing and revising his verse as he paced back and forth on the path at Rydal Mount. The "quondam gardener's boy" at Rydal Mount is reported to have said of Wordsworth, his employer:

He was ter'ble thrang [i.e. thronged] with visitors and folks, you mun kna, at times, but if he could git away from them for a spell, he was out upon his gres walk; and then he would set his head a bit forward, and put his hands behint his back. And then he would start a bumming, and it was bum, bum, bum, stop; then bum, bum, bum reet down till t'other end, and then he'd set down and git a bit o'paper out and write a bit; and then he git up, and bum, bum, bum, and goa on bumming for long enough[,] right down and back agean. I suppose, ye kna, the bumming helped him out a bit. However, his lips was always goan' [t'] whoale time he was upon the gres walk.[2]

Wordsworth, like his jolly creation, was a tireless "tinker" himself, and, indeed, "tinkering" became the family epithet for the recurring process of revision.[3]

I

When Matthew Arnold published his selection of *Poems of Wordsworth* for Macmillan in London in 1879 he did not include *The Tinker*, but he did hope to overcome the deleterious effects, as he saw them, of Wordsworth's constant mending of his verses. George Craik, a partner in the Macmillan firm, hoped the volume would create "a new and a large interest in Wordsworth." Arnold's own purpose, as he told his friend Mark Pattison, was "to make an acceptable book and to spread the reading of Wordsworth."[4] The *Poems of Wordsworth* appeared in two formats, one in the Golden Treasury Series in small octavo, at the beginning of September 1879, for 4 s. 6 d., and the other at 9 s. in a limited "Large Paper Edition," with a few corrections, about three weeks later, dated 20 September 1879. A printing of 3500 copies was agreed upon, though copies seem to have been run off in lots of 750 to allow for corrections in press to the stereotype plates. In November of the same year the small octavo issue was reprinted with more corrections and two additional poems. George Craik's prediction that the volume would do well was borne out by steady demand: the later issue of 1879 was reprinted in 1880 and 1882. Arnold then made corrections and additions in 1884 which saw print in 1886; and "slight alterations" were made in 1888, the year of Arnold's sudden death. In its first 110 years the book has been reprinted more than forty times and is still in print with its original publishers.[5] *Poems of Wordsworth, Chosen and Edited by Matthew Arnold*, with its Preface, which first appeared in *Macmillan's*

Magazine in July 1879 to draw notice to the volume, was widely distributed in England and in North America, and, as we all know, gained considerable influence over readers' perceptions of the poet and the poet's work for many years after.

One might suppose from Arnold's and Craik's comments that editions of Wordsworth's poems had disappeared from the bookstalls and that general interest was slight. This seems not to have been the case, for since the poet's death in 1850 his heirs and his own publisher, Edward Moxon, had alone produced a dozen or so printings of the collected works, one version with and one without the Fenwick notes. The making of selections of various kinds, begun while the poet was alive and usually with his permission, was a popular activity as well, generating in 1857 the first edition of "early" Wordsworth, a selection by William Johnston of poems from the 1815 edition.[6] But by the 1870s the tone and appearance of the editions being produced took a definite turn. Elaborate bindings of full calf with gilt edges and a central crest were not uncommon and were usually supplemented by engravings to illustrate the poems and to enhance their drawing-room appeal.[7]

Even more curious, however, is the volume edited for Moxon by William Michael Rossetti, brother of Dante Gabriel and one of the seven Pre-Raphaelite "brothers." This handsome Victorian edition, with gilt and embossed cover and elegant engravings by Edwin Edwards, contains a Prefatory Notice by Rossetti in which he charges Wordsworth with being "too conscientious and too little instinctive for a poet." The result, according to Rossetti, was that "with all his imagination, all his intimate knowledge of Nature, all his deep pure feeling, all his command of poetic resource, he is not, in the large sense, a fascinating or attractive writer." He goes on to list among Wordsworth's "blemishes," in a kind of crescendo of aesthetic wrongdoing, "occasional triviality, more frequent bathos, and prosing lengthiness more frequent still." He finally does grant Wordsworth to be "a most true poet – indeed, a very exalted and a great one," but only if all of his flaws can be "excluded altogether in our minds." Yet, paradoxically, the volume, thus introduced by Rossetti, reproduced the complete poetical works.[8]

It is against this double vision of an exalted poet with serious flaws that Arnold appears to launch his own Preface and selection. Taking a positive view of what he thought Wordsworth did best, he built his selection accordingly, without lingering to berate the poet's faults. He placed him high, as a sixth in the company of Dante, Shakespeare, Molière, Milton, and Goethe, and praised by illustration the strength and variety of his lyric, narrative and elegiac voices.[9] Qualities Arnold points to in his Preface – Wordsworth's capacity to "deal with life," his access to "joy," and his "austere naturalness" of expression – have all long been prominent features of most critics' assessments of Wordsworth since Arnold wrote the Preface (pp. xvi–xxiv) or are part of the ongoing "Arnold Controversy." It is Arnold's view, not Rossetti's, that has prevailed.

But this influence has not gone unchallenged. Indeed, Arnold-bashing has been an academic sport for some time. Fifty years after *Poems of Wordsworth* appeared, Lane Cooper complained bitterly against Arnold's assessment of Wordsworth in his Preface. Cooper catches Arnold in error and overstatement, chastising him for not even reading carefully the poems he chose for his own edition. He repeats Edward Dowden's criticism that, in choosing other than the final lifetime edition of *Poetical Works* (1849–50) as the basis for his text, Arnold produced an "illegitimate" edition, and that, furthermore, Arnold "silently manufactured a text of his own, such as Wordsworth had never sanctioned or seen, by piecing together readings from more editions than one." Besides these editorial blunders, Cooper noted the further liberty Arnold took in "naming poems as their author did not wish to name them," raising through this string of scholarly sins, Cooper believed, "a presumption against his critical method as a whole."[10] Cooper's diatribe was "answered" by others, notably by G.G. Sedgwick, who gave credit to Arnold for aiming well at a "general" audience.[11] But apart from R.H. Super's excellent remarks on the "Wordsworth" essay in his edition of Arnold's prose,[12] no one has tried to determine what Arnold's "method" was, critical or otherwise. What principles guided him as he chose, edited, and arranged Wordsworth's poems? And what were the consequences?

It is clear that Arnold did not aim his volume at the parlour-book trade. He may have appreciated a book that was compact enough to be carried about easily, as did Wordsworth, who was fond of the small octavo 1832 edition for this very reason. It is also clear that Arnold did not wish to produce either a "complete" or an "authorized" edition, preferring both earlier versions and a narrower corpus, as we shall see in a moment, and aiming at what he fondly called the "General Public." In discussing with Macmillan a prefatory "notice" for the volume, Arnold said he wanted a brief one, adding, surely with tongue in cheek, "not such an introduction as those which Jowett and Green bury their authors in."[13] Macmillan approved and added that he should annotate "only to the extent of common intelligence" (*Arnold's Books*, pp. 132–3).

Once this Preface had appeared in *Macmillan's Magazine* in July, Arnold wrote to Pattison to ask his advice on whether or not to expand it to include a detailed "Etude on Wordsworth's poems," a change strongly recommended by Francis Taylor Palgrave, the general editor of the Golden Treasury Series. But in Arnold's view such a poem-by-poem study would be "out of place." He thought it "enough to say what I believe his rank among poets to be, and what, stated briefly, it is which makes his greatness." And he added that "the poems must justify and illustrate this themselves."[14] Arnold's correspondence before and after publication reveals how seriously he tried to avoid pleasing only "Wordsworthians." He at first yielded to pressure from a friend, Frederick Myers, who urged him to find a place for the *Evening Ode, composed upon an Evening of Extraordinary Splendour and Beauty*. But he thought better of this plan, as he told Lady Richardson, after asking R.W. Church, the Dean of St Paul's, to read Wordsworth's *Evening Ode*. It was a poem, Arnold felt, which did not "lay hold of any but the initiated." When the commonsensical Dean told him that "it seemed always something very good was coming, but it never came," Arnold ruled out including the *Ode* as likely to elicit the same response from other readers of "common intelligence."[15]

Finally, with an eye on his very practical-minded audience, he shrewdly mixed economic with literary motives when he defended his choice of poems to Willy Wordsworth, the poet's son. After publication, Arnold wrote to Jemima Quillinan (daughter of Edward Quillinan and stepdaughter of Wordsworth's daughter Dora), with whom the younger Wordsworth had registered his complaints about Arnold's selection, "What I had to think of, both in the preface and in the Selection, was the great public; it is this great public which I want to make buy Wordsworth's poems as they buy Milton's."[16] Time has proven him successful in this enterprise.

II

To begin with, as he approached the task at hand, Arnold disliked Wordsworth's arrangement of his poems in "classes" for the collections of 1815 and after. He told his sister, Fan, as he was working out his selection, that Wordsworth "will come out better, and more effective in my arrangement, I think, than he has ever come out before." He explained further that he had

gone on the plan of throwing pieces of one poetical *kind* together, not of classifying them, in Wordsworth's own intricate way, according to the spiritual faculty from which they are supposed to have proceeded.[17]

In his Preface he was more severe, calling Wordsworth's plan a "scheme of mental physiology," and finding his categories "ingenious but far-fetched" and the "result of his employment of them ... unsatisfactory." In defence of his own groupings and juxtapositions, he added that in Wordsworth's scheme "poems are separated one from another which possess a kinship of subject or of treatment far more vital and deep than the supposed unity of mental origin" (Preface, pp. xii–xiii). Arnold's arrangement of Wordsworth's poems was intended to reveal such kinship.

The poetical "kinds" of Arnold's own devising were developed for Wordsworth's poems in imitation of Arnold's sense of the Greek "kinds" of verse, which, in fact, had guided his grouping of his own poems a decade earlier for his selection for the *Poems* of 1869. There he arranged his poems in the classical rubrics of Narrative, Elegiac, Dramatic, and Lyric Poems, emulating what he came to regard as the "infallible ... tact of the Greeks in matters of this kind" (Preface, p. xiii). But despite his remark to Alexander Macmillan a few days after his letter to Fan, that he had "always wished to arrange these poems in some natural and logical order" (*Arnold's Books*, p. 136), *and* his insistence in the earliest version of the Preface that Wordsworth's poems were now "naturally grouped" (a phrase he later deleted),[18] his choice of "kinds" for the Wordsworth volume was something of a compromise. "Narrative" and "Lyrical" poems follow classical categories and "Poems of Ballad Form" may be seen to correspond to the "Dramatic" class. But Arnold came close to imitating Wordsworth's variable and inclusive manner of classifying poems in two new groupings: Arnold's title, "Poems Akin to the Antique, and Odes," in its odd inclusiveness, suggests Wordsworth's "Poems of the Imagination"; and Arnold's "Reflective and Elegiac Poems" is a blend of Wordsworth's "Poems of Sentiment and Reflection" and "Epitaphs and Elegiac Pieces." Just as Arnold later found it expedient to add to the groupings in his own *Poems*, for the edition of 1885, a category for "Sonnets," so he provided a generous sampling of Wordsworth's sonnets beneath that rubric in the 1879 volume. Under the guise of imitating the traditional genres of Greek poets in order to group the poems "more naturally" ("Preface," p. xiii), Arnold in some degree remade Wordsworth in his own image – an unspoken kinship of another kind.[19]

The idea for the volume came from his publisher, Alexander Macmillan, not from Arnold, in January 1877, and Arnold responded with interest. But not till two years later, in February 1879, after several reminders from Macmillan, did Arnold settle down to the task (*Arnold's Books*, pp. 132–3). His method was to use an interleaved copy, sent him by Macmillan, of "a recent one Volume edition to mark" – that is, presumably, to both select and emend the poems to be included. But Arnold persuaded himself and then Macmillan of the superiority of the 1832 edition of Wordsworth's *Poetical Works* over any other and "marked" the interleaved copy accordingly. In what seems to modern editors a curious method indeed, this marked text was used by the printer to set up the type and the first proofs were then read against a copy of the four-volume edition of 1832 borrowed from Macmillan's partner, George Craik (*Arnold's Books*, pp. 134, 135).

Though Macmillan offered to free Arnold from the task of reading proof, assenting to Arnold's earlier condition that the "printer will read from the 1832 edition & follow all the punctuation &c he finds there," Arnold nevertheless insisted on undertaking the proofreading himself (*Arnold's Books*, p. 136). He argued, "I shall not invariably keep to the text of the edition of 1832; and then, too, there are some explanatory headings of Wordsworth's own to be introduced from the edition of 1858." As a reader of proof he slipped badly at least once, as he learned to his horror when he discovered the sonnet *After-Thought* read "We Men, who in our morn of youth *defiled* / The elements, must vanish; – be it so!" instead of, properly, "defied / The elements."[20] As we shall see, he did depart from the 1832 edition, but he included only one of the "explanatory headings" introduced by John Carter from the Fenwick notes in his edition of Wordsworth's *Poetical Works*, published first in 1857 and reprinted in 1858.[21]

Arnold was given a surprising degree of control over the design of the volume, control Wordsworth himself achieved only through a lifetime of dealings with his several publishers. Arnold suggested the frontispiece, a vignette based on Benjamin Haydon's portrait of Wordsworth; it was engraved for the book by Charles Henry Jeems. He wanted the sonnets to appear "in that close order which [Wordsworth] always used himself – not in the open Italian order," and he selected the type, preferring the smaller "Golden Treasury" type to a larger one chosen by Macmillan which gave fewer lines to a page. Arnold's choices gained him additional space, but they reflect as well his sense of his audience for the volume – a book of poetry he wished to aim at "common intelligence" not at the specialist or the scholar. He was not always successful in shaping the appearance of the text, however; after more than half of the book was set in type he asked to change titles from roman to italic type. The alteration was politely refused by Craik, who pointed out that the roman caps were "the same as your own selections which is a beautiful book and one we wished to copy" (*Arnold's Books*, pp. 133, 136, 139). Arnold did not insist on italics. But when he learned that the publisher had performed the "horrible out-rage" of "sticking my name in huge letters on the back of the volume," he "stopped this when only 750 sets of boards had been printed."[22] Arnold's sense of propriety won out over Macmillan's stratagem to sell copies on the strength of Arnold's name on the spine.

As he had warned Macmillan, Arnold did not rest content with the 1832 readings. In April of 1879 Arnold wrote to Jemima Quillinan, to ask her to recover readings from Wordsworth's edition of 1815 for him. As Arnold explained it,

I am making a selection from Wordsworth's Poems, and I want to restore some of his lines to what they were before he, as dear Mrs. Wordsworth used to say, "tinkered" them. (*Letters*, 2:182 [21 April 1879])

Though, as we shall see, he did not strictly adhere to the 1832 text for his authority, we can appreciate the significance of his choice once we recall that for the stereotype edition in six volumes of 1836 and again for the one-volume edition of 1845 Wordsworth undertook extensive revisions of many of his poems. Arnold selected many of these revised poems for his edition but reprinted them in the unrevised state of 1832, leaving unrepresented Wordsworth's later choices.[23]

Chronology is masked by Arnold's arrangement of the poems in "kinds" and by his almost complete omission of any information on their dates. But Arnold's much deliberated selection itself is a less obvious but no less certain mark of his preference for early poems.[24] Of the 176 poems Arnold placed with such care in his edition (including those added to its several reissues), 104 were published by Wordsworth before 1808, the year Arnold mentioned in his Preface as the end-date for the decade of his "really first-rate work" (Preface, p. xii).

Of the remaining poems, forty-two were published before or in the 1832 edition, the one Arnold would have known as a schoolboy, and as a neighbour of the poet from 1834 when Dr Thomas Arnold, Matthew's father, purchased property at Rydal to provide a place for family holidays but also to be near the now famous Wordsworth.[25] Indeed, there were frequent walks with his father and the poet and visits to the drawing room at Rydal Mount – only a short ramble from Fox How, the home Thomas Arnold built – at first with his family and later alone or with his brother Thomas. Such intimacy no doubt contributed to making Arnold the "Wordsworthian" he confessed himself to be and introduced him to new work by Wordsworth during these years.[26] His sense of closeness to the Wordsworths may also account both for his frequent inattention to his unqualified claim about the "single decade" and for his inclusion of quite personal poems which pay tribute to Wordsworth's family members and friends whom the young Arnold came to know during his stays in the Lake District. Perhaps in his own form of tribute he expanded initials and blanks in poem-titles to identify the subjects whose names Wordsworth kept dark: *To H.C.* became *To Hartley Coleridge, To* ——— became *To Mary Wordsworth*, and so on.

As we would expect, all but two of the twenty-two "Ballads" and "Narratives," in Arnold's arrangement, appeared first in *Lyrical Ballads* (1798 and 1800) or in *Poems, in Two Volumes* (1807). Nor is it surprising that thirty-three of forty "Lyrical" poems originate in these publications. The other three "kinds," "Sonnets," "Poems Akin to the Antique, and Odes" and "Reflective and Elegiac Poems," draw more evenly from the span of Wordsworth's career. The claim that Arnold ignored "major" works like *The Excursion* (1814) and *The Prelude* (1850), a view encouraged by Arnold himself in his Preface, is not entirely true: they are represented, respectively, by *Margaret*, a "Narrative" which Arnold drew from the first book of *The Excursion* by excising the lines about the Pedlar and giving Margaret's story a new title, and by printing the excerpts from *The Prelude* which Wordsworth himself cut from the poem and published separately in *Lyrical Ballads* and Coleridge's *The Friend*. It is true, however, that Arnold's volume gives no sense of the full shape or argument of these long poems.

Arnold's respect for Wordsworth's skill with the sonnet form is expressed in the large number he included (sixty-six) and in his careful selection of them. A significant block of twenty-two sonnets justly comes from the two fine sequences which appeared in 1807 in *Poems, in Two Volumes*, "Miscellaneous Sonnets" and "Sonnets Dedicated to Liberty." For the rest Arnold chose four to ten sonnets from each of the subsequent sequences or collections through 1842, and continued to refine his selection as he added six and dropped eight sonnets through the 1886 issue (see *Arnold's Books*, pp. 144–5). In this way, he produced a selective record of the poet's lifetime use of the sonnet form, a record which clearly belies the "single decade" theory.

III

How did Arnold treat the texts of Wordsworth's poems? We can best see what Arnold did, and why, if we have some sense of what his contemporaries were doing. In 1859 George Routledge published *Poems of William Wordsworth*, selected and edited by Robert Aris Willmott (brought out again in London and New York in 1866). Willmott, doing what many like him had done before, made new poems by excerpting passages from longer pieces and assigning them titles, as in *A Cottage Girl, The Rivulet, Greek Superstitions*, and *The Deserted Cottage*,[27] all from *The Excursion*, and he named or renamed others at will as in *Daffodils, An Evening Scene* (that is, *Expostulation and Reply*), *A Calm Evening* (the sonnet "It is a beauteous Evening, calm and free"), *The Mother's Song* ("Her eyes are wild"), and so on. In such a context, one in which, as Alexander Macmillan put it, "Wordsworth's poems" were "open to be made money of[,] or mincemeat of, by any publisher who chooses to be reckless in what he does, provided only he does business,"[28] we can now examine Arnold's treatment of titles and texts.

Hardly straining contemporary editorial convention, Arnold gave titles to seven untitled poems by printing the first line or part of it above the text in capitals, though he took care to surround it with quotation marks to show its origin ("My heart leaps up when I behold," "I wandered lonely as a cloud," and the five "Lucy" poems). As mentioned earlier, he filled in blanks where Wordsworth had chosen not to give full names. Besides those cited already, he expanded the titles of *Composed at Neidpath Castle* and *To Lady Fitzgerald* to make identities explicit. He shifted or altered titles of paired poems when only one of the pairs was wanted or the pair was to be separated, as in *September 1819* and *Tribute to the Memory of a Dog*. He added subtitles with additional information in some cases, explaining the original context of *To the Rev. Dr. Wordsworth* and providing the date of *Extempore Effusion upon the Death of James Hogg*, and in one instance he recovered a discarded subtitle, probably with the same motive (*A Farewell. Composed in the Year 1802*). Oddly, in one famous poem he shifted Wordsworth's own title to subtitle status, and recalling perhaps the Wordsworths' informal name for the poem, retitled *Resolution and Independence* as *The Leech Gatherer, or, Resolution and Independence*.[29]

But Arnold was not averse to inventing his own titles for several of Wordsworth's poems which the poet left nameless. I've mentioned *Margaret*, Arnold's title for her story excerpted from *The Excursion*, the only such "poem" excerpted by Arnold from a longer work.[30] After first discarding it, Arnold placed the lyric "Yes, it was a mountain Echo" after *To the Cuckoo* and dubbed it *The Cuckoo Again*; "When, to the attractions of the busy world," Wordsworth's prelusive elegy for his sailor brother John, was titled *The Fir-Grove Path*; and Sara Hutchinson's favourite sonnet, "Methought I saw the footsteps of a throne," became, unequivocally, *Death*. Perhaps most interesting of these exercises in naming the nameless is Arnold's inventing a title for Wordsworth's "Calais Beach" poem – "It is a beauteous Evening, calm and free." Though Wordsworth experimented with the first line, eventually restoring the original, he never titled the sonnet. Arnold's title, *Composed Upon the Beach Near Calais, 1802*, is accurate, of course, and analogous to the title of the contemporary sonnet Wordsworth called *Composed By the Sea-side, Near Calais, August 1802*. But Arnold's title draws attention as well to *his* play upon Wordsworth's poem in his own *Dover Beach*. The octave of Wordsworth's sonnet describes what lies before him to the west:

> It is a beauteous Evening, calm and free;
> The holy time is quiet as a Nun
> Breathless with adoration; the broad sun
> Is sinking down in its tranquillity;
> The gentleness of heaven is on the sea:
> Listen! the mighty Being is awake,
> And doth with his eternal motion make
> A sound like thunder – everlastingly.

Compare these lines with the opening of Arnold's poem (published in 1867) in which he looks eastward toward France:

The sea is calm to-night.
The tide is full, the moon lies fair
Upon the straits; – on the French coast the light
Gleams and is gone; the cliffs of England stand,
Glimmering and vast, out in the tranquil bay.

But Arnold's "eternal note of sadness" and his sense of the duplicity of Nature ("which seems / To lie before us like a land of dreams, / So various, so beautiful, so new"), is in stark and deliberate contrast to Wordsworth's hope-filled sestet, addressed to the "Child" – his daughter Caroline:

Dear Child! dear Girl! that walkest with me here,
If thou appear'st untouched by solemn thought,
Thy nature is not therefore less divine:
Thou liest in Abraham's bosom all the year;
And worshipp'st at the Temple's inner shrine,
God being with thee when we know it not.

Following the same structural pattern, Arnold addresses *his* "love" in the final stanza, but only to emphasize their isolation "on a darkling plain / Swept with confused alarms of struggle and flight, / Where ignorant armies clash by night."[31] Naming Wordsworth's poem to echo his own echoing poem is a fine Arnoldian irony.

In another move reminiscent of his own habits of poetic composition, Arnold gathered up what subsequently came to be known as the "Lucy" poems in a single sequence to tell a story. He seems to have been the first editor of Wordsworth to do so in this complete form.[32] Wordsworth himself *never* did so. Four were composed in 1798–99 in Goslar, Germany, and the fifth in 1801, two years after his return to England. The first four were probably composed in this order: "A slumber did my spirit seal," "She dwelt among th'untrodden ways," "Strange fits of passion have I known," and "Three years she grew in sun and shower." They were printed in the second volume of *Lyrical Ballads* (1800), not in their chronological order, but in a rearranged grouping of three ("Strange fits," "She dwelt" and "A slumber") with the fourth ("Three years") appearing separately later in the volume. When he wrote the fifth ("I travelled") Wordsworth told Mary Hutchinson it was to follow "She dwelt" but later told the printer to place it after "A slumber." He then cancelled this instruction and published the poem in 1807 among a miscellaneous group of lyrics. Thus, even prior to inventing the idea of classes for his poems, Wordsworth did not think of keeping the "Lucy" poems together in any continuous narration.[33]

Wordsworth first gave shape to his plan to classify his poems in a letter to Coleridge in 1809. In this arrangement he placed the poems "about Lucy" among those that "relate to the fraternal affections to friendship and to love and to all those emotions, – which follow after childhood in youth and early manhood." Thus, while implying that they participated with other poems in a narrative of growth and change, he did not specify which "Lucy" poems he meant to include.[34] In a more fully developed manuscript list of the "classes" of poems which he drew up in 1811–12, Wordsworth placed four of the poems (excluding "A slumber") in three different classes: Affections ("Strange fits"), Imagination ("Three years"), and Elegiac poems ("I travelled" and "She dwelt"). In the 1815 *Poems*, where the classes were introduced, he printed only three of the five, in two classes, omitting the two he designated as "elegies," retaining "Strange fits" in Affections and "Three years" in Imagination, and adding "A slumber" to Imagination. And finally, in 1820 he arranged all five as they were to stand through his lifetime – "Strange fits," "She dwelt," and "I travelled" in Affections and "Three years" and "A slumber" in Imagination – without ever marking them as a free-standing sequence of "love poems."[35]

In Arnold's own *Poems* ("First Series"), published in 1853, he included a sequence of six love poems addressed to "Marguerite" called *Switzerland*. In his collected *Poems*, published in 1869, he retitled and rearranged the set, now a sequence of eight poems. The new arrangement, with the added poems, tells a story that spans ten years: the titles are *A Memory Picture, Meeting, Parting, A Farewell, Absence, Isolation. To Marguerite, To Marguerite – Continued,* and *The Terrace at Berne (Composed Ten years after the Preceding)*. Again, in the 1878 *Selected Poems* (the volume Macmillan was using as the pattern for *Poems of Wordsworth*), Arnold dropped the first poem from the sequence and moved *Absence* to follow *To Marguerite – Continued*, keeping this trimmer story-line through subsequent editions.[36] As an editor, though he does not extend his storyteller role so far as to *name* each of the "poems about Lucy,"[37] Arnold clearly drew them out of their quite distinct sequences in Wordsworth's two "classes" to make a connected narrative that Wordsworth himself chose *not* to make. As Arnold's arrangement tells the "story," "Strange fits of passion have I known" introduces the speaker and his attitudes toward Lucy; "Three years she grew in sun and shower" tells Lucy's story from "Nature's" point of view; "She dwelt among the untrodden ways" retells her story from the narrator's somewhat distanced view; "A slumber did my spirit seal" returns us to the narrator's feelings and perceptions; and "I travelled among unknown men" is, like Arnold's *The Terrace at Berne*, the narrator's retrospective musing upon his experience. While he played no active part in initiating the search for the identity of "Lucy," the implicit narrative derived from Arnold's arrangement of the five poems contributed to their popular reception as a continuous story of developing love and the lover's ensuing grief over his loss of the beloved.[38]

IV

Even by the editorial standards of his day it was a serious lapse on Arnold's part not to point out in his Preface that he was presenting "early" texts by more or less following the 1832 readings. Because Wordsworth did not alter them after 1832, in more than a third of the poems Arnold's chosen copy text does not differ from Wordsworth's final text, but in some, "Strange fits of passion have I known" and *Song of the Feast of Brougham Castle*, for example, Arnold's 1832 text preserves a state very close to the first printing and presents a text startlingly different from versions Wordsworth produced in 1836 and 1845 when he undertook extensive revision before going to press with new printings. Less dramatic perhaps, but hiding radical changes nevertheless, is Arnold's choice of the 1832 version of *The Brothers*, a poem that in 1820 and 1827 underwent much revision, which is reflected in Arnold's text, and again in 1836 considerably more reworking, which is not.

More curious than these revivals of early versions are the many texts which can only be called eclectic in make-up. Arnold's *Laodameia* (improving on Wordsworth's spelling of the title character's name, "Laodamia") follows the 1832 readings throughout except for lines 158–63, the few lines from 1815 which he requested from Jemima Quillinan, despite the fact that the 1832 printing departs from those of 1815 and 1820 in yet another half-dozen lines. Indeed, Arnold's preference for early readings was less than a consistent principle, for he brought back the poem *Alice Fell*, omitted by Wordsworth from 1820 through 1832, by adopting the 1845 version, much revised. He was not above "tinkering" a fair number of Wordsworth's poems himself, not by inventing new lines as he did titles, but by mixing disparate printings in one poem. In *To the Daisy* ("In youth from rock to rock I went") he adopted 1845 readings for the first seventy-two lines, 1832 for the next four, and 1845 again for the last four. Other such mixed texts are *The Green Linnet, To a Highland Girl, The Solitary Reaper, Ode to Duty, To Thomas Clarkson, The Trossachs, Lines Left upon a Seat in a Yew-tree, Beggars* (with readings from three different editions), *Sequel to the Foregoing (Beggars), A Poet's Epitaph*, and *Elegiac Stanzas*. Indeed, for most of the poems Wordsworth published after 1832, Arnold did not exercise his preference for choosing "untinkered" texts at all, going to the versions in the 1845 one-volume edition (or later) for poems first published in the collections of 1835 or 1842.

As an editor of Wordsworth, so R.H. Super has said, Arnold "was fussy but not scientific" (*Prose*, 9:337). But no editor operates in a vacuum, however scientific. So basic a matter as whether to choose an early or late form of the poetic text is still hotly debated by modern editors, and the decision reached cannot be free of the editor's (or reader's) personal predilection and theoretical bias. And even though editorial standards have long surpassed Arnold's eclectic methods, as both poet and editor he provides a rich example of a reader's role, and something of his motives, in shaping the text he reads. Considering the results of Arnold's work on the selections overall, we can go further. Anxious to influence Wordsworth's reputation as the fine lyric and narrative poet he saw him to be, Arnold built up his text accretively, if not systematically, to that end. He saw Wordsworth as a fellow poet suffering from neglect and misreading. Not surprisingly he thought the older man's work looked the better the more it resembled his own. Knowing precisely where on Harold Bloom's "map of misreading" Arnold's "transumption" of Wordsworth falls is less important, perhaps, than recognizing Arnold as a poet/scholar defending himself by literally and imaginatively reshaping his poetic precursor.[39]

4 Women and Words in Keats (with an Instance from *La Belle Dame sans Merci*)

RONALD TETREAULT

It has become commonplace to praise Keats as a moral hero, bravely enduring the ravages of disease and disappointment until he makes his awkward bow from the stage of the tragedy that can be constructed from his life. His writing, however, is a different matter, for it offers no cathartic reconciliation. That calm of mind with which he faced his death ("Now you must be firm," he reassured Severn, "for it will not last long")[1] is missing from a text marked again and again by passion and uncertainty. Yet these, rather than any faith he may have achieved, may be the very values which make Keats still worth reading. We could not care less today whether the Romantics spilled their religion or merely tried to put it into new bottles. The product seems to matter less than the process to readers who turn to poetry not to find a testament of belief, or even to meet with a record of experience, but to delight in the play of a complex structure that seeks – never with total success – to master anxiety.

One of the many things at stake in the game of Keats's text is whether to prefer the spirit or the flesh, the mind or the body, a conflict whose trace is sufficiently evident throughout the history of Western civilization. This clash is apparent in the varying responses of his readers no less than in the "poet himself." On the one hand, something of a puritan strain in American criticism during this century has elevated consciousness over the senses in Keats, perhaps in justifiable reaction to the Pre-Raphaelite taste for the sensuous in his poetry. Amy Lowell's detection of a religion of beauty and "the wisdom of virtue" in his text helped establish Keats as a serious thinker, an author who in Lionel Trilling's words "was nothing if not a man of ideas," a writer whose "heroic vision" was blessed with the "wisdom of maturity";

such a reading is canonized in Aileen Ward's claim that one of the "central motives" of Keats's poetry is "the attempt to reach a transcendent realm of the spirit through poetry."[2] A concomitant of this body of criticism is the belief that Keats developed as a poet precisely to the extent that he was able to outgrow mere sensation and surmount it by reaching for a higher kind of truth intuited by the imagination.

Recent British criticism, however, has given a renewed emphasis to sexuality in Keats's poetry, most evident in John Bayley's contention that "the body ... is the centre of Keats's poetry."[3] This re-evaluation of the erotic in Keats's poetry quite naturally finds a focus in his relations with women and his attitude toward them. Keats had a profound need to love and be loved, but he found immense complications in the economy of desire. Accordingly, this view of Keats stresses not his achieved (or even projected) certainties but his uncertainty, not his wisdom but his anxiety and guilt.

As usual, the critics fail to agree. One school, and that a very influential one, locates the centre of Keats's poetic project in a spiritual quest for goodness, truth, and beauty; the other sees the centre in the urge to satisfy more immediate physical and psychic needs. Whether Keats's poetry is brought into focus more clearly by the supposition of his moral idealism or by the force of his sexual desire defines the terms of a dispute that is not easy to settle. At first sight these two views seem poles apart; reconcile them how we will, whether through a progression from sensation to thought or through a marriage of coexisting principles, the tension between them remains. Perhaps the difficulty arises from the attempt to locate a centre to Keats's poetry at all, for once we do we seem compelled to determine which of the two is primary and to privilege one over the other. In the process, the play between them is too easily lost. On second look, we may be able to see that neither moral idealism nor sexual fantasy is the real problem, but rather the medium in which they are expressed. Keats is after all a poet, and one who furthermore is dying: language and time are his limiting factors. Putting into words the fleeting moment inevitably creates distortions and disjunctions, so that it may be well to read the text of Keats neither as coming from an origin like "the body" nor working toward the end of "a transcendent realm of the spirit." We may read it instead as the fruit of an unresolvable tension, taking our cue from Walter Jackson Bate's evocative and carefully phrased characterization of Keats's poetry as "the drama of the heart's debate with actuality."[4]

The kind of reassurance that allowed Keats to say that "fine writing is next to fine doing the top thing in the world" (*Letters*, 2:146) comes into question when we examine other passages in praise of reading and writing with the problem of language in mind. Moved to emulation by the examples of Shakespeare and Milton, Keats rejoiced in the prospect of becoming a great author himself:

I am convinced more and more every day [he wrote Bailey] that (excepting the human friend Philosopher) a fine writer is the most genuine Being in the World – Shakespeare and the paradise Lost every day become greater wonders to me – I look upon fine Phrases like a Lover. (*Letters*, 2:139)

The qualifications that make writing and writers somehow second best to active benevolence are in themselves troubling, for they hint at an ambivalence toward language. Nor should we be so misled by the ease and charm of his own picture of himself as a lover of the word that we overlook the implications of the trope (and a very common one it is in Keats) that draws a likeness between using language and being in love. Loving and reading, loving and writing, are so often associated in Keats that it is worth considering what they can have in common.

For Keats, reading was not just an activity but also a way of trying to understand the world and an attempt to get a grip on his experience of it. But often that experience was one of a fleeting actuality, where his reach exceeded his grasp. A passage from an early poem supplies an example:

> Stop and consider! life is but a day;
> A fragile dew-drop on its perilous way
> From a tree's summit; a poor Indian's sleep
> While his boat hastens to the monstrous steep
> Of Montmorenci. Why so sad a moan?
> Life is the rose's hope while yet unblown;
> The reading of an ever-changing tale ... (*Sleep and Poetry*, 85–91)[5]

The thought of the transience of life is a venerable commonplace, but when Keats introduces images of falling or a potential fall, especially when it is unanticipated, the topos becomes coloured by his recurrent anxieties. The dew-drop cannot foresee its end, but the picture of the Indian unconsciously drawing toward a precipitate death has at once urgency (for he could awake and try to avert his fate) as well as a profound existential terror *lest* he awake and see that his fate is inevitable. The passage places life thoroughly in the context of time, with an insistence on time running out, and sees reading strictly within these same temporal limits. A change of mood is suggested in the later lines, for to say "Life is ... the reading of an ever-changing tale" is to comprehend life through the metaphor of reading as a process of incessant deciphering of meanings, taking delight in their play. But the fact of death lingers from the preceding lines, casting a pall over the pleasure of pursuing ever-changing meanings, and renewing the urgency of a demand for the recovery of truth. Still the lines seem to ask whether any truth can compensate for the truth of death, any more than the Indian awake would be better off than the Indian asleep. Even if "Life is ... the reading of an ever-changing tale" to Keats, both terms of the metaphor remain highly problematic and troubling.

Nevertheless, reading was an essential activity for Keats, as necessary to his soul as food was to his body. He stands out among the Romantics in so clearly attributing his awakening as poet not to an epiphany of nature but to an epiphany of reading. His sonnet *On First Looking into Chapman's Homer* not only tries to recover this moment, but reminds us how much Keats's responses to experience were mediated by words, both by those he read and by those he wrote.[6] Just how vital reading was to Keats is recalled by Cowden Clark, who frequently observed him in the act: "He devoured rather than read." It is strange how metaphors of eating constantly seem to intrude themselves into descriptions of those most characteristically Keatsian activities, reading, loving, and writing. The figure hints at a need for sustenance, a drive toward something that would appease a hunger not just for pleasure but for truth, permanence, and creative energy. "How many bards ... have ever been the food of my delighted fancy" exclaims Keats in a sonnet, using the metaphor to trope his love of reading toward his desire to write.

Ever since the psychoanalyst Stephen Reid pointed out that "ingestion is Keats's primary mode of experience," images of eating have been objects worthy of attention in Keats's poetry.[7] Let us examine them, however, not as expressions of some kind of Keatsian psychopathology, but for the patterns of figuration they generate in his text. As a metaphor for reading, eating figures a need for spiritual sustenance as an urgent quest for a food that will satisfy the hunger for experience. As a metaphor for loving, eating figures the desire for woman as an all-consuming passion to encompass and control. And as a metaphor for writing, eating figures the quest for truth as an act of appropriation, an attempt to absorb the substance of the world into the self. Reading as eating implies the desirability of finding the right food, which is to say not just the right books but the right meaning in what is read. Seen in this way, the dangers of misreading and misunderstanding are every bit as grave as the effects of a bad diet. Loving as eating implies the reduction of the beloved to the status of mere object without needs and desires of her own, existing purely to satisfy the needs of her lover. The risk of misreading the lady is a hidden peril in Keats's text, then, of which *La Belle Dame sans Merci* is only one instance. Writing as eating implies the recovery of a fleeting presence which is represented by the word even as it disappears into time. Such a process may be at work in the great odes, and is explicitly featured in the act of bursting "Joy's grape" in the *Ode on Melancholy*. Someone who "lov'd the principle of beauty in all things" (*Letters*, 2:263) in quite this way is in danger of killing the things he loves. Thus, women and words are constantly jeopardized in Keats's text.

The association of reading, loving, and writing as acts of possession first comes into focus in Keats's writing about his reading of Milton. One of his annotations in his copy of *Paradise Lost* draws the connection in most vivid terms:

Milton [writes Keats] is "sagacious of his Quarry," he sees Beauty on the wing, pounces upon it and gorges it to the producing his essential verse.[8]

Such a predatory approach to the otherness of Beauty introduces a note of violence into the relation between the artist and his materials that is not altogether missing from Keats's work, though carefully held in check. His poetry seldom attacks the other so directly, seemingly preferring seductiveness in its hunt for both truth and the ideal female counterpart. More to Keats's taste is the manner in which Milton's Adam gains his Eve, an episode in Milton's poem that obviously made as deep an impression on Keats as it has on his commentators. His letter on Adam's dream has become a fulcrum for more than one interpreter who has sought to locate the essence of Keats in the visionary imagination:[9]

I am certain of nothing [he confessed to Bailey] but of the holiness of the Heart's affections and the truth of Imagination – What the imagination seizes as Beauty must be truth – whether it existed before or not – for I have the same Idea of all our Passions as of Love they are all in their sublime, creative of essential Beauty. ... The Imagination may be compared to Adam's dream – he awoke and found it truth. (*Letters*, 2:184–5)

Since what he finds is Eve, his dream come true in waking life, Adam's dream may serve as a provisional literary origin for Keats's tendency to figure truth as a woman. What must be stressed, though, is that both here are objects of love and desire. In the eighth book of *Paradise Lost*, God promises Adam to form Eve "exactly to thy heart's desire" – she will be

Thy likeness, thy fit help, thy other self,
Thy wish, exactly to thy heart's desire.   (8:450–1)

As much as the depiction of woman as projection of the heart's desire suggests narcissistic self-deception, so the identification of this woman with a literal truth risks failure to seize reality as anything more than the fulfilment of a passionate wish. To capture such a truth in words adds a further dimension of complexity. No less than true love and true meaning, the beauty of women and the truth of words remain elusive quarry for Keats.

However much Keats might seek to tolerate their elusiveness, his pursuit of Beauty and Truth was troubled by quite human and understandable acts of appropriation. His insistence that "what the imagination *seizes* as Beauty must be truth" is very much at odds with the attitude formulated only one month later as "Negative Capability" ("that is when a man is capable of being in uncertainties, Mysteries, doubts, without any irritable reaching after fact & reason," *Letters*, 1:193). Though he acknowledged the wisdom of surrendering his desire for the beautiful woman and the true word, he often in practice surrendered *to* it. Nor can he be blamed for violating his own theories, for the surrender of desire is, after all, akin to the surrender to death. Torn between his best intentions and the pressing demands of his finite existence, Keats's poems burst with an intensity created by this tension between the ideal and the real.

Any suspicion that Keats might follow Milton's example and "gorge" upon otherness seems at first an unworthy one. Keats's tendency to idealize women should be obvious, especially to anyone who has managed to read all of *Endymion*. The youth's devotion to the moon-goddess Cynthia, who first visits him in a dream as Eve does Adam, is total. Hailing her as "that completed form of all completeness ... that high perfection of all sweetness" (1.606–7), he embarks on a quest for his true love that is fulfilled when he recovers in a mortal woman the ideal he has sought. This awe of female perfection is evident in a more clearly erotic moment in an early poem where he meditates on "the soft rustle of a maiden's gown":

> How she would start, and blush, thus to be caught
> Playing in all her innocence of thought.
> O let me lead her gently o'er the brook,
> Watch her half-smiling lips, and downward look;
> O let me for one moment touch her wrist;
> Let me one moment to her breathing list;
> And as she leaves me may she often turn
> Her fair eyes looking through her locks auburne.   (*I Stood Tip-Toe*, 99–106)

His reiterated requests to touch her, watch her, and listen to her breathing hint at guilty pleasures, but the maiden departs with all her attractive innocence intact.

This chivalric attitude toward women, typical in one of Keats's era and class, conceals a difficulty, for though it often pictures women as better than they are it can as often paint them as worse. In another early reflection on the female sex, Keats's yearnings acquire a tinge of literary convention:

> Heavens! how desperately do I adore
> Thy winning graces; – to be thy defender
>   I hotly burn – to be a Calidore –
> A very Red Cross Knight – a stout Leander –
> Might I be loved by thee like these of yore.
>   ("Woman! when I behold thee flippant, vain," 10–14)

Though expressing the code of knightly behaviour, these lines assume an air of patronizing condescension by implying that the lady stands in need of defence at all. This reduction of woman to inferior status is clinched later in the verse when Keats exclaims, in a tone that may as well be exasperation as admiration, "God! she is like a milk-white lamb that bleats / For man's protection" (31–2). Keats's guardian urge here relegates woman to the level of helpless and dependent beast, one to which a sentimental attachment might be formed were it not that lambs are too often led to the slaughter. Such unpleasant associations are inevitable in this clumsy apprentice piece when Keats reaches for a simile to express his desires toward the lady:

> ... when I mark
>   Such charms with mild intelligences shine,
> My ear is open like a greedy shark,
>   To catch the tunings of a voice divine.   (25–8)

Predation, however repressed, returns in this violent image of desire, and with it the terror of being eaten whole. Fortunately, ingestion as a figure for love is never so blatant and repelling in his better-known poetry. Keats is usually capable of representing love-play in subtler terms, as this favourite extract indicates:

> O for ten years, that I may overwhelm
> Myself in poesy. ... First the realm I'll pass
> Of Flora, and old Pan: sleep in the grass,
> Feed upon apples red, and strawberries,
> And choose each pleasure that my fancy sees;
> Catch the white-handed nymphs in shady places,
> To woo sweet kisses from averted faces, –
> Play with their fingers, touch their shoulders white
> Into a pretty shrinking with a bite
> As hard as lips can make it ...   (*Sleep and Poetry*, 96–109)

There is an easy and assured movement in these lines from eating fruits to catching elusive beings to kissing quite tangible girls to biting their shoulders with aroused passion. Yet this is an aspect of Keatsian sexual fantasy no less prominent than that of vulnerable innocence. Living in an age that had no clear concept of independent adult womanhood, Keats can only picture woman in extreme terms.[10] Whether goddess or nymph, angel or demon, virgin or whore, woman has an ambiguous status in Keats's text. It is small wonder that Keats sometimes worried, as he confided to Bailey, that "I have not a right feeling towards women" (*Letters*, 1:341).

The fact that Keats could be deeply concerned about his "feeling towards women" must restrain any urge we may feel to take him to task for what many would identify as a sexist attitude. And even if he didn't struggle against it, his masculinity is hardly his fault. Keats's view of women, after all, is less diabolical than it is commonplace; he had merely assimilated the discourse of love current in his age. The phallocentric gestures of objectification, possessiveness, and jealousy typify much male writing (and thinking, too), and in this regard it must be admitted that Keats's was by no means the worst. He had the sensitivity to be disturbed when these tendencies asserted themselves in his writing, and he had the imagination to offer them resistance, but assert themselves they all too often did, and in a way that contradicted his better instincts. His habits of loving, as well as of writing, often seem to be in tension with his theories and wishes. But that tension was a creative one, a source of his intensity, and a reminder that our aim as critics ought to be not to pass moral judgment on Keats but to examine how his text functions.

The anxieties about women that pervade Keats's text were by no means absent from his relationship with Fanny Brawne. Although he found in her a rare combination of a maiden he could worship with a woman who could return his affection, his passion for her so far outstripped anything that so young and inexperienced a girl could be expected to comprehend that she was sometimes frightened by it. "Why may I not speak of your Beauty," he implores her in a letter of 1819, "since without that I could never have loved you – I cannot conceive any beginning of such love as I have for you but Beauty" (*Letters*, 2:127). More than embarrassed by his ardour, Fanny seems to be desperately trying to defend herself from his all-consuming passion for her. "I kiss'd your writing over in the hope you had indulg'd me by leaving a trace of honey," the same letter concludes, playing once again upon the metaphor of loving as eating.

As one might say to a child in jest, "I'll eat you up, I love you so," Keats in deadly earnest might have swallowed up Fanny Brawne if he could. No less than his letters, his love poems to Fanny sometimes express a possessiveness that is very disturbing. One sonnet, written late in 1819 and usually taken to be addressed to her, insists:

O, let me have thee whole, – all, – all – be mine!
    That shape, that fairness, that sweet minor zest
Of love, your kiss, those hands, those eyes divine,
    That warm, white, lucent, million-pleasured breast, –
Yourself – your soul – in pity give me all,
Withhold no atom's atom or I die ...   ("I cry you mercy," 5–10)

These lines express more than a desire to have the woman physically: they disclose an impulse to take possession of her soul, her "self," a drive to swallow up her very identity. The speaker would deny his beloved virtually any independent existence, seeking to assimilate her being into his. The metaphor of eating that figures the lady as vital food for the lover surfaces again, this time explicitly, in the ode *To Fanny*, a poem that Robert Gittings places in the context of Keats's raging jealousy:[11]

> Who now, with greedy looks, eats up my feast?
>   What stare outfaces now my silver moon!
> Ah! keep that hand unravished at the least;
>   Let, let the amorous burn –
>   But, prithee, do not turn
> The current of your heart from me so soon.   (*To Fanny*, 17–22)

Keats here ravenously asserts his exclusive claim to Fanny's nurturing power; she is his feast, and should be his alone. He deeply resented the slightest indication that Fanny might feel less strongly about him, or that she might occasionally allow herself the smallest pleasure apart from him. Similarly, the tone of his letters to her can suddenly turn from affection to high-handed accusation:

I have heard you say that it was not unpleasant to wait a few years – you have amusements – your mind is away – you have not brooded over one idea as I have, and how should you? You are to me an object intensely desireable – the air I breathe in a room empty of you is unhealthy. I am not the same to you – no – you can wait – you have a thousand activities – you can be happy without me. Any party, any thing to fill up the day has been enough. How have you pass'd this month? Who have you smil'd with? All this may seem savage in me. You do not feel as I do – you do not know what it is to love ...   (*Letters*, 2:304)

Though Keats's emotional excess may have stemmed from the onset of his illness, frustration and hypersensitivity only served to intensify a tendency to misread the lady already latent in his writings. If his idea of "what it is to love" could approach a fantasy of total possession, it is a tribute to Fanny's gentle nature and her real feelings for him that she was able to put up with the extravagance of his demands.

Fanny Brawne, of course, was not without resources of her own. Though he often saw her as a substitute for the mother he had lost in childhood, a devoted presence from whose breast he could draw psychic as well as physical nourishment, he sometimes found that the obverse of this relationship was his total dependence upon her. She exercised a power over him, a power to dominate his complete attention and absorb his total being, a power that threatened the power he sought to exercise over her. At such moments as he acknowledges it, he is the one to feel as if he were being swallowed up:

I cannot exist without you [he wrote to her late in 1819] – I am forgetful of every thing but seeing you again – my Life seems to stop there – I see no further. You have absorb'd me. I have a sensation at the present moment as though I was dissolving. ... You have ravish'd me away by a Power I cannot resist.   (*Letters*, 2:223–4)

Having sought to master her, her moods and her movements, Keats finds himself being mastered by her, or, more precisely, mastered by his passion for her. Alarmed by her power, he encounters in his love for Fanny something it is beyond his power to control, a power resident in the other to which he seeks to assimilate himself. If he cannot possess, he is willing to be possessed; either way, he identifies otherness with self.

Now this drive to appropriate the other pervades his writing no less than it troubles his relations with women. Keats's inclination to "look upon fine phrases like a Lover" is the key to a whole system of substitutions in his text which draws a likeness between loving and writing and treats woman as a trope for the truth of language. When he wrote as he loved, his text was driven by an insatiable hunger for beauty and truth. That these might serve ends of their own quite apart from the satisfaction of his own desires seems unnerving to Keats; that women might have desires and that words might have powers beyond his control is a prospect he wants to deny because it brings his own power as a man and a poet into question. More than killing the things he loves, he fears being consumed by them. He locates a desire in woman and an energy in the word which threaten to overwhelm his own. Yet when he tries to fix women or words for his own purposes, he finds them slipping away into time. Through the being of one and the medium of the other, he reaches out to grasp an eternal presence only to meet with a baffling absence. The pathetic gesture by which the epistolary Keats seeks to recover Fanny's presence and sustaining powers by kissing the words of her letter over and over is re-enacted by the poetic Keats in search of his muse.

As is customary, Keats's muse is portrayed as female in his text, and the tensions we have been tracing mean his relations with her are troubled. The difficulties he encountered in relating to women seem compelled to repeat themselves in his struggle to come to terms with his poetic ambitions. Sometimes, he would court poetic inspiration like a fickle (and even darkly threatening) mistress:

I know not why Poetry and I have been so distant lately [he writes to his brother George] I must make some advances soon or she will cut me off entirely.   (*Letters*, 2:74)

How to win her compliance deeply concerned this lover of the fine phrase. Curiously, his meditation on how to recover creative energy moves almost immediately in this same letter to an association of poetry and power:

> The language of Poetry naturally falls in with the language of power. I affirm, Sir, that Poetry, that the imagination, generally speaking, delights in power ...

Whether the power that poetry delights in is her own or whether it is the power of the poet who seeks to control her is unclear here, and points to Keats's deep ambivalence as both lover and writer. He loves both women and words at the same time as he fears and mistrusts them. He cannot master his anxiety over the possibility that the poet's power, like the lover's, is merely borrowed, and arises from the assimilation of himself into the power of the other. The possessor now fears being possessed.

The will to possess operates no less in writing than in loving, and manifests itself in Keats's text as a drive to appropriate otherness, this time as meaning, into the self. This urge to mastery emerges in one of Keats's earliest poetic statements of intention:

> ... the events of this wide world I'd seize
> Like a strong giant, and my spirit teaze
> Till at its shoulders it should proudly see
> Wings to find out an immortality.   (*Sleep and Poetry*, 81–4)

Later in the poem, this attitude to the poet's power is qualified by the attribution of gender to his instrument, poetry:

> A drainless shower
> Of light is poesy; 'tis the supreme of power;
> 'Tis might half slumb'ring on its own right arm.
> The very archings of her eye-lids charm
> A thousand willing agents to obey,
> And still she governs with the mildest sway.   (235–40)

Poetry is imaged as both Zeus and Danaë, an accommodating female who at the same time possesses a masculine "might." But her "supreme of power" operates in a very different way from the strong-arm tactics of appropriation. She governs with subtle gestures, and her "mildest sway" seems a resource of female power that remains mysterious to the poet. Once again, trying to master both women and words, Keats has difficulty reading the lady.

The identity of poetry was as elusive to Keats as Fanny Brawne's real intentions. He wanted to be absolutely certain that he possessed knowledge of both, but the true meaning in each case evaded his grasp. The woman who thus escapes like literal truth is multifaceted and changeable, possessing in her transformations a demonic power. It is little wonder then that

Keats should find his muse troublesome when, as in the *Ode on Indolence*, he depicts poetry as female:

> One morn before me were three figures seen ...
> The first was a fair maid, and Love her name;
>   The second was Ambition, pale of cheek,
> And ever watchful with fatigued eye;
> The last, whom I love more, the more of blame
>   Is heap'd upon her, maiden most unmeek, –
> I knew to be my demon Poesy.   (1, 25–30)

We can surmise from his famous journal-letter that Keats saw Ambition as a man (*Letters*, 2:78–9). This figure of masculine power is oddly "pale," like the knight in *La Belle Dame sans Merci*; perhaps his fatigue results from being "ever watchful" to catch beauty and truth on the wing. Love and Poesy are both enticingly female, though the latter bears a demonic aspect. "Demon Poesy" is addressed as "maiden most unmeek," a phrase Bush points out is an inversion of an epithet normally applied in prayer to the Virgin Mary.[12] Far from being a pure, nurturing, and ever-present mother, then, Keats's "demon Poesy" is unmeek in her assertion of her independence from his demands and mercurial in her fleeting visitations. He loves her in spite of her inconstancy, though, for he still believes it possible to recover the presence that is marked by her absence. Trying to possess her, he has become possessed by her.

Keats's attitude toward women is thus reinscribed as an ambivalence toward poetry by the substitution of writing for loving. Just as women must be one of two types for him, so poetry must be either daemon or demon, muse or succubus. She appears to him sometimes in the guise of an otherworldly tutelary genius, sometimes as vexatious sprite, the "deceiving elf" of the *Ode to a Nightingale*.[13] A lover of beauty and truth, Keats can never capture the fleeting moment of their presence in words, for signs can only supply a presence that marks an absence. In the act of writing down, even in the act of speaking the word, the order of the signifier is always already "discrepant by the time of a breath" from the fleeting signified.[14] It is the dimension of time, together with the change and loss temporality entails, that frustrates the poet and the lover alike and drives both, not just to phallic, but to phallogocentric excess. Keats's passionate effort to conjure up Fanny's presence by kissing her writing comes to mind. But Keats can find in those words no simple presence or absence that will satisfy his craving, for everywhere there are only traces, and traces of traces that vanish all too quickly.

La Belle Dame sans Merci can thus be read as an epitome of Keats's relations with women and words.[15] A poem of the erotic imagination, it is as much about poetry as it is about love. From firmly within the perspective of time it calls into question an imaginative experience that seems to transcend time, and conceals a subtext in which language is subject to temporal limits. Above all, it is a poem about loss.

As a poem about love, though, it draws upon the courtly conventions of its medieval literary ancestor. Like Chartier's fifteenth-century work, Keats's poem opens with a description of a love-lorn knight, "so haggard, and so woe-begone," awaiting the renewed favour of his mistress "alone and palely loitering." He bears all the marks of the abandoned lover on his face, though the "fading rose" of his cheeks suggests that the last embers of passion still smoulder within. He tells of his encounter with the now vanished beloved:

> I met a lady in the meads,
>   Full beautiful, a faery's child;
> Her hair was long, her foot was light,
>   And her eyes were wild.

The wildness of the lady's eyes may indicate a passion of her own that would at once answer that of the knight and threaten him with its own power; at the same time, her "wild" eyes might suggest an untameable quality about this lady, like a wary animal unwilling to be caught, or an elusive fairy. We cannot read what her eyes signal any more than the knight can. Her appearance, her actions, and her intentions are all conveyed from his point of view in the poem, and she is subject to his interpretation before she can become available to ours.

Whether we can trust his version of events, which after all is designed to gain our sympathy, is uncertain. Parts of his testimony, indeed, sow doubts. That he met this lady "in the meads" may be innocent enough; but the topos of a man of superior social station who preys upon country maidens is a familiar one. Once again, the garland, the bracelets, and the "fragrant zone" he makes for her seem endearing tokens; yet as images of encirclement they suggest some attempt on his part to capture and even to fetter her. She looks at him, he says, "*as* she did love," but her inarticulate moan may only *seem* sweet to him. After all, sweeping her up onto his horse may be an act of ravishment as much as one of love, a gesture of power as much as one of affection. Her sidelong bending and incomprehensible song might equally be signs of some impulse to escape on her part.

Nevertheless, although the lady can hardly be called the aggressor in this affair, she does seem to co-operate. She feeds the knight on "honey wild," perhaps wild as herself, and "manna dew," a sustenance with divine overtones. And she avers her faith:

> And sure in language strange she said –
>   I love thee true.

She takes him to her home and, though she weeps and sighs, seems to permit his advances. Despite her declaration, the lady seems unreadable, or at least in grave danger of being misread. That is why his description of the onset of their love-making is so troubling:

> And there I shut her wild wild eyes
>   With kisses four.

This moment is reminiscent of the advice to the lover in the *Ode to Melancholy* to "feed deep, deep upon [his mistress's] peerless eyes." The act of possession in Keats's text is imaged again and again as a swallowing up, an overcoming, or at best an indifference to, the conflicting feelings of the lady. The manner of somehow cancelling the expression in the eyes of the beloved suggests an urge to deny female subjectivity, or perhaps to encompass and assimilate its power. What occurs in *La Belle Dame sans Merci* is certainly not a rape, but even so hints at the way an act of love, like an act of reading or writing, is always caught up in the complexities of desire and power.

By his status as warrior, Keats's "knight-at-arms" is a man of power. In his post-coital slumber, the knight dreams of men of superior power, "pale kings and princes," who like him have found disappointment in love. They inform him ominously: "'La belle dame sans merci / Hath thee in thrall!'" But have we at last learned the lady's true identity? Once again, the information the poem provides is backed only by male authority, which is normally enough in a phallocentric tradition where men control the power of naming. But the lady escapes such male determinations. She never identifies herself in the poem, and her silence on this point baffles interpretation. If the lady as signifier is perfectly identical with what the men believe is signified by her behaviour, then she is indeed a *femme fatale*. But the sign is mute. The only power the lady retains in the poem is the power to withdraw, and with her departure the true meaning of the knight's experience is also withdrawn.

Even if we allow the lady an active power of seduction in the poem, her identity as an evil demon who strives to place men "in thrall" is not assured. It is noteworthy that, in commenting on this poem, the major critics to a man insist on placing the lady outside the human circle. This gesture of exclusion applies whether she is viewed negatively (as she is by one extremely distrustful writer who calls her "a fairy mistress from hell") or with greater sympathy as one who bears the knight no malice.[16] It is as if every one agrees that no human being could behave in this way, and certainly no woman. But women have been seduced and abandoned before this, and a reluctance to admit that any woman would dare to turn the tables on her lover perhaps conceals a fear of woman as independent and self-determining subject. The men in the poem find their power challenged by such a personality, and having failed to retain her they languish in their futile hope that she will someday return to their influence. But the lady can be read as a power that defies the male will.

Just as the woman escapes, so words are elusive in this poem. After all, the beautiful lady might be "sans merci" in several senses at once. To be *sans merci* usually means to be merciless or pitiless, or at best "without kindness." It can also mean to be without thanks, suggestive of the lady's abrupt departure without so much as a farewell while the knight sleeps. In another turn of phrase, *se rendre à merci* means to surrender oneself unconditionally, or, more literally, to place oneself at the pleasure or discretion of someone, which of course is precisely what this beautiful lady does not do, hence the negating *sans*. She undermines his act of masculine possession by playing the role of beloved at the same time as she withholds something of herself; hence she survives by playing his game up to a point, but finally asserting her independence of it. The knight, who seems woefully ignorant of such strategies, is left distraught by nostalgia and guilt.

His wish for the lady's return is paralleled in the poem by an urge to recover meaning from words that like her seem to slip beyond reach. Though the lady's former presence is the motive of desire in the poem, her absence is the crucial fact in determining the mood of the poem. Its melancholy, its longing, and its lament for what might have been all stem from the lack of her. The knight's dream, "the latest dream I ever dream'd / On the cold hill's side," is a bitter parody of Adam's dream, for he awakes to find her truth false. He had taken her avowal, "I love thee true," as absolute. But she may have been lying, if only to appease him. Even if she had meant it, though, offering him her love at the time does not guarantee that she would love him for all eternity. She speaks her love "in language strange," a language whose present meanings slip away into time past as quickly as they are uttered, which is the condition of all language and our tragic estrangement from it.

If the knight-at-arms is the phallocentric focus of male will in the poem, it is the poem's narrator who introduces the note of phallogocentric desire into the text. He after all is the one who raises the possibility of a true and permanent meaning at the poem's very outset. "What can ail thee, knight-at-arms" he twice asks, as if the pale lover could fully comprehend what has happened to him. This naïve speaker can only try to shame the knight by drawing analogies from mute nature:

The sedge has wither'd from the lake,
　And no birds sing.
... The squirrel's granary is full,
　And the harvest's done.

In a supposedly simpler world than the human one, there is either depri-
vation or plenitude; to the narrator's understanding, there is either pure
presence or pure absence. But the knight has found that in the world of
time every presence implies an absence, while absence painfully bears the
trace of lost presences. The knight has tried to retain the lady's presence by
setting her on his "pacing steed," an image that can suggest the metre of
poetry; he tries to control her with "kisses four," a number that also hap-
pens to be the number of beats in three out of four lines in the poem. But
still she, together with what she signifies, escapes his acts of appropriation.
Thinking that both meaning and the lady can sometime be recovered is
what "ails" the knight, according to his own opinion: "And this is why I
sojourn here"; but what "this" can mean and what comfort it can offer the
narrator remain uncertain.

It may be said that Keats's celebrated "negative capability" is the cure for
what ails the knight. He must gain a respect for otherness, and school him-
self not to appropriate his poetic object by recognizing that representation
involves a recognition of absence and an acceptance of the necessary fig-
urativeness of all language. He must not search for literal meaning, but
instead enjoy the play of possibilities, becoming (in his famous definition
of negative capability) "capable of being in uncertainties, Mysteries,
doubts, without any irritable reaching after fact & reason" (*Letters*, 1:192).
But was the luxury of incessant deciphering something a dying poet
could afford? The detachment from final meaning Keats seems to rec-
ommend in theory was not always carried out in his poetic practice.
Though he might wish to give women and words free play, and occa-
sionally succeeded, a contrary urge to appropriate and control often
asserted itself in his text. Perhaps he adopted negative capability as a
defence against this tendency in his work, or maybe as an evasion. Or per-
haps Keats simply asked for too much. Given the failure to recover either
the Woman or the Word, negative capability may be only one side of a
heart's debate with actuality.

5 En-Gendering the System: *The Book of Thel* and *Visions of the Daughters of Albion*

TILOTTAMA RAJAN

I

Until recently Blake criticism has conferred a systematic coherence on his work through a canonical reading that contains the errancy of the early texts by making them experiments with or types of the later system.[1] The Bible, which Blake describes as the great code of art, has been the model by which both we and he have read his secular scripture. Assembled out of the writings of many men, and conjoining two cultures, it provides analogies not only for a unification of the authorial canon but also for a hermeneutics of cultural history that we may now recognize as imaginative imperialism. In the later prophecies Blake does indeed experiment with a self-canonization that relies on the hermeneutic code of the Bible to eliminate those differences from himself that he dismisses as self-contradiction (E520;l.92).[2] Thus in *Milton* he develops rules of exegesis, such as the distinction of contraries from negations, to limit the dissemination of meaning in his canon. This interpretive grammar, moreover, is developed within a scene of reading that combines Christian typology with post-Kantian hermeneutics. The Puritan poet revisions his past so as to become his own prophetic reader. Likewise Blake's poem revisits the site of his early work, beginning with a reduced repetition of *The (First) Book of Urizen* that announces *Milton* as the second or perhaps the third book, redeeming the first one from a higher perspective on the spiral of understanding.

But the early texts are very different from *Milton*. We must remember also that the authorized version was not unchallenged, and that the same Blake who used the biblical paradigm to limit reading was profoundly influenced by gnostic heresies that questioned it. Gnosticism made possible Blake's radical humanism as well as his belief that the individual was the source of a knowledge to which the institutional church was a hindrance. This emphasis on the individual challenged belief in a single scriptural canon, and in the hermeneutic fiction that we all understand things in the same way. For as Elaine Pagels suggests, the Gnostics, while they were not relativists, regarded all doctrines including their own "only as approaches to truth."[3] Given the existence of the heresies, the forming of a scriptural canon had been the scene of a struggle in which doctrinal questions were entwined with political issues such as the status of women and the democratization of the structures by which knowledge was transmitted. Blake encountered these problems both explicitly, through his interest in heterodox thought, and as part of the archaeology of the scriptural genre. As he composed his secular scripture he faced the dilemma of whether it was legitimate to construct a canon, and of whether there were not voices excluded by canon formation.

The forming of a canon is part of a cultural strategy that effaces the origins of truth in a moving army of metaphors and metonymies that are sublimated until, as Nietzsche suggests in the well-known passage from "Truth and Falsity in an Ultra-Moral Sense," a people considers them as canonical and unavoidable. Yet Blake's own critique of the canon in *The Marriage of Heaven and Hell* involves a semiological dismantling of terms like good and evil, and not simply an ideological critique of such terms. It is accomplished, in other words, through a revolution in poetic language that gives his own truths an unstably and consciously linguistic existence. This essay considers how the *figure* of woman in two early texts becomes a mirror of the text's cultural production. It does so by looking at Blake's construction of a mobile text that can be read from more than one perspective, as part of the canon and as a heresy against it. By writing these texts as inside views of a female character, Blake enters them as his own reader. He inscribes in them a canonical reading that is in turn subject to questions of cultural hermeneutics: questions about whether everyone does indeed understand things in the same way. Moreover, Blake's early texts differ from the later prophecies in form as well as focalization. Briefly, they use a modular form which juxtaposes discontinuous discursive segments, sometimes spoken by different voices. Though we encounter these segments in a different order, they do not simply unfold into each other: they function as mutually reflecting mirrors that make the reading experience recursive.[4] Most commonly Blake will surround the text with a preludium and a further preface or motto. Often the meaning of the framing or preliminary components is less clear than their structural function, so that there is a defamiliarizing of this function in which the text's form becomes its content. Thus a motto does not simply provide guidance but raises the question of whether there *is* a key to the text's meaning. An introduction does not simply lead into the narrative but makes us reflect on whether the narrative is shaped by the point at which we enter it. The resulting reflection on perspective is encouraged by the relative spatial autonomy of these segments. Because the text marks the seams between its parts, we are aware of the structurality of what we assemble out of it. The parts are foregrounded in a challenge to the hermeneutic circle, with its organicist notion of a correspondence between part and whole. The whole, instead of being what the parts fit into, becomes a shifting effect of the particulars through which we view it.

The oversignification of part over whole marks the text's resistance to totalization, by indicating the priority of a particular perspective to the systems and syntheses created to contain it. That Blake presents events from different perspectives has often been observed. Thus in *Milton* we see events both from the viewpoint of Eternity and from that of Milton as he descends into Generation. But traditionally these perspectives have been aligned in terms of the hermeneutic schema of single to fourfold vision, so that the layering of perspectives in a time that is visionary rather than linear creates a hierarchy that distinguishes partial from complete vision.[5] Yet perspectives in the early texts are juxtaposed rather than cinematically superimposed, so that their relationship is dialogic rather than anagogic. If they form a whole, it is a cubist rather than a visionary whole. Jean Metzinger points out that the aim of cubism is not to recompose the six faces of the cube into an organic whole: "An object has not one absolute form, it has several ... As many images of the object as eyes to contemplate it, as many images of essence as minds to understand it."[6] Augmenting the perspectivism of the early texts is their mobile construction in terms of plates that are left unbound and whose order varies. Blake thus creates what Barthes calls a "writerly" text,[7] denying to it a canonical form and making us aware of its truths as a field of metaphors that we ourselves structure by inscribing in it our own further metaphors. The mobile structure of the text unmakes what H.R. Jauss calls the "substantialist idea of the self-contained work."[8] The text, to accommodate Blake's own term, exists in different "states," accommodating but always situating the perspectives of author and reader.[9] Blake's new practice of reading has two consequences that this essay attempts to explore. It creates a dialogue in which readers do not simply find an ambiguity which is in the text, but open up from different historical vantage-points possibilities that "Blake" may not have foreseen but that nevertheless follow from the overdetermined nature of the text. At the same time by making us aware of how we construct the text from the perspective we bring to it, it also compels us to historicize that perspective, and to recognize it as constituted on the traces of other horizons of expectation inscribed in the text and its reception-history.

Our first text will be *The Book of Thel*, a poem that is often read canonically in the light of Blake's later attacks on the selfhood, as a critique of its virginal protagonist, whose fear of losing her identity prevents her from making the psychological crossing from innocence into experience.[10] In the course of the poem Thel has a series of conversations with a lily, a cloud, and a clod of clay, who reassure her that entry into Generation, which seems like death from her point of view, is from an Eternal perspective part of a regenerative process. The cloud points to the cycle of condensation and rarefaction and argues that when he seems to pass away it is only to be absorbed into the continuum of nature. Similarly the disintegration of the human body as it becomes food for worms fertilizes the earth and nourishes those future generations in whose life the individual lives on.

For those who see Thel as wrong to flee back to the vales of Har, she thus becomes a figure in the argument that the entry into experience is a fortunate fall that will lead to "organized innocence." But whether the cloud and the clod adequately represent "Blake" is far from clear, given that the clod appears in the *Songs* as a figure not just for generosity but also for naïveté. The problem of the signifier, an unmarked problem in any text where one voice speaks for another, is explicitly marked in this poem by the presence of natural objects which serve as figures for "Blake's" voice, and which thus raise issues of representation: whether it be "Blake's" representation of Thel, Thel's representation of herself, or the critic's representation of "Blake." Figures are at the heart of the text's mode of argument: as the highly stylized personification of natural objects suggests, the cyclical construction of time that allows Thel's conversants to imagine organized innocence is linked only *metaphorically* to a human world that may be irrevocably linear in its movement toward death and decomposition. But the poem not only uses figures, it is also about the figures that it uses.

Crucial to our sense that the poem can be read heretically as well as canonically is precisely its use of metaphor or figure as transposition, as a perspective shift that tries to transform one position into another. An initial example is Thel's description of how the lamb "crops" the lily's flowers, a curiously gentle term for what (given Thel's identification with her) is actually the flower's death. The word "crops" picks up the lily's own description of herself as "melting" in the sun, and adds to the metaphorization of withering a disturbing sense that it is not just death that must be refigured, but death caused by others, unnecessary death. In one sense the substitution of the cut flower for the violated person asks us to change our perspective and to see what is horrible to us as natural. But in another sense metaphor suspends this cleansing of the doors of perception at the site of language, making us aware that it is safe to change our perspective only because the poem is a pastoral that constructs an artificially stylized world. And pastoral, as Blake suggests in the *Songs*, may itself be a political convention used to cloud our perception of social violence.

Some sense of a violence that exceeds the ability of Blake's system to contain it emerges in Thel's final monologue, which is the scene not only of her figures but also of ours:

> Why cannot the Ear be closed to its own destruction?
> Or the glistning Eye to the poison of a smile!
> Why are Eyelids stord with arrows ready drawn,
> Where a thousand fighting men in ambush lie?
> Or an Eye of gifts & graces, show'ring fruits & coined gold!
> Why a Tongue impress'd with honey from every wind?
> Why an Ear, a whirlpool fierce to draw creations in?
> Why a Nostril wide inhaling terror trembling & affright
> Why a tender curb upon the youthful burning boy!
> Why a little curtain of flesh on the bed of our desire?   (E6;6:11–20)

Two assumptions have informed commentary on this passage. Although the language is completely inconsonant with any she has used hitherto, we assume that the lines are spoken by a self-projected spectre of Thel rather than by a collective unconscious that might lend them authority. We also assume that "Thel's" questions refer to her fear of "normal" sexual experience, and that since virginity is "wrong" her horror can be dismissed as hysteria. But the referent of the traumatic images is far from clear, for a "thousand fighting men" may just as well refer to war as to sex. In copies that eliminate the last two lines of the passage, with their reference to the "youthful boy" and the "curtain of flesh," the lines point more directly to some amorphous form of social violence the source of which seems lost somewhere in the political unconscious. While the poem leaves us free to think that this unconscious is another figured curtain (perhaps a screen for Thel's sexual fears), its obliteration of precise referents also raises the possibility that our dismissal of her fears may be a screen for our own fears. In other words, the passage also asks us to enter the space Thel flees and to construct what might be there that so violently negates the language of (un)organized innocence.

At the heart of this poem is a deep uncertainty as to whether there is innocence after experience. This uncertainty can be located in elements of the poem's discourse and construction that mark its indeterminacy as deliberate. For one thing, there is the division of a relatively short text into chapters that mark off different discourses from each other, a feature that limits the authority of each character to the chapter that it dominates.

What results is a juxtaposition of different perspectives on the poem's central problem, rather than a continuous narrative that builds up authority for the perspective of eternity and reaches a crisis at which Thel denies that perspective. If Bogen and Erdman are accurate about the chronology of composition, Blake may actually have written the poem in segments marking his own shifts in perspective. Thus it seems that chapter 3 (on the clod and the worm) was executed separately from the first two chapters, and that the final chapter was composed later (no earlier than 1791) as an "'Experience' climax and commentary attached to what may in 1789 have been more purely a poem of 'Innocence.' "[11] The perspectivism of the poem is further emphasized by the motto. Providing us with questions rather than moral prescripts, the motto does not valorize any one point of view. For while the eagle cannot know what is in the pit in the way the mole does, neither can the blind mole wholly see what is there. But while the eagle may see more than the mole, that does not necessarily change the mole's world, which is constituted by its blindness. That wisdom cannot be kept in a silver rod suggests, moreover, that understanding must not be codified in closed forms that provide one law for mole and eagle alike. Each speaker, including Thel, claims such closure, although the dialogical form of the poem belies it. For the lily and the cloud, having delivered their message, retreat to a "silver shrine" and an "airy throne" respectively (E4;2:2, E5;3:24). Only the clod invites Thel into her home, thus potentially opening herself to another perspective which she too avoids by disappearing from the poem thereafter.

By composing the poem in perspectival segments Blake creates a text that exists in different "states," so as to accommodate but always situate the perspectives of both author and reader. As in many of these texts, variant orders for the plates are of symptomatic rather than determinate significance. The existence of offset numbers for the plates that include the narrative prevents us from literally rearranging Thel's history. But the free-floating status of the text's margins (motto, illustrations, etc.) has a suggestive function, in reminding us that even fixed narrative orders can be seen in more than one way: the entry into the graveplot can be seen as a crisis in which Thel refuses wisdom, or it can be viewed as a *peripeteia* that exposes the hollowness of what has gone before. This sense of the poem as existing only in states is reinforced by the most noticeable variant: the relocation of the motto from the beginning to the end in copies N and O. Those who see the motto as a "moral" see it as counselling Thel to accept experience (like the mole), and not to protect herself with symbols of privilege like the rod and the bowl. Shifting it to the end would then reinforce a reading of the poem as a critique of Thel, and would place a space between us and the sympathetic impact of her final speech. But we can also read the motto existentially, and see it as dismissing the visionary eagle in favour of the mole, who understands that there is no "vision" beyond "experience." In that case Thel, who has entered the darkness in which all transcendental consolations are dissolved, would actually have lived by the motto whose location at the end would refigure it as a confirmation of nausea. As the significance of the shifts depends on the meaning we attribute to the individual segment, so the mobile structure of the text generates a radically perspectival reading experience.

Perhaps the most disturbing aspect of the text has to do with the deferral of authority for the credal passages. For these passages are either not spoken by the characters to whom they pertain, or are dubiously authorized by an anthropomorphism that makes voice a figure. Thus the conversation with the lily breaks up into two discursive segments, repeating itself so as to produce differences within the creed of self-sacrifice, and displacing the enunciation of that creed between the lily and Thel in such a way that it is finally spoken by no one. The lily begins by pointing out that she too is vulnerable, but that God watches over her, and when she "melts" in the summer (a pointedly gentle word for "withers") it is "To flourish in eternal vales" (E4;1:24–25). The notion of a lily having an afterlife is of course a pathetic fallacy, and that fact is registered in the transference of the discourse to Thel, who sustains the fiction that death is not painful, but with complications that betray an increasing anxiety. This time the lily's death is not part of a natural cycle but is produced by others: by the lamb "cropping" her flowers (E4;2:6). There is also no reward in eternity, nothing being posited beyond the natural world. The continued pastoralization of death masks a displacement the significance of which Thel herself may not grasp. The consolation of "eternity" has been dropped because it has not satisfied Thel's desire for reassurance about *this* world. And the lily has not dealt with the problem of unnecessary suffering implicit in the fact that the lamb eats the flower. In the second set of lines the lily is still described as smiling in the face of her sorrows (E4;2:6). But then these lines are not spoken by the lily herself, but by Thel, nervously voicing what may be the conventional wisdom. When Thel asks the lily to reconfirm her aestheticization of suffering, the latter does not answer but refers her to the cloud. The cloud in fact does take Thel's suggestion for re-visioning death as mutability to the appropriately pietistic conclusion. But the cloud is also the only male character in the trio who speak to Thel, a fact which is of significance in terms of the gendering of voices which (as we shall see) plays so important a role in this poem.

Perhaps the most disturbing of these deferrals comes in the final chapter, where the clod, a female character, seemingly confirms the cloud's wisdom. In response to Thel's identification of the worm with unaccommodated man, "an infant wrapped in the Lillys leaf" (E5;4:3), the clod assures Thel that God cherishes even the most ugly of things (E5;5:1–4).

Whether the clod's reassurance that God values the worm who will eat her properly answers Thel's fear of becoming fertilizer is not something we shall explore. But it is also notable that the worm, who lacks the cloud's airy throne and lives in a house of clay, never adds its voice to the chorus of reassurances. Instead the clod speaks for the worm, who simply weeps. Thus when Thel finally decides to confront experience, she does so from within a network of evasions and on the basis of what can be no more than a representation of the worm's condition as a metaphor for her own, the worm's silence marking a certain resistance to metaphor and thus to the idealizing imagination. Or it may be that the clod does not even claim to speak for the worm. It may be that because Thel has addressed herself to the worm, she *takes* the clod's reassuring words as applying to the worm and concludes that God cherishes it "With milk and oil" (E6;5:11). But while the clod is said to bend over the worm in "milky fondness," it is on the clod's head that God pours "his oil" (E5;4:9, 5:1). Whether the clod's words of wisdom refer to herself or also to the worm is thus unclear. And functions like reference and metaphor are in fact at the heart of this poem, which is set up as a conversation with natural objects figured as speaking, and which thus brings to the foreground the problem of how we perceive the world through language. What is clear from the way dis-courses are juxtaposed and characters are made to speak for each other is that in the lived world reference operates through metaphor and is thus fundamentally ambiguous. We make one situation refer, by metaphorical extension, to another. The ambiguity generated in the gap between the clod's words and Thel's understanding of them raises a larger problem about the reference of the abstract to the concrete. Can the clod's experience stand for that of the worm or for that of Thel, and can credal abstractions refer to concrete existential situations?

The poem's self-reflection on its figures, and its operation as a semiotic screen on which readers must view their figures, is mobilized around the central figure in the text, Thel. In both *Thel* and *Visions* Blake focuses on female characters and both women use a language that is highly figurative, naming their experience in terms of something else, as though they lack unmediated access to their own lives. The depiction of understanding as en-gendered through the intermediary of figures is particularly striking in *Thel*, where the protagonist invents three figures for herself – a flower, a cloud and a clod – and where she often speaks of herself in the third per-son. The poem, of course, is not about female identity in the way Mary Wollstonecraft's novels are. Rather it is about an aborted transition from innocence to experience that Blake *represents* through a young girl. The questions it raises thus pertain first of all to the *semiotic* status of woman in the economy of mythmaking. Or more precisely, we can read woman as both a signifier, a figure for a certain life situation, and as a suppressed referent, someone who must be figured in certain ways to construct her as the appropriate signifier. This crossing of figure and referent has the effect of interrupting the unambiguous functioning of the signifier, and of making it the site of a resistance to any attempt to fit it into the system. The female figure – for she is always a figure – thus becomes a mirror that reflects back the metaphors used to compose her identity. And because she is a figure in an argument that the poem puts into action but also textualizes, the text's reflection on its own mode of production has two consequences. It draws attention to the figures that support its argument, and it makes us consider the visionary arrogance of using people as figures without regard for their experience. In using woman to promote a certain relationship between innocence and experience, the poem raises the question of how we figure women, and thus allows us to question the legitimacy of the way the relationship is being constructed and evaluated.

In using a female figure to embody his "myth," Blake chooses an over-determined figure – one that is the site of cultural tensions – and he thus engenders a dialogue between hegemonic and oppositional readings of the myth. Blake would have been aware from Joseph Johnson's radical circle that the rethinking of female identity was being done partly in linguistic terms: that writers like Mary Wollstonecraft thought of women as constructed by language and reading, and of women writers as limited by the genres of experience available to them. By focusing on a young girl at the point in cultural history when he was writing, Blake suspends the ratification of any normative identity he or we might construct for her through the use of culturally en-gendered figures. It is probably no accident that the poem is called "The *Book* of Thel." The protagonist is on the threshold between innocence and experience, but also on the threshold between receiving an identity from others and constructing one for herself. As Thel proceeds through a landscape that is obviously symbolic rather than real, and thus the scene of various cultural inscriptions, she tries to read her identity in the book of nature, and thus to accept as natural the identity modelled for her by others. But we are all the time aware that the book of nature is a reversible trope: that the natural may be something written. Thel's behaviour is characteristically female. She does not assert her identity like the Bard of *Experience*, or even like the ungendered child of *Infant Joy*, who says with innocent directness, "I happy am" (E16; l.5). Instead she asks others to tell her who she is and what she should do. This linguistic detour creates a space between Thel and the identity offered her. Her own uncertainty about accepting the prescription of the lily, cloud, and clod is evident in the fact that she must hear it three times. And because we are aware that her passivity is gender-specific, we are hesitant to ask that she identify with roles that she wants to assume yet projects as other. What is most striking about the figures who try to reassure Thel is that they are all feminine, behaviourally if not pronominally. The lily who suffers herself to be eaten by the "innocent" male lamb follows the feminine path of self-sacrifice. The clod is associated with nurturing and pitying. Only the cloud is male, and Blake's identification of him as such, in contrast to his use of the figure elsewhere,[12] marks his desire to normalize a pattern that demands the sacrifice of selfhood. It marks, in other words, the difficulty of placing "Blake," who seems to raise and suppress the question of gender, who wants Thel to follow the advice she is given and who also seems sensitive to her doubts. We should not minimize Blake's own commitment to the "message" of Eternity. Yet the very attribution of gender to natural objects suspends this message in an anthropomorphism and raises the question of whether "eternity" itself is not a cultural construction. And paradoxically it is the fact that Blake makes one of these characters male instead of making them all female which raises the question of gender as a point of anxiety.

If this approach to the poem constructs a feminist reader, it does so partly as a paradigm for avoiding an archetypal reading that would protect the text from any insertion into history. Blake's use of a female protagonist allows him to experiment with a creed he could not otherwise promulgate. The clod could not have offered the same advice if the protagonist of the poem had been Orc. But in so far as the female figure facilitates the articulation of this creed, the interruption of figure by referent that occurs when we consider Thel as a "real person" configures a larger interruption of visionary argument by social and historical considerations. To put it differently, "Blake" argues for an approach to experience that he seems to naturalize by associating it with traditional female virtues, but he does so at a point when people are beginning to question the nature of woman. He also makes his protagonist ambiguously silent in the face of the female roles offered her by the figures she finds in the book of nature. The result is that the text becomes a site for the reader to produce a genealogy of its morals: an analysis of the historicity of values that is not dissimilar from the one Blake himself performs in *The Marriage of Heaven and Hell*.

Such a genealogy involves historicizing not only the poem but also contemporary readings of it. The normalization of experience as something Thel ought to face comes from an effacement of its social dimension that makes it simply a temporal category, a stage of life. This effacement occurs through a placing of Thel's "virginity" within a horizon of expectations that is both male and modern. Thus one possible reading might reclaim "Blake" as an advocate of free love by assuming the healthiness of (sexual) experience, and thus the regenerative role of all "experience" for achieving emotional wholeness. But how the reader is to place herself in relation to Thel's virginity may well seem clearer now than it did at the end of the eighteenth century, when "sex" was interimplicated in its social construction and had not yet been reconstructed as "natural." Blake often does advocate an open embrace of sexual experience, and yet the consequences of that experience in a poem like *Visions* seem to justify Thel's fears. In so far as virginity plays a symbolic role in the economy of the poem – which we literalize in using it to prescribe Thel's conduct – Thel's desire to remain a virgin suggests that sometimes experience may be unavoidably, yet irrevocably, crippling. It does not dogmatically suggest that, however. For Blake not only focused on Thel at a threshold in her life that looks both backwards and forwards; he also focused on a female figure at a threshold in women's history. The semiotic function of the female figure is to be an open signifier in a way that a male figure could not have been. Because of the increasing consciousness among women writers about social conditioning, woman had become a *tabula rasa* cleansed of previous cultural inscriptions and open to new formulations of her identity. On the one hand the liminal status of woman at this point in history allows us to see trauma itself as socially engendered rather than as a deep structure, a Freudian absolute. On the other hand, the text raises the question of whether there is such a thing as virginity, in the sense not of sexual innocence but of not yet being written on. Already Thel seems inhabited by experiences she has not had, by some collective unconscious that occupies the void of her not yet having become anything. Her sense of nightmare is generated by a temporal metalepsis in which the future is already past. And in a larger sense this metalepsis is a cultural structure that calls into question not only virginity but any form of newness or origination, be it regeneration in eternity or historical renewal.

III

In *Visions of the Daughters of Albion* Blake again contextualizes his reflection on organized innocence through a character whose gender raises questions of cultural inscription. The narrative begins, like *Thel*, with a dialogue between Oothoon and her figured self, in which the marigold responds to her reluctance to pluck it: "pluck thou my flower Oothoon the mild! / Another flower shall spring" (E46;1:9–10). Most critics see the hopes Oothoon projects onto the flower as enshrining the poem's wisdom, and assume that the world of experience will include (re)generation. Oothoon, as is well known, is raped by Bromion and then rejected by Theotormon as soiled, on the basis of a classification of woman as property. At first she internalizes the latter's standards, but then she counters them by refusing to treat *him* as property, offering instead to procure girls for him and watch them copulate (E50;7:23–6). This generous offer supposedly marks her emotional regeneration, for she has now entered the gift economy of feminists like Cixous, and sees beyond the narrow perceptions of selfhood disdained by "Blake."

Given the way he later writes her into his dictionary of symbols,[13] some part of "Blake" clearly does see Oothoon as achieving wholeness in a poem that authorizes its myth by claiming to be a radically feminist statement. But the early poem is also distinguished by an individual focus that makes us see the system from the viewpoint of its participants. As a mobile text that does not put wisdom in the "golden shrine" of the marigold (E46;1:10), but exists only in its reading, the poem situates "Blake's" perspective against its own margins. These margins emerge first of all in the discrepancies between juxtaposed segments that repeat and displace each other. Thus the argument might seem to duplicate the narrative. But in beginning with Oothoon's love for Theotormon and ending with her rape, it summarizes only the first seventeen lines of the narrative. One way of viewing this discrepancy is to say that it juxtaposes the merely factual account of Oothoon's experience with the much longer inside view which focuses on what a person creates from the events that bound her life. Oothoon in the narrative deals constructively with the rape, while in the argument she simply says, "But the terrible thunders tore / My virgin mantle in twain" (E45;iii:7–8). But then the fact that it is the argument, not the narrative, that is spoken by Oothoon herself raises the possibility that the narrative does not develop beyond line 17, but continues the rape by dramatizing the rending apart of Oothoon's psyche. Discrepancy is likewise the subject of the poem's motto: "The Eye sees more than the Heart knows." Does this mean that the reader's eye can see more than Oothoon's heart knows, and what in turn does she know? Does the heart know only the pain of rape, while the visionary eye can see beyond this experience? Or does the empirical eye see things to which the heart, with its will to vision, is justifiably blind? To interpret the motto is irrelevant, because we need to see it not as a hermeneutic key but as a grammar of understanding. As such, it provides verbs which lack predicates as well as personal subjects. It thus produces perceptual positions that can be occupied by anyone and that will accordingly change in the perceptions they generate. But it produces them in such a way that the positions are diacritically constructed, and qualify or reverse each other so as to keep the meaning of the poem open.

At the heart of the poem's indeterminacy is Oothoon as a figure for organized innocence. Leopold Damrosch is one of an increasing number of commentators to note the Urizenic images in which her generosity is described:[14]

> But silken nets and traps of adament will Oothoon spread,
> And catch for thee girls of mild silver, or of furious gold;
> I'll lie beside thee on a bank & view their wanton play
> In lovely copulation bliss on bliss with Theotormon.   (E50;7:23–6)

"Nets" and "traps," images even in this poem of dissimulation (E49;5:18,6: 10–12), mark Blake's awareness that there is something not quite right in the representation of Oothoon as emancipated. Significantly, several lines after she is thought to have unbound herself from Theotormon's standards, she is still described as "reflecting" his "image pure" (E47;3:16), as culturally constructed by what she so passionately resists. To oppose the designation of women as private property by becoming a procuress is hardly liberated behaviour even in terms of the ethic dubiously described as "free love." Not only does Oothoon still conceive herself as an instrument of male pleasure; she also visits on other women a version of her own fate. We could (and to some extent we probably do) argue that she is only a flawed type of organized innocence. But to abstract from the material circumstances of Oothoon's response something of which it is a sign is a kind of essentialism. Moreover, it is questionable whether a woman, once she allows herself to read as a woman, would not see Oothoon's "generosity" as a notion conveniently en-gendered within a male discourse. Read psychologically rather than typologically, Oothoon's solution may well be a symptom of deep trauma. One could speculate that her fantasy about other women copulating "openly" is a way of justifying to herself the enormous cost of *her* having been open to the world of experience. Thus she imagines a scene in which her openness is refigured so that it no longer opens women to male compulsion, because their entry into the economy of pleasure is voluntary. But it is significant that she does not participate in this scene, marking both a silent doubt about her fantasy and the fact that she has been emotionally crippled by the rape. Of significance here is the ambiguity raised by Oothoon's openness, as to whether she is actually raped in a legal sense.[15] Oothoon had imagined a world in which that ambiguity could not exist because there was no rape: a world in which she could be open without opening herself to exploitation. At the end it may be that she reverts to that utopia in a voyeuristic fantasy that sees exploitation as innocent openness.

The problem of how to read Oothoon's cure throws into relief the larger question of how the text's figuration of her discloses the genealogy of its own visionary morality. On one level the poem enacts a familiar Blakean pattern: the story of how a fall from innocence becomes the dialectical ground for the imagining of a more genuine innocence. But it is also a defamiliarization of that pattern: a pattern which operates by substituting symbolic referents for literal referents, the spiritual story of Oothoon's suffering and regeneration for the more disturbing physical story of her rape. If the text dramatizes the power of imagination it is significant that the "reality" it tries to transfigure is a rape, an event whose sheer physicality thwarts attempts to read it figuratively. By figuring the Blakean paradigm through the story of a rape the poem calls into question the very making of figures, crossing aesthetics with ethics, and asking us whether it is right to use rape as a figure of something else. Blake's own complicity in this displacement is marked by the curious fact that Oothoon's rape is not simply refigured; it is never actually named in the poem. It enters the poem not only as a figure for other violations that are similarly unnamed, but also through a figure: the figure of Bromion's thunders which Oothoon says tore "My virgin mantle in twain." Indeed the narrator's repetition of this figure, "Bromion rent her with his thunders" (E46;1:16), goes even further toward naturalizing the event, by effacing any mention of virginity or of the violent removal of clothing. That the rape is from the beginning poeticized is what makes it possible to compare Oothoon's loss of innocence to the plucking of a flower. And the fact that the unnatural is uneasily represented as natural is what makes it possible to see Oothoon as responding positively to an "experience" Thel could not see as normal.

This representation of Oothoon is in a sense a second rape: a linguistic rape that repeats the original violation even as it criticizes it, by denying Oothoon the right to speak her pain as it is. For Oothoon has not found a language to express her emotions. Trying to articulate what she *is* in her words, she also expresses that identity as something she is not through the gaps between her words, through her cries and silences. Though she speaks for most of the poem, unlike Thel who is represented by others, Oothoon's language is opaquely symbolic, as though she has lost the literal referents of her words:

> With what sense is it that the chicken shuns the ravenous hawk?
> With what sense does the tame pigeon measure out the expanse?
> With what sense does the bee form cells? have not the mouse & frog
> Eyes and ears and sense of touch? yet are their habitations.
> And their pursuits, as different as their forms and as their joys:
> ...
> Ask the blind worm the secrets of the grave, and why her spires
> Love to curl round the bones of death; and ask the rav'nous snake
> Where she gets poison: & the wing'd eagle why he loves the sun ...   (E47;3:2–12)

The hysterical crescendo of questions does not clearly say anything, though valiant attempts have been made to explain them in terms of the "system." In the first passage it seems that Oothoon is attributing to each creature a sixth sense that makes it unique, thus asking Theotormon to see her on her own terms by perceiving her through the organ of perception unique to her. Yet the impression of a series of analogies accumulating conviction for this point of view is belied by the heterogeneous jumbling together of everything from chickens to snakes. Even as we look for the common denominator in this chaos of analogies, we are distracted by the resonances of individual analogies. Can Oothoon praise the chicken for shunning the hawk, yet also view the fact that she did not shun Bromion as a fortunate fall that allows her to see new possibilities? If the "night is gone" that closed her "in its deadly black" (E47;2:29), why does she image her new-found identity in terms of poison and death as well as in terms of the wild ass refusing burdens? How we construe the images is less important than the pathology of their form. For Oothoon says nothing directly. Instead she refers to chickens and bees, creatures who do not so much provide her with useful analogies as suggest that she cannot speak literally about what she feels. What she feels is not of course clear, for the distance of her language from any literal referent is symptomatic not only of a distance between conventionalized language and inward experience, but also of her alienation from herself. Allowed to name her experience only symbolically, Oothoon is cut off from her own body, not simply by a patriarchal order but also by her own trauma, which leads her to seek figurative displacements and ultimately to "heal" herself in ways that perpetuate that order. She has, as it were, a symbolic body, a body of metaphors and metonymies that we should not too easily take for truth. And the renovation of that body projected by "Blake" may likewise be symbolic, disembodied.

The fact that organized innocence may still be unorganized is marked for us by the moveability of the frontispiece depicting Bromion and Oothoon still invisibly bound together, with Theotormon on one side of the entrance to a cave, his face averted. None of the characters face each other, and the plate thus represents the traumatized stasis produced by the rape, in which Oothoon's position is still determined by that of her oppressors. Whether the transposition of the plate to the end in one copy (A) and its repetition at both beginning and end in another (F) was an accident is irrelevant. Clearly these shifts represent someone's sense of another way the poem asks to be read, and clearly the way Blake produces his texts allows them to exist in more than one version. Placing the plate at the beginning seems to allow that the narrative develops beyond its initial stasis. Placing it at the end gives a certain finality to its bleak image of a psychologically frozen world. Because the plate in copy A is actually more brightly coloured than in some other copies the pessimism of the final placement is subject to revision.[16] But the point is that its moveability allows the meaning of the poem to be constructed by the reader in a field of intertextual possibilities.

It would be easy to condemn Blake for imposing a male discourse on the poem, or to concur in what seems a celebration of free love. But the author in this text is self-critically evasive. David Punter has pointed out that the trauma is also Blake's: the trauma of a man who does not know how to deal with what his culture has done to women.[17] It is interesting in this context that Ortega y Gasset should relate metaphor to "the spirit of taboo." Metaphor, he says, "substitutes one thing for another – from an urge not so much to get at the first as to get rid of the second."[18] But

significantly, while Blake presents the rape figuratively, he does not efface
its violence. Indeed the tendency to naturalize rape is crossed and sus-
pended by a desire to dramatize other modes of exploitation such as
slavery and capitalism, by figuring them as forms of rape. The fact of
violence structures critically the space in which Blake must move as
reader of his own text. For violence constitutes its object as other, removes
it from the sphere of our own experience and thus of our understanding.
In dealing with someone whose experience is unutterably more painful
than anything we ourselves know, the immediate response is to find
analogies from our own experience that will heal the rupture created in cul-
tural understanding. Not only must we explain an alien experience to
ourselves; we must also explain ourselves to the other person, contending
with an obscure sense of complicity in her pain. This complicity (which we
also feel in the face of natural occurrences such as death) may not stem
from anything we have done, but simply from a sense that we have hith-
erto been insensitive to what has now ruptured our security. Breaking the
social hermeneutic in which we all thought we understood things in the
same way, violence forces us to use language to re-establish a sense of
shared values, but compels us to recognize the tenuousness of the bridges
thus constructed. Blake is nervously aware that images of plucked flowers
and thunderstorms, with their attendant promise of regeneration, are
analogies that do not identify Oothoon's experience so much as refigure it
as Blake wishes it were. This awareness surfaces in the imagery of nets and
traps, and in the fact that the frontispiece can be relocated as a coda. It also
surfaces in the poem's recourse to silence and cries. Oothoon "howls" and
"laments" (E47;3:1). She is silent for periods of up to a day (E47–8;3:14,4:25)
and is supported by a non-verbal chorus: the daughters of Albion, who
echo back her "sighs" but not her words, as though her words are really cir-
cumlocutions for sighs. It is all too easy for us to read the poem instead of
hearing it, as the daughters do, and thus to reduce the duration of its
silences from a day to a line. But these silences manifest the gaps in the text
where language cannot reach and force Blake's ideology to know its own
margins.

What I have suggested is a different perspective on the poem from the
visionary reading that we assume "Blake" to want. But Blake may also be
uneasy about a reading that would incorporate Oothoon into his corpus,
fixing her in her symbolic body. As in *Thel* the double reference of the poem
– both visionary (to Blake's system) and historical (to specific events of the
kind detailed in Stedman's narrative)[19] – produces a crossing of figure and
referent in which the typological reading of Oothoon is interrupted by a
psychological and social reading that reconstructs her as person rather than
sign. This crossing becomes an occasion for us to reconsider the kind of
reading necessary to sustain Blake's system. Leslie Tannenbaum suggests

that for Blake typology is "synonymous with the creative process itself" and that by "defining Christ as the Imagination Blake adopts as his subject the typological process itself."[20] Or to put it differently, by placing Christ at the centre of his phenomenology of spirit Blake represents imagination as typological and demands, for that representation to be sustained, an archetypal reading that translates individual experience into a central paradigmatic story. But the early poems are too close to their social referents not to be aware of the cultural imperialism that informs such reading as a will-to-power over the text's own uncertainties. By writing for an audience composed of men and women instead of sheep and goats, Blake calls into play instead of effacing the cultural differences that the "romantic imagination" tries to dismiss. And inasmuch as rape is contiguous in this poem with other acts of psychic and political seizure, its resistance to being read figurally marks a certain limit to the attempt to silence other forms of social violation through imaginative transfiguration.

6 Romantic Aversions: Apostrophe Reconsidered

J. DOUGLAS KNEALE

This is a figure which less than any other would bear abuse.
Wordsworth, 5 May 1814

Yet whence this strange aversion?
Wordsworth, *The Borderers*

According to certain recent publications, the figure of apostrophe or *aversio* has become something of an "embarrassment." Jonathan Culler, in an essay entitled "Apostrophe," claims that whatever else apostrophes may be, "above all they are embarrassing: embarrassing to me and to you." Because it is allegedly so embarrassing, the figure, Culler asserts, has been "systematically repressed or excluded by critics"; more specifically, Mary Jacobus argues, it has been "regularly ignored by writers on the ode."[1] In another essay Culler repeats his thesis: "Apostrophes are awkward and embarrassing. ... Critics either ignore them or transform apostrophe into description."[2] And once more, in the *Yale French Studies* memorial volume *The Lesson of Paul de Man*, Culler restates his case: "Apostrophes are embarrassing, and criticism of the lyric has systematically avoided both the topic of apostrophe and actual apostrophes."[3] The reason given for such regular or systematic avoidance is that apostrophe represents something "which critical discourse cannot comfortably assimilate" – that is, Culler suggests, "some innate hostility to voice" (*Pursuit*, 137, 136).

Perhaps it comes as a surprise nowadays to be told that discourse has an "innate hostility to voice." Voice, as Jacques Derrida has shown, has always been privileged in Western culture as a guarantor of truth, consciousness, and being – while writing has been repressed as secondary and derivative.[4] To resolve this confusion we need to rehabilitate our historical understanding of apostrophe by demonstrating that, far from being "systematically" or "regularly" avoided by critics, the figure has a distinguished tradition of commentary, beginning with the classical writers Cicero and Quintilian, and moving through the Renaissance and eighteenth-century rhetoricians. For example, Sherry, Peacham, Fenner, Fraunce, Puttenham, Day, Hoskins, Blount, Smith, and Blair – to name more than a few – all regularly and systematically discuss apostrophe.[5] In addition, we need to reconsider apostrophe in relation to the figures of prosopopoeia and ecphonesis in order to view its particular function within a larger oratorical structure of address. What we discover when we pursue this sort of *aversion therapy* is that apostrophe does indeed represent something which discourse cannot comfortably assimilate: not voice as such, however, but what I shall call the passing of voice, its want or lack, even its sudden removal.

My position may be stated briefly. The current problem with apostrophe stems from associating it with voice rather than with a movement of voice, and the reason for this error, I think, lies in a misunderstanding of rhetoric. Classical rhetoric is fundamentally a vocative form of discourse, always explicitly or implicitly involving a second-person "thou" or "ye" – what Roman Jakobson calls the "conative" function of language.[6] Thus classical rhetoric has no trope or scheme of address as such because, being derived from forensic oratory, it is intrinsically vocative. It does not, therefore, see its own essence as a trope or deviation. Erich Auerbach, writing on apostrophe and address, puts it this way:

The theorists have never described or listed the address to the reader as a special figure of speech. That is quite understandable. Since the ancient orator always addresses a definite public – either a political body or the judges in a trial – the problem arises only in certain special cases, if, with an extraordinary rhetorical movement, he should address someone else, a *persona iudicis auersus*, as Quintilian says.[7]

Rhetoric does, however, distinguish types and conditions of address – such as, in the Tudor rhetoricians' terminology, the "outcrie" or the "exclamation," and the "turne tale" or the "aversion." I shall attempt to distinguish this latter figure, apostrophe or *aversio*, from its related forms of address, including exclamation or ecphonesis, and then demonstrate its operation through a close reading of Wordsworth's text "There Was a Boy." By doing so, I hope to show that the central problem with Culler's argument lies in his failure to distinguish, on either historical or theoretical grounds, between apostrophe and address. To put that claim a different way, I mean to show that what Culler's influential essay is really about is not apostrophe, but prosopopoeia.

I

Quintilian discusses the figure of apostrophe at some length in book 4 (1.63–70) and again in book 9 (2.38–40; 3.26–8) of the *Institutio Oratoria*.[8] In

the first of these instances he argues against certain "cautious and pedan-
tic teachers of rhetoric" (4.1.70) who forbid the use of apostrophe in the
exordium, or introduction to an oration, not "because they regard [apos-
trophe] as illicit, but because they think it useless" (4.1.65). Quintilian's
counter-argument pragmatically seeks to demonstrate the utility of the fig-
ure through a series of examples from Cicero and Demosthenes. But what
interests the reader more is Quintilian's first definition of apostrophe:
"The figure which the Greeks call *apostrophe*, by which is meant the diver-
sion of our words to address some person other than the judge, is entirely
banned by some rhetoricians as far as the *exordium* is concerned" (4.1.63).
Two aspects of this definition require comment, since they reappear in
nearly all discussions of apostrophe down to the nineteenth century. The
first is the notion of apostrophe as a "diversion" of speech (*sermonem a
persona iudicis aversum*). The second point, necessarily related to the first, is
that this diversion redirects the speech to someone other than the original
hearer – in this case, since Quintilian is dealing with forensic oratory,
someone other than the judge. The positing of what later rhetoricians
would call the "proper" or intended hearer, and the oratorical diversion
from that person to another person, constitute the two chief characteristics
of the figure.

In book 9 Quintilian offers a more elaborate definition, still within a
forensic context: "*Apostrophe* also, which consists in the diversion of our
address from the judge, is wonderfully stirring, whether we attack our
adversary ... or turn to make some invocation ... or to entreaty that will
bring odium on our opponents" (9.2.38). Quintilian reminds us of the
pragmatic, as distinct from ornamental, function of apostrophe in judicial
rhetoric: like all figures, its effect is supposed to persuade. Once again the
two key points of a *proper* listener and a *diversion* from that listener are
present.

That is not the case, however, in the pseudo-Ciceronian *Rhetorica ad
Herennium*, where the following definition of apostrophe appears in
Caplan's translation: "Apostrophe is the figure which expresses grief or
indignation by means of an address to some man or city or place or
object" (4.15.22).[9] While this definition intimates the close relation between
apostrophe and prosopopoeia – by addressing "man or city or place or
object" the orator implicitly or explicitly invests the addressee with the ani-
mate faculty of hearing – there is a confusion of terminology, because in the
original Latin text the word translated by Caplan as "apostrophe" is actu-
ally *exclamatio*.[10] As future rhetoricians would insist, exclamation is not the
same as apostrophe, though they are indeed similar, both being moti-
vated by passion and having the potential to address people or objects
either present or absent, alive or dead.[11] The difference between these
two figures, however, is that exclamation does not necessarily contain a
turn or diversion from the original hearer; a text may be a consistent

exclamation to a reader, and yet still not an apostrophe. By contrast, apostrophe always depends on a pre-text.

II

Apostrophe is literally a turning away, an aversion, as both Richard Sherry and Henry Peacham call it. It is, Peacham says, "a forme of speech by which the Orator turneth suddenly from the former frame of his speech to another ... which is no other thing then a sudden removing from the third person to the second." "The most usual forme of this figure," he continues, "is in turning our speech from the third person to the second" (116). But Sherry locates the turning elsewhere. "*Aversio*, aversion," he says, is "when we turne our speche from them to whom we dyd speake to another personne, eyther present or absent" (60). It is for Sherry thus a turning from one second person to another second person, in an intersubjective or intertextual movement between vocatives. Of the three traditional divisions of rhetoric – forensic, epideictic, and deliberative – forensic rhetoric illustrates this intersubjective movement most clearly, as when the orator turns aside occasionally, as Hoskins put it in 1599, "to some new person, as, to the people when your speech before was to the judge, to the def[endan]t, to the adversary, to the witnesses" (48). At first glance, Peacham does not seem to agree with Sherry's intervocative definition, as he suggests that the shift of address is from third- to second-person discourse, from "it" to "you." This is not really a disagreement, however, for what Peacham assumes but does not make explicit here is the *intrinsic* second-person form of address in rhetoric, always involving a "proper" listener from whom the speaker can turn to confront an invoked listener.[12]

Other Renaissance rhetoricians concur in these definitions. In *The Artes of Logike and Rhetorike* (1584) Dudley Fenner writes: "Apostrophe or turning to the person, is when the speach is turned to another person, then the speach appointed did intend or require. And this Apostrophe or turning is diversely seene, according to the diversitie of persons. Sometimes it turneth to a mans person. ... Sometimes from a man to God ... Sometimes to unreasonable creatures without sense" (chapter 8).[13]

Angel Day, in the list of tropes, figures, and schemes added to the 1592 and later editions of his *English Secretary*, has the following entry:

Apostrophe, or Aversio, when wee turne our speeches from one person or thing to another, as if having spoken much of the vanitie of the worlde shoulde thereupon turne and saie unto the world, O world, how sweete and pleasant are the shewes of those things which thou producest: but in taste, how full of too much bitternes? Or in speaking of the certaintie of death, and the little respect thereof had, to turn a mans speach to death it selfe and saie, O death, how bitter is thy remembrance to a man having peace and plenty on his riches, &c. (90)[14]

Eighteenth- and nineteenth-century rhetorical treatises are similarly consistent in their definitions of apostrophe. Thomas Gibbons, in *Rhetoric; Or a View of Its Principal Tropes and Figures* (1767), writes: "Apostrophe is a Figure in which we interrupt the current of our discourse, and turn to another person, or to some other object, different from that to which our address was first directed."[15] Citing Quintilian, Gibbons claims that "this Figure is of admirable service to diversify our discourses, as we direct ourselves to different objects from those we first addressed" (221). Other rhetorical handbooks and treatises follow suit – for example, John Holmes's *The Art of Rhetoric Made Easy* (1766), Hugh Blair's *Lectures on Rhetoric and Belles Lettres* (1783), and John Walker's *A Rhetorical Grammar* (1822), partly cribbed from Gibbons's *Rhetoric*.[16]

A number of twentieth-century critics and theorists have discussed apostrophe – for example, Sister Miriam Joseph in her exhaustive catalogue of tropes and schemes in Shakespeare, Paul Fry in his splendid study of the English ode, Annabel Patterson in her work on Hermogenes and Renaissance style, Paul de Man on Michael Riffaterre, and Riffaterre on de Man.[17] Here, however, is Derrida in *The Post Card*, offering a thoroughly historical and conventional definition of apostrophe. Derrida writes:

The word – apostrophizes – speaks of the words addressed to the singular one, a live interpellation (the man of discourse or writing interrupts the continuous development of the sequence, abruptly turns toward someone, that is, something, addresses himself to you), but the word also speaks of the address to be detoured.[18]

Taken together, these texts from the sixteenth to the twentieth century represent a tradition of definition, example, and commentary on the figure of apostrophe or *aversio*. A similar tradition could be mapped out here for the figure of exclamation, or *exclamatio*, or ecphonesis, "the outcry," as it is variously called. Significantly, the rhetoricians do not include a diversion of speech as part of their understanding of the figure. Peacham once again offers a useful, representative definition:

Ecphonesis of the Latines called *Exclamatio*, is a forme of speech by which the Orator through some vehement affection, as either of love, hatred, gladnesse, sorrow, anger, marvelling, admiration, feare, or such like, bursteth forth into an exclamation or outcrie, signifying thereby the vehement affection or passion of his mind. (62)[19]

The motive for exclamation must always be passion – it is "not lawful but in extremity of motion," Hoskins says (33) – though this passion must be "simulated and artfully designed," else the outcry is not a figure, as Quintilian stipulates (9.2.27). One of the most common rhetorical signposts for exclamation is the word "O." Thomas Wilson, in his *Arte of Rhetorique*

(1560), gives the following instances: "Oh Lord, O God, O worlde, O life, O maners of men? O Death, where is thy sting? O Hell, where is thy victorie?"[20] In *The Mysterie of Rhetorique unvail'd* (1657) John Smith says that exclamation "is expresst or understood by an Adverb of crying out, as Oh, alas, behold; which are the signs of this figure" (140).

It is important to cite these definitions of apostrophe and exclamation more to distinguish their rhetorical differences than to demonstrate their syntactical affinities. We no longer can say, for example, that Wordsworth's line "O there is blessing in this gentle breeze" is an apostrophe *automatically* because of the telltale "O."[21] Only if it were a "turne tale" O, one depending on a rhetorical pre-text or prior discourse, would we be correct in making such a statement. But I wish to turn back to Culler's text before going on to Wordsworth's, to develop some of the larger implications of my brief survey.

III

What is at stake in such a reconsideration of apostrophe? One concern is obviously historical: we discover, as de Man once said of allegory, "a historical scheme that differs entirely from the customary picture."[22] But another interest is theoretical. By describing apostrophe as a turning from an original (implicit or explicit) addressee to a different addressee, from the proper or intended hearer to another, we emphasize the figure as a *movement* of voice, a translation or carrying over of address. This understanding is crucial if we are to distinguish simple direct address from the turning aside of address, from the rhetorical and temporal movement of apostrophe. In Culler's essay "Apostrophe," however, this distinction is missing; curiously, no definition of apostrophe is given there, despite Culler's admission that a study of apostrophe should require it:

If we would know something of the poetics of the lyric we should study apostrophe, its forms and meanings. Such a project would confront at the outset complex problems of definition and delimitation, which I here leave aside in order to focus on cases which will be apostrophic by any definition. (*Pursuit*, 137)

"Which I here leave aside": yet whence this strange aversion? Culler seems to assume the straightforwardness of apostrophe. But in fact his choice of texts "apostrophic by any definition" is problematic: "O Rose, thou art sick!"; "O wild West Wind, thou breath of Autumn's being!"; "Thou still unravished bride of quietness"; and "Sois sage, ô ma douleur!" (*Pursuit*, 137). While doubtless many teachers, myself included, have called these examples apostrophes, not one of them, by definition, qualifies; there is no vocal turn involved, no "sudden removing," in Peacham's phrase (116): they are all direct exclamations, or ecphoneses, occurring in the *first line* of their respective poems, with no preceding speech, no pretextual basis from which to turn, no discourse to "interrupt," as Gibbons (213) and Derrida (4) put it.[23] Blake's lyric is addressed to the rose; Shelley's ode is addressed to the west wind; Keats's text is addressed *to* a Grecian urn as much as an ode written "on" it; and Baudelaire's meditation is spoken uniformly to the single addressee Sorrow. It might be argued that if language is originally figurative, always already tropological, then these examples do contain a turn, a trope that animates each of the non-human subjects addressed – a rose, a wind, an urn, sorrow. But such a figure is not apostrophe, of course, but prosopopoeia, which does not depend on a rhetorical aversion. My interest, however, is in the *turn of voice*, not the turn or deviation of another figure within voice.

Simply put, the problem is a confusion of apostrophe and address. In his analysis of de Man's essay on Riffaterre's poetics, Culler repeats his error. He misses the turn. Renewing his argument about the systematic exclusion of apostrophe in criticism, Culler attempts to bring de Man on-side by noting that he "takes a considerable interest in apostrophe and some interest in other critics' inclination to avoid and ignore it" ("Reading Lyric," 99). This seems to me to be a crucial misreading of de Man, for what Riffaterre avoids and de Man takes an interest in is not in fact apostrophe. Indeed, the passage from de Man that Culler cites to substantiate his point about apostrophe is actually about something else. Culler quotes: "'Now it is certainly beyond question,' de Man writes ... 'that the figure of address is recurrent in lyric poetry, to the point of constituting the generic definition of, at the very least, the ode (which can, in its turn, be seen as paradigmatic for poetry in general)'" ("Reading Lyric," 100). The "figure of address," not of apostrophe, is de Man's concern here. And de Man is surely right to claim that this rhetorical structure defines a paradigm for poetry. Yet why does he single out the ode with respect to the structure of address? Assuredly because of all poems, the ode is the type that frequently is explicitly addressed to someone: Psyche, Autumn, a skylark, the Confederate dead.[24] Of course, other genres do this too, addressing Penshurst, a coy mistress, Peele Castle, or intellectual beauty.[25] But we need to emphasize that this structure of address, this explicit directing of voice, is crucially different from the movement of apostrophe, the redirecting of voice.

This distinction should help to dispel Culler's perplexity in *The Pursuit of Signs* over the lack of discussion of apostrophe in many critics, especially in George N. Shuster's *The English Ode from Milton to Keats*, one work Culler singles out to prove his allegation of a systematic scholarly neglect of apostrophe.[26] "The problem of apostrophe ought to lie right at the heart of this book," Culler writes, "but from the outset Shuster engages in instructive maneuvers to exclude apostrophe from his domain" (*Pursuit*, 136). Yet the theoretical and definitional error exhibited in his analysis of de Man is present here: the passage Culler goes on to quote is not about apostrophe. Here is Shuster's "maneuver," as quoted by Culler:

"The element of address," [Shuster] notes in the introduction, "is of no especial significance, being merely a reflection of the classical influence. All the verse of antiquity was *addressed* to somebody, primarily because it was either sung or read and the traditions of song and recitation required that there be a recipient." (*Pursuit*, 136; my emphasis)

"Thus," concludes Culler, "*apostrophe* is insignificant because conventional" (*Pursuit*, 136; my emphasis).[27] Apostrophe? Could the confusion of terminology, the commentary at cross-purposes, be any plainer? No wonder, then, that Culler says "that one can read vast amounts of criticism without learning that poetry uses apostrophe repeatedly and intensely" (*Pursuit*, 136) – especially when what a reader thinks is apostrophe is not apostrophe, when the standard "element of address" is mistaken for the tropological diversion of address. Shuster's argument, perhaps a manoeuvre nonetheless, is that since classical verse – his focus, like de Man's, is the ode, the text "to" someone – is intrinsically vocative, its essence need not be taken as a deviation, the fundamental taken as "especial."

What really is de Man's interest in his reading of Riffaterre? Plainly, not apostrophe as such, but prosopopoeia, "the master trope of poetic discourse" (*Resistance*, 48). And when Riffaterre answers de Man's charges concerning his poetics of reading, he entitles his response simply "Prosopopeia." Apostrophe is related to prosopopoeia, as ecphonesis is, but it is not a necessary relation: one can apostrophize someone (such as a defendant in a courtroom) without using prosopopoeia; and conversely one can, as Riffaterre points out, conceive of a text in which, for example, a "beseiged city speaks its mournful dirge without having been apostrophized." Prosopopoeia, Riffaterre writes, "merely lends a voice to a voiceless ... entity" ("Prosopopeia," 108). Or even less: sometimes it merely lends an ear, in the way that Wordsworth lends an ear to nature in book 1 of *The Prelude*:[28] "to the open fields I told / A prophecy" (50–1) – a passage that anticipates in book 5 those other "open fields, which, shaped like ears, / Make green peninsulas on Esthwaite's Lake" (5.433–4).[29]

I V

Apostrophe is not a figure, that like Janus, carries two faces with a good grace.

Wordsworth, 5 May 1814

What are the consequences of such a theory of apostrophe for reading

Wordsworth? By understanding the figure as a "trope," as an arche-trope that literally repeats the "turn" of all figural language, we open up the concept of voice to the force of its differential structure and therefore to its deconstruction.[30] We also begin to perceive the relation between rhetoric and form in a poem such as *Tintern Abbey*, which Wordsworth regarded as affiliated with the ode through what he called its "transitions," or turns or strophes, which turn out to be apo-strophes or *aversios* invoking first the "sylvan Wye" (56) and then the "dear, dear Sister" (121).[31] Milton's *Lycidas*, as pastoral elegy rather than ode, organizes its three-part structure around a similar series of aversions that foreground the movement of voice: "Return, *Alpheus*, the dread voice is past ..."[32] And Coleridge typically structures his conversation poems and "Effusions" using apostrophes to create the present-past-future, or "out-in-out," transitions that M.H. Abrams has identified as a feature of the "greater Romantic lyric."[33] Some Wordsworthian texts, such as the "Poem ... Addressed to S.T. Coleridge," posit a larger structure of rhetorical address and its aversions. *The Prelude* has been called Wordsworth's best conversation poem, but at what point does apostrophe become conversation? Where does trope shade into genre? Or to put the question more directly: how many aversions does it take to make a conversation poem? Let me consider some of these issues in a brief close reading.

The case of Wordsworth is exemplary. As "a man speaking to men" (*Prose*, 1:138), the Wordsworthian poet by definition finds himself in situations of rhetorical address which are potentially apostrophic. I take as the locus classicus the text "There Was a Boy," in which the interruptive pause after the opening statement suggests a turning away:[34]

> There was a Boy: ye knew him well, ye cliffs
> And islands of Winander! (*Prelude*, 5.364–5).[35]

As an example of forensic rhetoric, Wordsworth's text illustrates the "sudden removing" of voice, as both relocation and deletion. Indeed, there may have been a boy, but the speaker is *non habeas corpus*, and so he turns from his initial auditor to invoke the corroboration of witnesses: "Ye knew him well, ye cliffs / And islands of Winander!" The vocative itself does not signal apostrophe so much as does the movement from the third-person formula "There was" to the second-person pronoun "ye." This turn or trope, at once apostrophic and prosopopoeic, swerves passionately from an epitaphic statement about the Boy's death to an immediate address to a personified Nature. In doing so it anticipates the subsequent rhetorical and thematic reversals in the episode, and implies an intertextual question: Who would not testify for the Boy of Winander? Who would not sing for him?

Seeking Nature's corroboration is not unusual for Wordsworth. In book 1 of *The Prelude* a similar moment occurs, with the important difference that no apostrophe is used:

> The sands of Westmoreland, the creeks and bays
> Of Cumbria's rocky limits, they can tell
> How, when the Sea threw off his evening shade,
> And to the shepherd's hut on distant hills
> Sent welcome notice of the rising moon,
> How I have stood, to fancies such as these
> A stranger ...   (1.567–73)[36]

No aversion here, not even in the appositional construction, but the powerful prosopopoeia still obtains. The assurance that the sands and creeks and bays "can tell" implies that the poet could turn to invoke their testimony, to call on these natural objects that they might answer him.[37] Their statements as witnesses would be to corroborate the poet's description of his response ("How I have stood ... ") to the action of Nature ("when the Sea threw off his evening shade ... "). There is a dialogue between addresser and addressee, between nature and humanity, carried in the "welcome notice" sent by the sea to the "shepherd's hut." "The earth / And common face of Nature," Wordsworth writes following this incident, "spake to me / Rememberable things" (1.586–8). In such a collaborative speech act the poet seeks for no trophies, not even apos-trophes. Though he does not use *aversio* here, Wordsworth achieves a rhetorical effect remarkably similar to that in the first passage: here Nature is personified by being charged with a voice that "can tell"; in the Boy of Winander text Nature is attributed with consciousness, or knowledge: "Ye knew him well!" But it is, Wordsworth fears, a knowledge purchased by the loss of power, which is to say, by the loss of voice: a power is gone, which nothing can restore. The apostrophic turning to Nature evokes "rememberable things," but also a guilty consciousness: Nature's response implies responsibility. For one can anticipate Wordsworth asking here the accusing question: "Where were ye nymphs ... ?" – even as he had done some thirteen years earlier in another poem:

> Where were ye, nymphs, when the remorseless deep
> Clos'd o'er your little favourite's hapless head?
> For neither did ye mark with solemn dream
> In Derwent's rocky woods the white Moonbeam
> Pace like a Druid o'er the haunted steep;
> Nor in Winander's stream.   (*The Dog – An Idyllium*)[38]

The conventional elegiac topos of the invocation to nature is described also by the Wanderer in book 1 of *The Excursion* (475–81):

> – The Poets, in their elegies and songs
> Lamenting the departed, call the groves,
> They call upon the hills and streams to mourn,
> And senseless rocks; nor idly; for they speak,
> In these their invocations, with a voice
> Obedient to the strong creative power
> Of human passion. (*Poetical Works*, 5:24)

"Nor idly": this is no mere pathetic fallacy.[39] The voice that speaks or calls to Nature obeys the "spontaneous overflow of powerful feelings" (*Prose*, 1:127, 149), resulting in apostrophe or exclamation, the voice by "human passion" moved.

The sudden removing of voice is related to a silencing of voice, an overdetermined muteness that is "redoubled and redoubled" (5.378) in "There Was a Boy." First there are the "silent owls" (5.373), then the "pauses of deep silence" (1805:5.405) that baffle the child, and finally the poet's "mute" address to the grave (5.397). Alternating with these silences is a succession of voices, sometimes choric, sometimes univocal, but always "responsive" (5.376) in their own answerable style. The text follows a sequence of aversions that thematize the adversarial aspect of forensic rhetoric: here, the Boy is stationed vis-à-vis nature in a way that reminds us of a subject-object dialectic, the mind versus the world. But the colloquy in the text troubles this opposition by textualizing it, making "The Boy of Winander" into a type of conversation poem, intersubjective rather than dialectical.

Intersubjective dialogue or familiar colloquy is implied also in the naturalized apostrophe near the origin of *The Prelude*. The sudden beginning in MS. JJ shows a rhetorical aversion from a third-person form of address to an immediate "thou":

> Was it for this
> That one, the fairest of all rivers, loved
> To blend his murmurs with my nurse's song ... ?
> ... For this didst thou,
> O Derwent ... ? (Norton *Prelude*, p. 1)

Recall Angel Day's example of *aversio*, "as if having spoken much of the vanitie of the worlde [one] shoulde thereupon turne and saie unto the world, O world" (90) – or, in this case, as if having spoken much *of* the River Derwent, Wordsworth should turn and speak *to* it. The 1798 passage continues the apostrophe, with additional notices of "thy silent pools" and "thy streams" (Norton *Prelude*, p. 1), and then just as naturally returns to the original discourse.[40]

The opening of the 1805 *Prelude* uses apostrophe in a similar way, turn-ing from a "there is" clause – "O there is blessing in this gentle breeze" (1.1) – to a series of apostrophes to Nature: "O welcome messenger! O welcome friend! / A captive greets thee" (1.5–6). In the 1850 edition not only are these apostrophes deleted, but the personal pronouns "he" and "his," referring to the breeze, are replaced (probably by Christopher Wordsworth; see Norton *Prelude*, p. 29 n1) by "it" and "its," as if to localize the differ-ential movement of voice, or to curb its animating power. But voice in Wordsworth cannot be contained so easily, or halted in one place for long; it is always on the move, even when engraved, like an epitaph, in rocks and stones and trees.[41]

I suggest that the Boy of Winander is a poet "sown / By Nature" and therefore lacking "the accomplishment of verse" (*Excursion*, 1.77–8, 80). Yet he engages Nature in what De Quincey was the first to see as a "contest" or challenge to nature, in the tradition, as Geoffrey Hartman has sug-gested, of the singing contest of classical pastoral (*Fate*, 183, 290).[42] In his recollections, De Quincey recounts how Wordsworth once described his imaginative processes, using as illustration his own text "There Was a Boy" – "that exquisite poem in which he describes a mountain boy planting himself at twilight on the margin of some solitary bay of Windermere, and provoking the owls to a contest with himself" (160). "Provoking" is just the word; as syllepsis it conflates literal voicing and figural confrontation. The Boy is not quite an *agent provocateur*, but he does like to set the cat among the pigeons.

Yet why should Wordsworth vex his own creation? "Like the innocent bird," he writes, the poet's mind "hath goadings on / That drive her as in trouble through the groves" (*Prelude*, 1.142–3). But to provoke the birds in such a way is going far to seek disquiet. In book 1 the poet steals birds' eggs, even steals the birds themselves, now tries to appropriate their voice. But repeatedly critics claim that the Boy is in a harmonious "com-munion" with nature.[43] Given the recurrent pattern in Wordsworth's poetry of an external act of violence followed by an inner sense of guilt, might we not read the Boy of Winander episode, not as an example of an exquisite harmony with nature but yet another muted or transmuted act of aggression against it? Even Wordsworth's phrase "redoubled and redou-bled" (5.378) has intertextual overtones of battle, as in the war in heaven in *Paradise Lost*, 6.370: "The Atheist crew, but with redoubl'd blow" (a line which Wordsworth explicitly echoes in *The Prelude*, 10.502: "Wielded the sceptre of the Atheist crew"); or as in *Richard II*, 1.3.80–2: "And let thy blows, doubly redoublèd, / Fall like amazing thunder on the casque / Of thy adverse pernicious enemy."[44] The Boy of Winander's "blows" surely belong here too. Still, other echoes trouble: when Eve says to the serpent,

"Redouble then this miracle, and say, / How cam'st thou speakable of mute?" (*Paradise Lost*, 9.562–3), we glimpse an intersection of battle, voice, nature, and muteness that operates in Wordsworth's text too. Challenge, tumult, and battle lead to bafflement, silence, and death, and show us just how high the stakes in this singing contest really are.[45]

Francis Jeffrey missed the pastoral conventions of the text when, in his review of Crabbe's *Poems* in 1808, he took Wordsworth's topos to be the "untimely death of promising youth" rather than of a promising poet.[46] The linguistic or "poetic" aspect, however, is difficult to avoid, for the opening apostrophe advertises its own intertextuality. The Boy stands with his hands pressed "palm to palm" (5.371) over his mouth in an attitude of devotion or nature-worship, but also in imitation of Juliet's "holy palmers' kiss." Or does he not rather play the swan and die in music? Mouth and voice seem linked to hands and writing by their very contiguity. The intervocative exchange begins, significantly, with the Boy:

>   he, as through an instrument,
> Blew mimic hootings to the silent owls,
> That they might answer him; and they would shout
> Across the watery vale, and shout again,
> Responsive to his call, with quivering peals,
> And long halloos and screams, and echoes loud,
> Redoubled and redoubled, concourse wild
> Of jocund din ...   (5.372–9)

There is a turn here so large as to be a complete reversal. We often think of Wordsworth as borrowing a voice from Nature to inform his poetry, to "naturalize" it as a language of things rather than of words. "Oh! that I had a music and a voice / Harmonious as your own," he says to the breezes and groves in book 12 (29–30). In this scene as well, the Boy's "mimic hootings" seem borrowed from nature: their mimesis, we naturally assume, is imitative of the owls' song. But the rhetorical structure of the passage creates interference with this reading, because here the direction is reversed: the Boy seems to confer the power of utterance on the owls; he gives away his voice to nature, and is silenced.[47] The sudden removing of voice comes as a "surprise," a "shock of mild surprise" that insinuates a deeper, usurping voice: "the voice / Of mountain torrents" (5.382, 383–4). The text establishes a series of acoustical oppositions between the Boy and Nature – sound/silence, source/echo, stimulus/response – in which the Boy appears to have the priority implied in the first term of each of these pairings. The owls "echo" the Boy: they "answer" him; they are "respon-sive" to his prior vocal stimulus. But is not this stimulus also a response?

The word "mimic" carries not only a temporal reference, alluding to recurrent, pre-textual encounters between the Boy and the owls ("many a time / At evening ... would he stand" [5.365–6, 368]), but also a proleptic force, anticipating the present and future exchanges. The Boy of Winander is a Boy Wonder: he is a source that is already an echo, a repetition of recurrence in a finer tone.

Robert Frost's poem *The Most of It* provides an intertextual gloss on the Boy's sound effects:

> He thought he kept the universe alone;
> For all the voice in answer he could wake
> Was but the mocking echo of his own
> From some tree-hidden cliff across the lake.
> Some morning from the boulder broken beach
> He would cry out on life, that what it wants
> Is not its own love back in copy speech,
> But counter-love, original response.[48]

As "original response," the Boy of Winander's calls foreground their textual self-reflexiveness, their difference from themselves. Whether we read the Boy's hootings as the call of the wild or "the call of the supplement," we are faced with a text redoubled with traces of other voices, other faces.[49]

The earliest version of the text, MS. JJ, with its wavering balance between first-person autobiography and third-person narration, contains a similar mimetic repetition in its description of the "pauses of deep silence" that "mocked" the Boy's skill (Norton *Prelude*, p. 492; 1805:5.405). "Mocked" becomes "baffled" by 1850, suggesting ridicule and usurpation, but "mocked" also repeats "mimic": silence imitates the Boy's song. To "answer" is not to mimic, unless the answer is echolalic, compulsively or automatically repetitive. The Boy's hootings, as onomatopoeic mimicry, are motivated. But they are also motivating: they stimulate both sound and silence. If we give linguistic and temporal priority to the Boy, however, we construct a hierarchy which is quickly undone by Nature; his voice is removed, suddenly deleted or overpowered by the silence of the grave. But even silence can be repeated: near his grave, Wordsworth writes, "A long half hour together I have stood / Mute" (5.396–7). The image of Wordsworth silently confronting a grave recurs throughout his poetry (for example, in both "spots of time," in the drowned man episode, even in the blind Beggar passage), and tells us what is different about this elegiac moment. Why is the poet mute? Is he "struck dumb," as de Man would say, because the poet is "frozen in [his] own death" as a result of being apostrophized by the Boy?[50] Yet how would this explain the animating power of the trope? The Boy experiences the ultimate aversion, like Lucy, being "rolled round in earth's diurnal course" (*A Slumber Did My Spirit Seal, Poetical Works*, 2:216), while the poet completes the circuit of address through his "mute dialogue" (2.268) with the grave. Instead of reading the Boy's epitaph, as we might expect him to do, he appears as if he were *listening* to it, quietly awaiting the Boy's call, like the silent owls earlier. The Boy's death is not the death of voice, but only a sleep and a forgetting of it: the personified church near which he "slumbers" is described as "forgetful"

> Of all her silent neighbourhood of graves,
> And listening only to the gladsome sounds
> That, from the rural school ascending, play
> Beneath her and about her. (5.402, 403–6)

"Listening only to the gladsome sounds": that is, not listening to the Boy, who nevertheless yet speaks? The "sounds" that "play," like music, about the "silent neighbourhood of graves" repeat the "jocund din" of the Boy's earlier colloquy. Death is not the end of voice for Wordsworth, but only another turning of voice – into stone or "speaking monument" (*Prelude*, 8.172), or the epitaphic "speaking face of earth" (*Prelude*, 5.13).

The conferring of speech on nature, anticipated in the personifying apostrophe to the cliffs and islands, implies that the poet calls on these natural objects to have them testify, to make them "responsive to his call" or invocation. Reiterating this movement, the Boy plays Narcissus to the owls' Echo, giving them a voice but half their own. The poet, through his poem, mutely "answers" the Boy, whose hootings are now "the ghostly language of the ancient earth" (*Prelude*, 2.309), *de profundis*. Gray's *Elegy*, with another mute inglorious poet in another country churchyard, reverberates in the mind: "Ev'n from the tomb the voice of Nature cries."[51]

The turning aside of address, even to the point of its turning around, carries us far into the interplay of voice in Wordsworth. In these "turnings intricate of verse" (*Prelude*, 5.603), directional shifts from cause to effect, or from expostulation to reply, become redoubled when we discover that the source is already an echo, self-mimicking in its repetition. Like the "dear Sister" in book 14 of *The Prelude* (265) or, even more, like Eve in another of Frost's poems, the Boy of Winander teaches the birds to sing: "Never again would birds' song be the same. / And to do that to birds was why [he] came."[52]

7 How to Do Things with Shakespeare: Illustrative Theory and Practice in Blake's *Pity*

DAVID L. CLARK

Fancy cannot be embodied any more than a simile can be painted; and it is as idle to attempt it as to impersonate *Wall* or *Moonshine*.
William Hazlitt, *Characters of Shakespeare's Plays*

What is an illustration, and what must a text be if it can be represented by an illustration? No English artist ever asked these innocent-sounding questions with the acuity and persistence of William Blake, and possibly at no point with more complex results than in some of the large colour prints of 1795. One print in particular (figure 1) stands in a strikingly revisionary relationship with its Shakespearean source, which it treats not as the representation of a perception – as is the case in conventional illustration – but as a field of rhetorical figures which can be detached from their original context and rearranged by the illustrator. The ensuing displacement between Blake's picture and his subject in Shakespeare may explain why the illustration lacks a title,[1] as if the artist were intent on marking his illustration's curious abstention from the text that it also figures forth. But partly because of a brief note scribbled by Frederick Tatham on the back of a pencil sketch now in the British Museum, we have known since the nineteenth century that the design illustrates a familiar, though notoriously difficult, passage from *Macbeth*. By convention the print is entitled *Pity*, after the soliloquy in which Macbeth, meditating on the consequences of his proposed assassination of the king, is transported by strange figures of pathos that rapidly assume an apocalyptic intensity. This is from Samuel Johnson's edition:

> Besides, this *Duncan*
> Hath borne his faculties so meek, hath been
> So clear in his great office that his virtues
> Will plead, like angels, trumpet-tongu'd again
> The deep damnation of his taking off;

1 *Pity*

> And Pity, like a naked new-born babe,
> Striding the blast, or heav'n's cherubin hors'd
> Upon the sightless couriers of the air,
> Shall blow the horrid deed in ev'ry eye;
> That tears shall drown the wind —[2]

The fact that Blake's illustration is at several points a scrupulously literal reproduction of Macbeth's similes for "Pity" has often been recognized.[3] But due attention has not been given to the disruptive implications of this literalness, not only for the Shakespearean text at hand, but also, more generally, for what I will call the hermeneutics of illustration. Because it "reads" the "real Surface"[4] of a single character's rhetoric, to the disadvantage of "seeing" the play's narrative context, *Pity* serves the disfiguring function of recalling the systematic effacement and displacement of language by which conventional illustration assimilates the written word to the order of sight. Binding the text to the turns of its language, *Pity* gives emphasis to its figural life but only at the notable expense of representing the "events" in Shakespeare's story. It could be argued that Blake's illustrative interpretation interrupts the play at the point dividing language as description from language as trope; in other words, the print disarticulates the work that it reproduces by exposing a gap between *Macbeth*'s referential and figurative functions. The epistemological stakes in this instance would appear to be quite high, if we agree with Paul de Man that "to understand primarily means to determine the referential mode of a text."[5] Indeed, in referring to Shakespeare's figures of speech Blake's print illustrates precisely that aspect of the text which always suspends its ability to be referential. The ensuing "failure" of *Pity* to "understand" *Macbeth*, that is, Blake's resistance to see "through" the text, and thus to reinforce the text's referential capacity, effectively leaves the play as such unreadable. Suddenly rendering *Macbeth* uncannily opaque to itself, *Pity* surprises the spectator by returning to view that which ordinarily undergoes a kind of repression or defacement whenever the process of *reading* writing is imagined to be one of *seeing* scenes. And like the uncanny, what returns is at once alien and familiar, Shakespeare's words and yet quite unlike anything we have previously seen of *Macbeth*. *Pity* consequently possesses not only a particular interest in relation to Blake's pictorial work but also a more general importance as the exploration of the nature of the relationship between words and images, reading and seeing. In approaching this painting, and in using it as a vehicle with which to explore the theory and practice of illustration, I will examine five closely related issues: Blake's literalist tactics in the context of the sister arts tradition; the artist's pictorial focus on the figure of personification; the relationship between pictures and the blank, literal, structures of apposition which underwrite Macbeth's soliloquy; literalism as a reflection on the difference between the cognitive and the performative aspects of language, between meaning and the rhetorical devices of meaning; and the implications of *Pity*, considered as the limit case of Blake's lifelong fascination with visualizing figures, for a hermeneutics of illustration in which the relationship of words to pictures is not simply one of seeing and re-presentation but, interminably, of reading and interpretation.

I THE ILLUSTRATION OF FIGURE
To Understand literally these metaphors ... seems ... absurd ...
Sir Joshua Reynolds, *Discourses on Art*

Blake painted *Pity* in an age when illustrations were expected to exhibit a "slavish fidelity" to the subject matter of the text and to the iconographic conventions that had come to govern its representation in pictures.[6] This was especially important for illustrations of Shakespeare, whose timeless themes were considered by England's intelligentsia to be the salvation of British art, an art – so Alderman Boydell complained – that had otherwise declined into "painting Portraits of those, who, in less than half a century" would "be lost in oblivion."[7] In this context, Blake's illustrative attention to Shakespeare's similes, rather than to his noble characters or exemplary stories, appears eccentric, even perverse. We might well ask: Where is Macbeth in this illustration of *Macbeth*? Unlike Shakespeare illustrations done before, or, for that matter, since Blake's composition, including most of those done by the artist himself, *Pity* treats the turns of Macbeth's anxious soliloquy as if *language* rather than a character were speaking, and thus the proper subject of the play's pictorial representation.

If Blake's curious design belongs to anything approaching a tradition, it is certainly not the familiar one which has always imagined the written text to be a conducive transparency to a visualizable referent that quite naturally lends itself to illustration. To be sure, *Pity* visualizes Shakespeare's words, but in a quite unconventional manner whose alertness to rhetorical language recalls the literalist strategies intermittently adopted in some medieval illuminations of the Bible. In the case of the ninth-century Latin psalter at Utrecht, for example, the illuminators take the Psalmist at his word and illustrate his plea – "Awake, why sleepest thou, O Lord?" – with a scene depicting God snoring comfortably in a tiny bed.[8] A similar fascination with what Walter Pater called "all that latent figurative texture in speech"[9] surfaces in more modern instances: in Freud and Benjamin, who in separate but complementary ways point to the profaning power of the literalist imagination at work in, respectively, the displacement of dream-thoughts and the translation of poetry;[10] and in Proust, Ruskin, and Pater, all of whom remark upon the "special temper" that Giotto exhibits in the representation of personified characters, figures whose literal vividness and grotesquery deflects and defers the unambiguous uptake of their allegorical significance.[11] If, as Pater claims, Blake is Giotto's artistic heir, then *Pity* represents a limit-case of that "special temper," fully exhibiting a "preoccupation" (as Pater says of Giotto) "with the aesthetic beauty of the image itself, the *figured* side of figured expression, the *form* of the metaphor."[12] What each of the examples that I have cited demonstrates is the allure of an interpretive move, at once original and unsettling, which articulates rather than effaces the difference between the materiality of the sign and what that sign is made to mean, whether by spectators or by readers. In the print at hand, Blake's studied focus on the figured side of Macbeth's figured expression puts to us that what the text literally says can and perhaps should be scrutinized without reference to the speaker or to the set of circumstances of his or her utterance – factors which ordinarily play an important role in determining both the meaning and the illustration of what is said. In quite specifically refusing to volatilize the letter of Macbeth's allegorical figures for pity, Blake's design reminds us that conventional illustration shares with conventional reading a constitutive disposition to treat *all* language in what could be called "allegorical" terms: as displaced figures for purely literal referents and as the written representation of an essentially visual perception.

Pity is by no means the only instance of literalism in Blake's illustrations. John Linnell, Blake's last important patron, once observed of the designs for *Night Thoughts* that "[Edward] Young ... seems almost the only poet who has had his mere metaphors illustrated and made corporeal."[13] Although Linnell's ambivalently complimentary remark underlines the originality of his visionary friend's technique, it is not altogether accurate: Blake also targets the rhetorical language of Bunyan, Milton, Gray, and, of course, Shakespeare, among others. In *A Sunshine Holiday* (figure 2), one of the illustrations in the *L'Allegro* series (c. 1816–20), for example, Blake's busy picture of the revelling townsfolk described in Milton's poem must compete with the phantasmagoric image of a naked giantess whose form blends imperceptibly into that of the mountain she sits upon. Two passages are conflated in this illustration, as Blake's manuscript notes make clear:[14] at one point Milton refers to the "Mountains on whose barren breast / The Laboring Clouds do often rest," and it is the dormant metaphor in this passage that Blake brings to life in the upper background of his illustration; the lower foreground, on the other hand, is taken up with a more conventional illustration of what is "happening," as it were, in the poem's narrative, the celebration of the "Sunshine Holiday." What is remarkable from the point of view of a hermeneutics of illustration is that Blake feels entirely free not only to disinter Milton's metaphor of the "barren breast" but also to "introduce" it (as he says) "into" a later point in the narrative account. In effect, he splices the personification of the mountain into the visual representation of the poem's ostensible subject matter, as if Milton's anthropomorphic figures were characters possessing the same referential status as the townsfolk. In his commentary Blake flatly states that the mountain and the townsfolk are identically "Humanized" (E683) – instinct with God – on this glad day. The assertion that all things manifest the "Human Form Divine" is a long-standing belief in Blake's myth, perhaps most fervently declared in the closing moments of *Jerusalem*. What should be emphasized here, however, is that the illustrator approaches Milton with the assumption that even his most unobtrusive metaphors express that fact. Blake's perfunctory explanation of his illustrative practice is helpful, but limited, to the extent that it familiarizes what is strange about this picture by too quickly reconciling its unusual visual details to the artist's larger mythic concerns. It is worth remarking that *A Sunshine Holiday* is not so much unaligned with Milton's poem as doubly aligned, treating the lan-

2 *A Sunshine Holiday*, illustration for Milton's *L'Allegro*

guage of *L'Allegro* as neither entirely descriptive nor figural but both at once. From the viewer's perspective, the illustration thus embodies a richly suggestive self-difference, one fraught with implications for the relationship between words and images.

It could be argued that Blake's literalist hermeneutic survives even to his last extended project, the illustrations to the *Divine Comedy*, especially the depictions of the various sinners and their punishments in hell. Blake reserves some of his most graphically disturbing pictures for those moments in Dante when the narrative accounts of life in the inferno are partly generated by the literalizing of a figure: for example, the theological discord of the Schismatics is punished by an eternity of butchery and self-mutilation; similarly, those lovers whose reason was swept away by lust are doomed to being thrown helplessly about in the whirlwind of a "hellish storm."[15] Less lurid but equally unusual are some of the illustrations which Reverend Joseph Thomas commissioned Blake to do a little more than a decade before the Milton designs. Of the six watercolours which eventually emerged, one in particular adopts a pictorial strategy which looks back to *Pity* and ahead to *A Sunshine Holiday*. *As if an Angel Dropped Down from the Clouds* (figure 3) visualizes a simile from *Henry IV, Part I*, in which Sir Richard Vernon enthusiastically describes how Prince Henry rose

> from the ground like feather'd Mercury,
> And vaulted with such ease into his seat,
> As if an angel dropp'd down from the clouds,
> To turn and wind a fiery Pegasus,
> And witch the world with noble horsemanship.

Blake literalizes Sir Richard's figure for Henry's stately confidence and royal power by painting a muscular male angel who descends, arms and legs fully extended, toward a steed that leaps strenuously upwards to meet him. Unlike the design for *L'Allegro*, Blake omits all representation of the text's narrative from his picture, and instead dwells exclusively on the illustration of Shakespeare's figure – as he does in *Pity*. But along the top of the picture the artist adds the image of a woman who reclines upon a cloud with an open book, as if to signal the artist's interest in the problematical difference between written signs and the scenes those signs are ordinarily said to describe. In other words, the image functions supplementally as an interior reflection on the fact that the object of illustration is here that which is *read* rather than seen, the text momentarily conceived as a tissue of figures and rhetorical positings rather than as the record of a perception. The cloud from which the angel drops is the same cloud that props up the woman's book, suggesting that she is in fact reading *Henry IV, Part I*, but it is a reading where the visualization of Shakespeare's rhetoric would seem to have overtaken the performance of the play in the theatre of her mind. Considered reflexively as a (literal) scene of reading, the figure of the woman thus functions in two ways: first, she points to the paradoxical relationship of Blake's literalist illustrations to his target texts, which "picture" reading precisely to disrupt the more conventional assumption that reading is simply a form of seeing; and second, she projects within the space of

3 *As if an Angel Dropped Down from the Clouds*

the illustration Blake's hope that his audience will respond to the play in the same unusual way.[16]

II THE PROPER LIMITS OF METAPHOR

In fact the metaphor ought to have an apologetic air, so as to look as if it had entered a place that does not belong to it with a proper introduction, not taken it by storm, and as if it had come with permission, not forced its way in.

Cicero, *De Oratore*

From the eccentric perspective of Blake's literalist illustrations, then, what is a text? We can approach an answer to this question by considering the rhetorical behaviour of the similes from *Macbeth* that *Pity* illustrates. It cannot be accidental that Blake focuses on a passage which is itself a highly conspicuous example of how figural language, far from being simply illustrative in nature, can interrupt and displace the conceptual meaning that it is expected to transport. Pity is like a "naked new-born babe, / Striding the blast"; alternately it is like "heav'n's cherubin, hors'd / Upon the sightless couriers of the air." As readers have often noted, Macbeth's similes are unlikely likenesses because their proper meaning, the totalizing term which should provide the basis of the resemblance between the parts of the analogies, is far from obvious. On what grounds, in other words, can Macbeth's analogies be made? Shakespeare's figures are meant to confirm and to reinforce the significance of pity through multiple illustration; yet the rhetorical *effect* is quite another matter, for in addition to gesturing from different directions at a common conceptual centre, the similes overlap and communicate between themselves, producing the curious confusions of sense which have always made the passage an equivocal subject of fascination in Shakespeare criticism.

In a famous essay from *The Well-Wrought Urn*, for example, Cleanth Brooks makes the most of the passage's rhetorical ambiguities: "Is the babe natural or supernatural?" he asks. Is it "an ordinary helpless babe, who, as a newborn, could not, of course, even toddle, much less stride the blast? Or is it some infant Hercules, quite capable of striding the blast, but, since it is powerful and not helpless, hardly the typical pitiable object?" "[I]s the cherubim comparison really any more successful?" he continues: "Would not one of the great warrior archangels be more appropriate to the scene than the cherub? Does Shakespeare mean for pity or for fear of retribution to be dominant in Macbeth's mind?"[17] To ask these questions is tacitly to confirm that figural language generates ambiguities which escape critical paraphrase. That Brooks will go on to expend considerable interpretive ingenuity answering them, thereby determining the *logos* or ground of the metaphors whose difficulty had attracted his interest in the first place, seems to corroborate de Man's observation that "Close reading ... cannot fail to respond to structures of language which it is the more or less secret aim of literary teaching to keep hidden."[18] Moreover, by delimiting the very aspect of the text which he also argues is the sign of its unparaphrasable literarity, Brooks betrays a hermeneutical anxiety which is hardly confined to twentieth-century formalism, for Macbeth's similes have been a notorious interpretive crux among close readers of Shakespeare since the earliest annotated editions.[19] In the eighteenth and nineteenth centuries criticism of these lines ranges from the censure of its "strained and unnatural imagery"[20] to the ambivalent responses witnessed by Horace Furness's

New Variorum, whose annotators fluctuate between denouncing the passage as "pure rant" and attributing its "wild, extravagant, phantasmagoric images" to Macbeth's paranoid dementia.[21] The argument that the "unrestrained imagination" of Macbeth's language embodies his unstable psychological state continues to have credence, perhaps because it claims to discover meaningfulness even and especially in that language's obscurity. In any case, the counter-argument that the soliloquy reflects a lapse in Shakespeare's creative intelligence has long since gone out of fashion. Only "a mind involved in the incoherent flow of its own ideas," to cite D.A. Traversi's fine phrase, can account for the "distortion and obscurity"[22] of Macbeth's soliloquy. I refer to these interpretations because they demonstrate in different ways and from different critical quarters how Shakespeare's rhetorical language consistently (and understandably) elicits from readers a desire to make it more narrowly referential and therefore to make sense of its seeming nonsense. It could be argued that Macbeth's language has so often been the subject of this sort of scrutiny because his tropes *must* be assimilated, since in fact they make salient and problematic the question of reconciling figures to their conceptual ground, the life of the letter to the idealizations of the spirit – the question, in other words, of the possibility of reading. The implied threat seems to be that unless the passage's figures are brought within what Brooks rather earnestly calls "the proper limits of metaphor," they will only mar the integrity of the text with "excrescences, mere extravagances of detail."[23]

Perhaps the most pertinent question here is not "what do these compounded similes for pity mean?" but "what does the fact that they have always been a troublesome issue mean?" Brooks's rhetoric of figuration, his characterization of uncontrolled figure as pure exorbitance, identifies him with an intellectual tradition which has always treated the trope as a turn away from truth, a turn, moreover, that harbours within itself the possibility of unruliness, even usurpation. Properly speaking, which is to say, within certain "limits," the rhetorical figure should illustrate, just as pictorial illustration illustrates: as a useful supplement to thought. But the hazard of the figure's errant powers is never far way, and indeed forms the horizon of impropriety against which the notion of a proper meaning defines itself. What modern readers like Brooks see as the menace of a certain linguistic unseemliness, Blake's contemporaries could feel more sharply as the threat of outright sedition. David Simpson points out that "the general tenor of eighteenth-century opinion is that metaphor can function as an illustrative strategy, in which case it is appropriate and desirable, but must never be allowed to question or unsettle the stability (ontological and visual) of that which it illustrates. It must be at the service of its employer, but must never raise its hand against him."[24] Such service may well be the object of conventional illustration, whether in pictures or in figures; but the effect can be quite different, as the curiously unstable nature of Macbeth's similes has consistently demonstrated. Blake is remembered for strongly mistrusting systems that exacted unquestioned obedience from human beings, and he worked always to unsettle hierarchical discriminations predicated on what was thought to be proper and improper. None of his illustrations, least of all his literalist designs, could be said simply to "serve" their target texts, a fact that made Blake's relationship with his real employers notoriously difficult, not to say unprofitable. What makes these designs unusual and disruptive, however, is that by illustrating the illustrative aspect of the target text's language, they bring out the interior distances that already divide the text from itself. As Tilottama Rajan has recently argued, "illustration and repetition make expression a differential process, by creating crevices between the parts of an analogy or between the different discursive planes (conceptual and figurative, abstract and concrete) that supplement and repeat each other."[25] In the case of the *Macbeth* print, it is precisely the extravagance and impropriety of Shakespeare's own figures that provide the artist with an illustrative opening, an occasion to intervene at the point where Macbeth's proper meaning is most at odds with his rhetorical expression. Opportunistically exploiting the text's self-differences, Blake's illustration is doubly improper: by picturing Macbeth's language rather than the scene that he occupies, the artist arrests the representation of the work as a continuously unfolding narrative; but in choosing to reproduce these particular figures, he also literalizes the interruptive effects already evident *within* Macbeth's similes, whose notorious resistance to reading blocks and complicates their efficient translation from figurative illustration to conceptual referent. In one move, Blake brings into the foreground what other readers of Shakespeare have systematically struggled to master, and, for reasons which have been no less systematic, what conventional illustrators of *Macbeth* have elided altogether.[26]

III   CONSIDERATIONS OF REPRESENTABILITY

But it cannot be ignored that Blake's print is characterized by its own revealing elisions and displacements. As we have already seen, Macbeth's similes are set up as alternate, contiguous illustrations of the same thing: pity is *either* like a "naked new-born babe" *or* like "heav'n's cherubin." Yet Blake signally disregards the discrimination urged by the passage's either/or structure – indeed, he has no choice in the matter, for how could apposition or contiguity as such be translated into pictures? Blake rather represents Macbeth's figures not only sharing the same pictorial "space," but making an ambiguous form of contact: the naked babe ascends purposefully above a supine woman and into the outstretched arms of a distracted cherub. To put it differently, *Pity* is constituted by the "fantastic" substitution of a visual, existential relationship *for* a rhetorical, metonymic one, whose fundamentally non-visual character makes it the other-scene of Blake's illustration, visible only because of the "prior" erasure of its invisibility.

I borrow the term "fantastic" from Freud, who uses it to describe what happens when the dream-work, which is primarily visual, and which he repeatedly compares to illustration, must contend with the rhetorical structures that underwrite the non-visual dream-thoughts: "'if,' 'because,' 'just as,' 'although,' 'either – or,' and all the other conjunctions without which we cannot understand sentences or speeches."[27] "Considerations of representability" compel the dream to "destroy" ("vernichten") – the annihilatory violence of Freud's German is revealing – these structures, and to replace them with "absurd" visual equivalents.[28] The rhetoric of the dream-content stands in a relation of inadequacy to its representation in images because, as Freud says, "from the point of view of the dream" all that can be pictured is "a thing that is *capable of being represented*."[29] For our purposes it is especially interesting that Freud immediately identifies the absolute heterogeneity underlying the dream with the paragone, the war of signs between the sister arts:

The incapacity of dreams to express these things [i.e., the "connections" necessary to the understanding of language] must lie in the nature of the psychical material out of which dreams are made. The plastic arts of painting and sculpture labour, indeed, under a similar limitation as compared with poetry, which can make use of speech; and here once again the reason for their incapacity lies in the nature of the material which these two forms of art manipulate in their effort to express something.[30]

By way of illustration, Freud suggests that "in ancient paintings small labels were hung from the mouths of the persons represented, containing in written characters the speeches which the artist despaired of representing pictorially." The art-historical accuracy of Freud's claim notwithstanding, the need for the supplemental insertion of written characters into the pictorial space raises important questions about the relationship between words and pictures. The eighteenth-century commonplace that pictures are "mute poems" suddenly takes on a more sinister pall, as if the silence of painting stood for a certain irreducible deprivation accompanying the translation of language into images – a loss whose impact Freud nicely contains by associating it with a primitive past.

"Considerations of representability" also oblige Blake to translate the rhetorical structures or "connections" of Macbeth's soliloquy into visual terms. But as Freud's remarks from *The Interpretation of Dreams* suggest, the fantastical result of this (mis)representation points to the incommensurability of language and pictures as much as to their interchangeability.

Pity discloses a deep displacement between the visual design and the unremitting and invisible structures which belong specifically to language in Shakespeare's text; but in a print whose literalism affirms the independent life of the letter this displacement seems only fitting, acknowledging as it does the radical difference between seeing and reading, a difference which conventional illustration works to efface in the process of treating language as description rather than language as trope. This effacement is an issue that will demand further consideration; let me stress for the moment that *Pity* is thus not only an illustration of figure but also an illustration of the figure of illustration, or more precisely, of the catachrestic borrowing of terms from an order that is alien to language to visualize that which has no properly visual configuration in language itself, namely the contiguity and apposition of Macbeth's similes. The unlikely likeness underlying Blake's illustration is thus catachrestic, or conspicuously "abusive."[31] And yet for at least one reason it is also strangely overdetermined: the relationship between *Pity* and the rhetorical devices underwriting the Shakespearean source text is structurally homologous to the personifications that the illustration literalizes in pictures. In other words, like the translation of pity into "heav'n's cherubin" or a "new-born babe," the print's visual (re)composition of Macbeth's contiguous similes *itself* amounts to a personification: by carrying over the text's inanimate, metonymic relationship to an apparently animate, and, as it were, metaphoric one, *Pity* gives a form and a face to what is radically formless and faceless.[32]

The composition which results from this exchange begs for a unified interpretation. Yet the cryptic details of the design make a conclusive explication difficult, to say the least. With her carefully placed fingers and her distracted stare, the cherub in the foreground appears to have had the experience but missed the meaning of her contact with the babe. Is her gesture one of redemption or of indifference? Who is the sepulchral figure at the bottom of the illustration? What do we make of the unaligned gazes of the cherub and the babe – or of the blankness of the courier's closed, "sightless" eye, a literal blind spot amid Blake's luridly visionary picture? As one might expect, the details of the design have prompted diverse, sometimes antithetical interpretations, many of them appealing to the larger clarity of Blake's myth because, it is assumed, the print says nothing coherent about *Macbeth*.[33] We know, for example, that Blake associated pity with death and the divisiveness of sexual reproduction, but these notions are only equivocally figured forth in the illustration.[34] It may not be an admission of critical exhaustion to suggest that the interpretive difficulties which characterize *Pity* lie at the heart of what the print is about. More than suggesting that the illustration is irreducible either to Blake's myth or to its Shakespearean pre-text, these difficulties disclose the design's deeper resistances, those inscribed even in its material status as a painting. Lacking its own title, and thus relying on readers other than Blake to identify its source in Shakespeare, *Pity* is excluded from the single most powerful means by which an artist might determine how a painting and especially an illustration is to be interpreted. Anyone who has struggled with Blake's painting knows the truth of Mark Twain's advice that "a good legible label is usually worth, for information, a ton of significant attitude and expression in a historical picture."[35] And yet *Pity* (or whatever more or less arbitrary label we give to the design) distinctly evokes the *possibility* of a unified interpretation, primarily because Blake is here so conspicuously responsible for fabricating an existential relationship between two figures where none had existed before in Shakespeare – except at the "literal" level of Macbeth's contiguous similes. Morton Paley's understandably impatient observation – that "it is *Blake* who makes the cherubin receive the 'new-born babe,' yet no symbolic meaning emerges from this"[36] – nicely evokes the underlying problem of the design, the hermeneutical lacuna between what Blake has *done* to Shakespeare and the expectation of meaningfulness that this doing raises in the viewer's mind.

The point is certainly not that the painting cannot or should not be interpreted for its "symbolic meaning." It is only that the difficulty in making such an interpretation exposes the arbitrariness of the design's crucial details with respect to the rhetorical structure which it represents *as* and *in* a picture. Paradoxically, it is in the total absence of continuity between the illustration and the source text that the other-scene of Blake's illustration, belonging to Shakespeare's language and lying utterly beyond the reach of pictures or picturing, makes its spectral presence most problematically felt. Both effacing and figuring forth the passage from *Macbeth*, the print's very substitution of pictures for words points to that passage's blankness or invisibility (which is the radical blankness of language and which would not require the supplement of illustration if it were already visible), and reminds us that the abusive exchange of a visual, existential relationship for a sightless, rhetorical one is contingently imposed, marking an absolute heterogeneity between the pictorial configuration of the design and its linguistic ground. Blake "*makes* the cherubin receive the 'new-born babe'": does the imposed nature of this pictorial meeting explain why the cherub and the babe do not look at each other, as if residually registering, from within the painting, the *resistance* of the linguistic material to its coercion into pictures? The composition which results from the exchange of pictures for language triggers the demand for the sort of symbolic interpretation whose specific details Paley finds lacking. For the conception of a significance that precedes its representation in pictorial signs Blake substitutes a referent which is *after the fact* vis-à-vis the text in *Macbeth*, produced or posited by the arrangement of these signs and therefore more properly not the cause of the illustration's composition but a compositional *effect*. But the gap between the meaning of *Pity* and the way in which it comes to mean discloses more than the contrived character of the world it seems to represent; it also makes explicit that meaningfulness itself must await the metaphorical transport of linguistic relations – which are radically sense-less – into relations patterned after those found in the phenomenal world, relations which are alone open to symbolic interpretation as, for example, "redemptive" or "indifferent." Seeing is thus linked to the apprehension of significance; but it is a significance that remains subtended by the prior blankness which it displaces and against which the form and content of what is brought to sight can only appear as a kind of visual hallucination. In this instance, then, it could be said that considerations of representability unavoidably make illustration into a *dream* of the text, or at least of the text's specifically rhetorical features. The deep truth of the design is dissimulative and self-consuming: at once a meaningful representation and exposed to disfigurement by the meaninglessness of the rhetorical armature of which it is a representation, *Pity* functions at two levels that are unaccommodated to each other and yet inextricably interinvolved. The terms "illustration" or "illumination" hardly seem adequate to describe *Pity*, since the "solar language of cognition"[37] that they fully imply fails to account for the way in which the print uneasily raises the question of language prior to its phenomenalization, that is, before the figural eclipse which brings the text into light and sense.[38] Whatever symbolic significance we attribute to the painting can thus appear not as a simple object of cognition but as a form of delusion, blind to the aporia lying at the heart of *Pity* in which illumination is indistinguishable from an originating concealment, visual composition from rhetorical destruction (*Vernichtung*), meaning from senselessness.

IV   THE FIGURE OF ILLUSTRATION

> It is a figure called illustration, by which the forme of things is so set foorth in words, that it seemeth rather to be seene with the eies, then heard with the eares.
>
> John Marbeck, *A Book of Notes ... and Commonplaces ...*

From Blake's manipulation of Shakespeare's similes in *Pity* we see that *Macbeth* presents itself to the artist not as the source of a sequential narrative awaiting its more or less faithful translation into pictures, but as a *resource* of perfectly detachable figures whose connotations are undetermined by the original text, and thus meaningful only according to how the figures are de-composed and recombined by the translation. The scandalous nature of Blake's literalist interpretive strategy here – but also at scattered points throughout his work – would be difficult to exaggerate in an age which had quite different ideas about the hermeneutics of illustration and about the relationship between words and pictures. Indeed, we would need to go as far afield as psychoanalysis to find a theoretical articulation of an analogously exorbitant hermeneutical model. As Geoffrey Hartman points out in a discussion of *The Interpretation of Dreams*, "analysis so invests and supplements an original version that it becomes less an object and more a series of linguistic relays that could lead anywhere – depending on the system and who is doing the switching."[39] Blake's "illustration" – in the present context, the term can hardly escape being placed in cautionary quotation marks – similarly rewrites and freely extends the target text, as opposed to reflecting, and, as it were, parasitically commenting upon it. Like the "illuminated poetry," Blake's literalist attention to the language of the "original version" would thus seem to embody a strong critique rather than a belated apotheosis of the sister arts tradition that so dominated eighteenth-century aesthetics. As W.J.T. Mitchell has conclusively demonstrated, Blake's illuminated poetry is less a felicitous union of words and images than a "composite" of vigorously independent modes of representation. Yet it is obvious that Blake's visual work is not entirely made up of the illuminated texts, as Mitchell defines them. For reasons that no doubt had as much to do with day-to-day survival as with visionary zeal, Blake continued to work primarily as an illustrator – that is, painting pictures *after* the words of other writers rather than combining the two to produce a composite art. How then to sustain a critique of the sister arts tradition when the illustrative gesture as such unavoidably presupposes that painting and writing are to some extent complementary? By illustrating texts Blake risks reproducing the very error of identifying words and images which his illuminated work complexly repudiates. How to illustrate the crucial differences between language and pictures in an illustration?

What I want to suggest is that Blake's literalist illustrative tactics signal the artist's awareness of this dilemma. In other words, literalist visualizations – *Pity*, as I have argued, is simply the limit case in Blake's work – augur the closest possible engagement with the sister arts tradition, since they displace and disrupt that tradition, with its identification of images and words, from *within*. The reasons that Blake found the ancient notion of *ut pictura poesis* ("as a painting, so also a poem") an unpalatable one are not difficult to imagine. The elision of the dissimilarities between the arts could only contribute to their domination by "bloated General Forms" (E184;J38:19), the abstract conceptions of unity for which Blake had a life-long revulsion. Moreover, the notion that the arts shared an underlying ground implied the givenness of the "objective" world, which in turn legitimated the evaluation of art according to the accuracy with which that world was imitated or reflected. For Blake these epistemological conditions reduced painting and poetry alike to what he calls, with a palpable sense of weariness, "the sordid drugery of facsimile representations of merely mortal and perishing substances" (E541:*DC*). More significantly, Blake challenges the pictorialist principle underwriting the sister arts tradition, the enabling belief that words are at root pictures and that good poetry is consequently composed of language evoking the clearest pictures in the reader's mind. Literary pictorialism accounts in part for the emphasis on picturesque or scenic verse in eighteenth-century writing, and for the prevalence of what Jean Hagstrum calls "visualizable personification" and "visually conceived allegorical personages."[40] Blake seems to have been constitutively incapable of writing the first kind of poetry; his geographies are almost exclusively mental and fantastic rather than pretty and familiar. But whether his undeniable interest in personified figures reflects an incipient pictorialism is open to question.[41] Mitchell for one rejects this possibility on the grounds that Blake's figures are deliberately non-visualizable. It is true that verbal figures like "Religion hid in War" (E231;J75:20) are impossible to visualize, but the anti-pictorialist argument seems harder to endorse when we consider the number of instances in the prophetic texts in which the descriptions of the Four Zoas (and their extended families) are supplemented with quite striking visualizations. Moreover, even if "Blake rarely describes his personae in visual terms,"[42] he is nevertheless captivated by visual possibilities of personification in the work of other poets, as we have seen in the case of his literalist interpretations of Milton and Shakespeare.

The designs for the poems of Thomas Gray (c. 1797–98) provide an instructive instance of the artist's focus on the trope of personification. Although substantially different in style and media from the colour prints of 1795, Blake's illustrations to the Eton ode, to cite one example, repeatedly target Gray's figures, visualizing not only the obvious allegorical characters – which abound in the narrative – but the poem's buried or partly buried prosopopeia. Thus Gray's somewhat tired reference to the passions as "vultures of the Mind" prompts Blake's startling depiction of a horde of bird-monsters swarming over the heads of a group of unsuspecting children (figure 4). As in the case of the illustration for *Henry IV, Part I*, the Gray design can be seen as self-consciously reflecting upon its status as a visualization of the target text's figures. The bird-monsters emerge from behind the text-box, as if to literalize how Blake's illustrative tactics have compelled Gray's language to yield up its hidden metaphors. In a certain way these creatures *are* things of language, inhabiting the Eton ode's verbal texture, rather than the world to which those marks refer; and so it is appropriate that they appear to tumble out of the space on the page that has been reserved specifically for Gray's *words*. That Blake chooses to make the monsters as menacing as he does suggests that the passions do more than intimidate the mind: here the artist may also be literalizing how his attention to the poet's "dead" metaphors threatens to disrupt the referential function of the text, opening it to pictorial interpretations which, from the perspective of conventional illustration, could only appear as aberrant, monstrous. At the very least, the sheer luridness of Blake's illustration puts to us that his handling of personification is not straightforwardly antipictorialist but pictorialist to an exaggerated, even grotesque, degree.

What are we to make of this curious crossing of picture and figure, this survival or perhaps revival of visualizable personification in the midst of Blake's usual impatience with pictorialist aesthetics? In her discussion of the Gray illustrations Irene Taylor argues that the artist visualizes the poet's "language to go beyond it, to make connections and arouse feelings only dimly present in some of [his] ... figures of speech."[43] But about the origins of Blake's idiosyncratic illustrative practice she is almost apologetic, speculating that "it may have been partly his very lack of sophistication that made him leap the bounds of tact"[44] when he chose to give pictorial expression to the poet's "metaphors and personifications." The faintly judgmental quality of Taylor's remarks is curiously reminiscent of more strident objections made by Blake's contemporaries, who warned that the illustration of personified figures was not only naïve or tactless but also ensured a profound loss in their rhetorical effect. As Burke writes in *A Philosophical Inquiry into the Origin of Our Ideas of the Sublime and the Beautiful*, poetry's "apparitions, its chimeras, its harpies, its allegorical figures, are grand and affecting; and though Virgil's Fame, and Homer's Discord, are obscure, they are magnificent figures. These figures in painting would be clear enough, but I fear they might become *ridiculous*."[45] Steven Knapp points out that Coleridge shared Burke's "sense of the inability of painting to match sublime personification,"[46] ready evidence of which lay with the illustrators of Milton who had endeavoured to depict the meeting between Satan and Death at the gates of Hell. Blake himself could not resist illustrating the same scene from *Paradise Lost*, although the result was not at all of the kind that Coleridge specifically criticizes. The artist's weirdly transparent figure for Death is the farthest thing from the "skeleton, the dryest and hardest image"[47] that Coleridge found objectionable in other illustrations. Yet Blake's original iconography might well have prompted similar criticism, for Coleridge's discomfort is not so much with a particular style of illustration as it is with the threat of ridiculousness posed by the illustration of figures as such.

Eighteenth-century readers that were less troubled by the rhetorical extravagance of Macbeth's soliloquy could praise it for the same reason that Milton's infamous scene was considered powerfully evocative: that is to say, for the unpicturable "obscurity" of its grand figures. An annotator in Furness's *New Variorum* briefly considers whether Shakespeare's apocalyptic scene was inspired by an earlier painting, for example, but he does so plainly in order to reaffirm poetry's power of sublimity: "what

4 "Yet see how all around them wait / The vultures of the Mind," illustration for Gray's *Ode on a Distant Prospect of Eton Collège*

[Shakespeare] ... has here said," he concludes, "no painter could so well express in outlines."[48] For Blake the argument that language, rather than images, possessed the capacity to excite a "sublime feeling of the unimaginable" – as Coleridge could suggest[49] – was to miss the point, since that which had no "outline" was simply without imaginative significance. Yet the question remains: what interdiction does Blake violate by painting the very picture that the *Variorum* annotator cannot imagine as Shakespeare's pictorial source? What exactly is risked by painting the figured side of allegorical figures?

That a risk of some sort is involved is evocatively implied by Hazlitt, who worried that the material representation of Shakespeare's "Poetry" on stage was absurdly reductive. "Fancy cannot be embodied any more than a simile can be painted," he writes in *Characters of Shakespeare's Plays;* "and it is as idle to attempt it as to impersonate *Wall* or *Moonshine*."[50] In other words, the performance of Shakespeare's fanciful play, and thus its translation from a world of words into so much stage business, is comparable in its dis-enchanting effect to the crude dramaturgy of Shakespeare's mechanicals, who break the dramatic illusion of the play by calling attention to the fictiveness of their roles. But what is the force of Hazlitt's simile of painting a simile? What is the analogous dis-enchantment in language, or more specifically, in the representation of similes in paintings? David Marshall's account of *A Midsummer Night's Dream* in the context of Hazlitt's remarks is helpful: "the threat of the mechanicals' literal-mindedness," he writes, "would be its reflection of the inevitable *disfiguring* inherent in presenting moonshine ... The question of the play is whether presenting and representing must mean misrepresenting; whether *figure* must be synonymous with *disfigure*; whether *figure* must mean or even might mean literalize, or literally, *de-figure*."[51] The equivalent threat of de-figuration posed by the representation of similes in paintings becomes clearer as we move the discussion of Blake's literalist strategy to a rhetorical context and thus away from a primarily psychological discussion having to do with the experience of the verbal sublime. Simply put, Blake is to illustrative practice what Wall and Moonshine are to dramaturgy; literalizing written figures in material images, he calls attention to the *un*likeness of the figures for their conceptual meaning, so that whatever likeness is suggested to the mind must compete with the difference that is everywhere presented to the eye. As J. Hillis Miller observes with reference to Giotto's unusual allegorical frescoes at Padua, "the more vividly and literally" the figured side of the figure is represented, "the more it brings out into the open the fact that the 'ethical' meaning – Temperance, Hope, whatever – has ... not been represented at all. It has only been indirectly named in a metaphor."[52] To the extent that *Pity* visualizes written figures it would seem to defy the linguistic bias of Burke and Coleridge, and to embrace the counter-argument, prevalent in the eighteenth century, that "pictorially conceived allegorical personages" were the most vivid embodiment of an underlying kinship, not incompatibility, between words and pictures.[53] But the very vividness of Blake's literalism invites us to consider not just the pictorial possibilities of personification, but the *indirectness* or aberrant turn of language by which the metaphor makes this visibility possible and brings the radically invisible concept of which it is a metaphor into sight. In so far as personification is paradigmatic of tropes that give a form to the formless, it is the exemplary instance of such making. Blake's literalist practice de-figures and marks the text *as* text, as a site of rhetorical positings or indirect namings which reflect nothing that is properly picturable and which consequently owe everything to the substitutive capacity of the trope, the figurality of the figure.

By painting personifications, which is to say by marking the total absence of continuity between sensible image and immaterial idea, Blake brings out what contemporaneous theoretical discussions of prosopopeia tacitly recognize: that consciousness and knowledge are irreducible to metaphorical transferences. As Earl Wasserman argues, in Blake's time the figure of personification was treated not simply as one trope among many but as the enabling condition of thinking itself; eighteenth-century thinkers, he argues, "recognized that of all the rhetorical figures, prosopopeia is precisely that one that best corresponds to the true nature of human abstraction, for it presents a universal in the corporeal substance by which alone it has existence for man and can be comprehended by him."[54] Wasserman cites the prominent educational theorist, David Fordyce: "what is *Sensible must*, by some Similitude or Analogy, represent what is *Intellectual*," he writes in 1786; "The Idea *must* be cloathed in a bodily Form, to make it visible and palpable to the gross Understanding."[55] Fordyce's imperatives – which I emphasize here – underline how the act of thinking is inseparable from the rhetorical substitutions with which it is carried out. (In an analogous way, Kant argues that since human beings are not perfectly rational creatures, knowing only by means of pure thought, there must be a faculty that enables them to refer concepts to what is given to the mind by sensible intuition; interestingly, although the German philosopher's work is more technically precise than that of his English counterparts, the specifically figural nature of this "referring" as a linguistic "making" or positing in the form of personification is not as explicit in *The Critique of Judgement* as it is in Fordyce's essay.) Blake's literalism similarly evokes the rhetorical basis of the mind's presentation of objects to itself, and does so by marking the sheer heterogeneity of conceptual abstraction and the means by which that abstraction is bequeathed a concrete immediacy through the necessary imposition of a figure: concepts cannot be embodied, they can only be indirectly named in metaphor.

But Blake's illustrative tactics go one step further than exposing the unlikeness of verbal figures for their abstract meanings. In *Pity* the figured side of Shakespeare's figures is brought into view to the exact extent that the figuration as such – which is to say, the positing or imposition of relation in language – is hidden: the gap between conceptual understanding and sensible intuition repeats another, deeper division, this one between the meaningfulness of Shakespeare's language and the literal, material constituents of that language. For as I have suggested, the tropological structure underwriting the passage in *Macbeth*, in which "pity" is analogous *either* to a new-born babe *or* to "heav'n's cherubin," has not been represented at all; the positing force of this either/or structure has only been fantastically effaced and displaced by a picture. If abstractions remain unavailable to understanding except through personification, then so too does the substitutive and appositional movement of the figure itself. To put it another way: Hazlitt's prohibition against painting similes, which *Pity* transgresses, is fundamentally a warning against de-figuring the radical unlikeness of the language's semantic and formal functions. The rhetorical structure of Macbeth's extravagant analogies is the blind, non-signifying aspect of language against which all visualized and symbolic representations must seem arbitrary and imposed, a mere "impersonation" of the text rather than its illustration. To paint a simile is *not* to paint a simile; in effect, it is to paint the impossibility of painting a simile, substituting pictures for the linguistic substitutions and structures which are themselves unpicturable. Similarly, to read a figure is to make "sense" of it, that is, to reconcile the sense-less, material, articulations of language to its meaning. Since the carrying over – *metaphorein* – of Macbeth's lurid figures cannot be pictured as such, its "annihilation" in the form of the picture that we actually get in *Pity* is as inevitable as it is aberrant: both aberrant *and* inevitable because the figurality of the figure is unpicturable and thus always only being pictured. How else to imagine the non-sensible articulation of the figure in anything but sensible terms, as a "literal," visual relation *like* the one between the cherub and the babe that is represented at the centre of Blake's painting? Paul Ricoeur points out that "the word 'metaphor' itself [is] a metaphor, the metaphor of displacement and therefore a transfer in a kind of space."[56] The figure of figure as a form of transference recalls how the compositional "space" in *Pity* is itself dominated by an ambiguously meaningful movement, a translation *from* the "mother" figure at the bottom of the design *to* the "couriers" or carriers whose eyes are "sightless." The carrying-over conceived as an irreducibly linguistic "phenomenon" cannot be seen; strictly speaking, it is not a sensible relation at all, but "considerations of representability" make it impossible to imagine the *relatedness* underwriting Macbeth's speech, or, for that matter, any of language's "forms" of articulation, in terms that are not already fully caught up in a metaphors relating to the senses.[57]

Ultimately, then, the exorbitant difference between picture and rhetoric in *Pity*, and the way in which the picture's visible form marks and blots out the source text's linguistic articulation, brings into view a breach or deep self-displacement that always and everywhere inhabits language as its constitutive feature. As Andrzej Warminski argues, language is "divided against itself ... as the *meaning* of words against the *order* of words, in short ... between language as meaning and language as syntax, articulation, non-signifying jointings or cleavings, a system of meaningless differential markings."[58] Though these "jointings or cleavings" are "the prop upon which meaning leans, and with which it is immediately confused,"[59] they remain necessarily illegible, in the same way that the sheer analogizing force of Macbeth's figures is itself unrepresentable in Blake's picture. In figuring forth rhetorical relation as literal, existential relation, *Pity* "pictures," as it were, what always goes-without-reading in language: the senseless, illegible cleft between the cognitive and performative aspects of language, between the meaningfulness of language and the irreducibly material elements (including the positing of analogies, but also, by extension, punctuation and syntax) that "act" at the level of the letter as the condition of the possibility of readable writing. By representing this cleft, Blake's tactics are structurally homologous to those adopted by Hölderlin in his bizarre, word-for-word "translations" of Sophocles. As Walter Benjamin points out, these necessarily unintelligible translations illustrate how literalist attention to the material constituents of the target text precipitates a sudden, "abysmal" loss of sense. All meaningful translation, that is, translation predicated on the communication of meaning (whether into another language or into pictures), opens itself up to the disfiguring power of this "monstrous" prospect, or to what Benjamin also calls "pure language" ("reine Sprache"), that which is *purely language*.[60]

V   TURNING READERS INTO SPECTATORS
> Written marks, to the extent that they are writing, are in some sense invisible – to be read, not seen.
>
> Cynthia Chase, *Decomposing Figures*

By literalizing figures which are "in" the language of a text but not in the realm of events to which that text refers, *Pity* throws into relief what conventional illustration suppresses or forgets in order to promote the conception that language is a serviceable transparency rather than a site of figural production, differential markings, and linguistic jointings. The notion that visualizations of texts consistently turn a blind eye to an irreducible element of the language that they claim to bring to sight returns us to the questions with which my remarks began: what is an illustration, and what must a text be if it can be represented by an illustration? The extent to which conventional illustration amounts to a form of literal deface-ment is perhaps summed up most forcefully by imagining an edition of *Macbeth* that was visualized in its entirety along the lines suggested by *Pity*. Blake's design puts to us that this "other" Shakespeare Gallery, presumably as alien and unhomely to our eyes as to those of Alderman Boydell's contemporaries, has been systematically elided in favour of illustrations which assimilate the Shakespearean text to the order of description. Perhaps the uncanniness and originality about *Pity* is a measure of how deeply inscribed the aesthetics of pictorialism have otherwise been in our conception of texts; indeed, the fact that readers continue to speak unreflectively of *Macbeth*'s *images* suggests a residual desire to think of Shakespeare's figures as pictures even when attention is paid specifically to the rhetorical elements of the text's language. When we also consider that a literally illustrated Shakespeare would amount to a series of disconnected visual scenes quite at odds with the coherent progression of the play's story, it becomes apparent that conventional illustration supplements the institution of the text's meaningful continuity. Illustration ordinarily refigures reading as a kind of seeing, and gives literal expression to the desire to see the text as an uninterrupted reflection of a fully formed world which is equally open to verbal and visual representation. Illustration accords a massive privilege to narrative because it so readily naturalizes the fiction that what is reported in the text is a series of successive events that have "occurred," whether in actuality or in the theatre of the mind. In other words, illustration hypostatizes the narrated by giving it the status of an existent reality whose givenness is precisely what enables any single "moment" of it to be brought into sight. But *Pity*'s sudden and arbitrary intervention at the point of the text's "real Surface" puts the text at odds with its own story, and thus disrupts the assumption that language is simply the making present of a pre-existing real. Blake's literalist attention to both the text's personifications and its non-referential rhetorical structures reminds us that the unity of the text (conceived as a continuously unfolding verbal replication of a visualizable world) is in fact a hermeneutical construction, a readerly invention which is necessary to the text's intelligibility as the narrative description *of* "something," but only possible at the cost of effacing the local effects of its non-referential, figural language.

In an age whose dominant aesthetic fostered – with an insistence which now appears somewhat overanxious – the hallucination that poems were "speaking pictures" and pictures "mute poems," it was perhaps inevitable that Blake's contemporaries sublated the difference between seeing and reading and thus the displacement effects generated by the substitution of one term for the other. As Mitchell suggests, the popularity of projects like Boydell's "Shakespeare Gallery" was "symptomatic of the belief that painting would be enhanced by an alliance with literature and that, despite some technical problems, translation from one medium to the other was possible and even inevitable."[61] In the days before he came under the spell of Lessing's *Laokoön*, even an artist as close temperamentally to Blake as Henry Fuseli could proclaim how exquisitely fitted words were to visual representation: "The excellence of pictures or of language," he writes in 1788, "consists of raising clear, complete and circumstantial images and *turning readers into spectators*."[62] Blake's tactics in *Pity* compel us to read this standard defence of the sister arts for the difference, for although Fuseli begins by asserting the equivalence of "pictures" and "language," he concludes by tacitly acknowledging that verbal images will need to be changed – "turn[ed]" is the word with some relevance here – from something that is *read* into something that is *seen* in order to secure that equivalence. Although the sister arts are equal, one is more equal than the other.

Pity addresses the hidden mechanism of this inequality, underwriting as it does the suspiciously easy effacement of language as language even amidst claims for the happy sisterhood of words and pictures. What needs emphasis from the start is that *Pity* does not then consist of a rejection of spectatorship. "Spectator" is the very word that Blake uses in *A Vision of the Last Judgment* (E560) to characterize the ideal viewers of his pictures, but, significantly, it is a term he associates with a process of active "entry" rather than passive reception. In the case of *Pity*, Blake's argument is not with the visualization of a text but much more specifically with the act of concealment by which the metaphorical basis of that visualization is hidden or disfigured. Readers *can* become spectators – *Pity* is the ocular proof – but "only" by means of the trope or rhetorical decree which translates the text into an image, the same trope that turns an invisible abstraction like "pity" into a new-born babe. The illustration of a figure from *Macbeth* unmasks both the figure of illustration and its disfiguring effects. For the pictured text engenders readers as spectators first by defacing the text and then by masking the rhetorical basis of its own engendering. When spectators fail to "enter" actively into conventional illustration, they cease reflecting upon the transfers and elisions which institute the text as description; readers thus turn into spectators, but blind themselves to their turning. Not to see this inescapable play of blindness and sight is to misapprehend illustration as the accurate and natural reproduction of the text: the viewer takes what is only a figure – the picture *of* the text – for its literal expression.

Of course, under the auspices of the sister arts tradition the conceit of illustration is that no such rhetorical subterfuge takes place. In this sense the relationship that pictures share with language is characterized by a duplicity and parasitism that Blake consistently identified with a particular kind of imaginative failure. Illustration affects a transparency to and dependency upon the text, claiming to repeat or clarify what the words have already made apparent. By bringing back into view that aspect of the text which is masked by conventional illustration, *Pity* suggests that matters are not nearly so genteel. Pictures are in fact ambivalently supplemental, both a self-effacing addition to the complete text and an invisible emendation of it, as if language suffered from a certain lack which its transport into pictures would remedy. Visual images hypocritically exercise a will-to-power over language, turning the text into something that it is not, *except metaphorically*. "Seeming a [sister], being a tyrant," to paraphrase *Milton* (E100;7:22), illustration demonstrates toward language precisely the disguised malice for which Blake had a single, bitterly ironic name: *pity*.

The pity that subtends the pictorialist conception of language can be expressed as outright rather than concealed contempt. Leonardo da Vinci, for example, dismisses poetry as "blind painting,"[63] as a language of images, in other words, which cannot be considered as actual pictures and so is bereft of sight. For Leonardo blindness is a figure for the radical imagelessness of writing. Poetic language as language is properly unseen, in the same way that it is mute: words are viewless and unheard until their irresistible translation into pictures and voice. Now the figural substitution of blindness for invisibility is not unfamiliar to Blake or Shakespeare, since Macbeth employs the same device when he compares pity to "Heav'n's cherubin horsed / Upon the *sightless* couriers of the air." Blake's illustration visualizes Shakespeare's metaphor for the invisible winds as horses whose eyes are blank, sightless. The couriers give the sightless winds a form and a face, but their blindness recalls the sheer aberrance and defacement of representing that which cannot be pointed to or seen. In these blank eyes *Pity* provides a paradoxical focal point for the hermeneutical problems that it raises. Invisibility is made visible as blindness, as though the bringing into sight brought with it a deprivation, a sightlessness. Are the blind horses then not an uncanny figure for illustration, whose function is to transport the invisible letter into visibility while itself remaining out of sight? The sightless couriers are clearly seen, yet do not themselves see, as if blind paintings of the double sightlessness that turns winds into horses and language into pictures: to begin with there is the blindness *to* the figure of illustration, the unreflected and therefore unseen linguistic moment which determines readers as spectators and words as images; and then there is the blindness *of* the trope (of illustration) as such, the radical invisibility of the very figure which brings language to sight. *The blank eyes, the literal, visible defacement of the horses is a figure for the invisible, figural defacement of illustration.* To put it another way: *Pity* makes us aware that illustration – including the illustration at hand – hides to the same extent that it reveals, and thus makes invisible the disfigurement for which it is itself responsible.

VI   THE TASK OF THE ILLUSTRATOR

Just as a tangent touches lightly and at but one point, with this touch rather than with the point setting the law according to which it is to continue on its straight path to infinity, a translation touches the original lightly and only at the infinitely small point of the sense, thereupon pursuing its own course according to the laws of fidelity in the freedom of linguistic flux.

Walter Benjamin, *The Task of the Translator*

In attempting to illuminate Blake's extraordinary print, we may find ourselves approaching a point which the artist would call the "Limit of Opacity." The only qualification is that, in the case of *Pity*, opacity (or blindness) shares with vision (or transparency) another and finer relationship than contrast. Though *Pity* (re)marks the text's figures in order to articulate the difference between reading the text and seeing the play, we remain spectators of a kind while Blake's illustration consists of pictures of language rather than language itself. Bound by the pictorialist conception of language that it interrogates, wholly disfigured by the disfigurement it outlines, *Pity* nevertheless has as its Shakespearean pre-text the sightless linguistic relations of Macbeth's language, "material" (to use Freud's term) whose "nature" it is to be irreducible to pictures. The fact that the print can only make this material "appear" in displaced form in a picture harbours a more general pathos: to the extent that legibility itself necessarily demands a similarly fantastic displacement of a text's stubborn structures, *all* texts are similarly "illustrated" and pictorialized, their intelligibility resting with the possibility of their literal senselessness being assimilated, by a sustained act of figuration, to the phenomenal order of light and sense. Illustration might then be said to be a figure for the more general process of comprehension and effacement called *reading*.

But where conventional reading institutes the text's intelligibility by privileging its referential meaning, *Pity*'s disruptive negotiation with *Macbeth* augurs a form of interpretation for which there is no obvious name. "Translation" might well suffice, though translation understood not as the stable carrying over of ideas from one language to another but as the radically revisionary engagement that Benjamin imagined to be the true "task of the translator": a brush with the target text at the point of its linguistic surface, a momentary point of contact and a veering away, like a tangent's intersection with a circle, to use his own illustrative metaphor.[64] In this obliqueness, in this scattering disregard for the "accurate" transmission of meaning, he suggests, lies the possibility of articulating "reine Sprache" ("pure language"), that which is purely language. The exorbitant relationship that *Pity* shares with *Macbeth* would seem to be an exemplary case of Benjamin's notion of "übersetzung," which is to say "at the furthest remove from paraphrase."[65] What is evident is that Blake's literalism, which renders Shakespeare's play strangely opaque to its own narrative, has important hermeneutical consequences, since interpretation, like illustration, depends on the text's transparency to its referents, whether historical, psychological, or aesthetic. For de Man this almost inescapable dependency has always made literary history into the history of what literature is not:[66] that is, into a systematic avoidance of the "structures of language" which de Man identifies with the literariness of "literature." But *Pity*'s reproduction of *Macbeth* affirms Roland Barthes's claim that "the space of writing is to be ranged over, not pierced."[67] And if ranged over, then also rearranged, the rhetorical features of the text's "real Surface" subject to the same de(con)structive forces that the dream-thoughts must bear under pressure of the dream-work: as Freud writes, these thoughts "are turned about, broken into fragments and jammed together – almost like pack-ice."[68] Blake's design surprises us with the dis-closural possibility that the humanist, meliorist notion of the line of vision is open to such deformation and displacement quite literally at every rhetorical turn by a kind of dream *re*vision that traces and effaces the "infinite inflexions" (E550;*DC*) of language. From the point of view of Blake's design, the relationship between poets does not amount to the gathering of a visionary company but a splintering of sense along the figurative axis of language. Disseminative, proliferative, jagged: sudden in its violent disfigurements, and hallucinatory in its abusive translations: *Pity* is what literary history looks like from the perspective of pure language.

AFTERWORD

Prometheus Bound:
The Case for Jupiter

ROSS G. WOODMAN

When, in the early 1950s, I began working on Shelley, among the models I used was Dante's notion of four levels in his *Convivio* by which, in Shelley's words, he "feigns himself to have ascended to the throne of the Supreme Cause."[1] To feign oneself meant to me at the time in some sense to fool oneself. Shelley, I knew, did not believe in a Supreme Cause. He was, as C.E. Pulos has demonstrated, sufficiently a Humean sceptic to question the very idea of causality, finding the only empirical evidence for it in the associational workings of the human mind.[2] In a state of vivid excitement, to use Wordsworth's phrase, associations are more immediate and original than under normal or habitual circumstances. They produce and perpetuate new metaphors described by Shelley as "before unapprehended relations of things" (*Defence*, p. 482). Once perpetuated, however, the metaphors become with time "fixed and dead."[3] When this happens, as indeed it must, new poets, Shelley argues, must arise not only to liberate metaphors from their assigned or fixed meaning but to create new ones. Shelley thus conceives of a vast poem built up since the beginning of the world, the author of which is the one great self-renewing mind through which "the everlasting universe of things" (*Mont Blanc*, 1) flows and to which certain individual minds in a fleeting state "beyond and above consciousness" (*Defence*, p. 486) are momentarily attached. Assigning himself a role in the making of that one poem, he sought to restore to life the epic poetry of Dante and Milton, the energy of which had, in his view, hardened into a system, degenerated into a form of worship, solidified into a canonized state.

In his Advertisement to *Epipsychidion*, Shelley includes a stanza in his own translation from Dante's *Convito*. It begins:

My Song, I fear that thou wilt find but few
Who fitly shall conceive thy reasoning,
Of such hard matter dost thou entertain.   (373)

To release the energy locked up in the hard matter of his favourite poets became for Shelley one of his chief missions not only as a critic but as a poet. Matter, he knew, was convertible into energy. New poets must arise to release it. This energy neither increases nor diminishes. It is constant. It both kindles and sustains and it is called by many names. Power is one. Love is another. Demogorgon is a third. In itself this energy is image-less; it has neither form, nor shape, nor outline. And yet, if it is to be harnessed, it must be given a form, a shape, an outline.

The danger is Incarnation: the identification of energy with the fixed form it appears to take under the influence of the shaping spirit of the imagi-nation, the plastic stress inherent in energy itself. Like the Gnostics, Shelley rejected this identification, though he did not, at least initially, go as far as many Gnostics and declare that the fixed forms of energy are evil. And yet, from the very beginning – or at least from *Alastor* onwards – he was at once confronted and haunted by the recalcitrance of matter, a "slow stain" whose "contagion" (*Adonais*, 356) turned life ("the eclipsing Curse / Of birth" [*Adonais*, 480–1]) into a universe of death, a "colossal Skeleton" (*Alastor*, 611).

This "colossal Skeleton" was for Shelley opaque matter or material-ism. It was the identification of energy with its accidental forms to the point where nothing but the forms were thought to exist. Reduced to matter, energy, he suggests, turns against itself to become in *Prometheus Unbound*

Thrones, altars, judgement-seats and prisons; wherein
And beside which, by wretched men were borne
Sceptres, tiaras, swords and chains, and tomes
Of reasoned wrong glozed on by ignorance.   (3.164–7)

Belonging to a generation that witnessed with a combination of wonder and horror the release of atomic energy, I thought I understood what Shelley meant by imaging the poet as the "hierophant" of an "unappre-hended inspiration" (*Defence*, p. 508) when, indeed, that "unapprehended inspiration" was, like Shelley's west wind, at once the destroyer of an entire order of society and, aided by its "azure sister of the Spring" (*Ode to the West Wind*, 9) the announcer of a new one. Thus, when Shelley in *Mont*

Blanc muses upon the river Arve as it flows from the glacier peak of the mountain into the "Dizzy Ravine" (34), he images at work an indifferent power bringing with it a flood of ruin not unlike the chariot of life in his final fragment, *The Triumph of Life*. Robert Oppenheimer, when he witnessed the first atomic explosion, quoted the *Bhagavad-Gita*: "I have become Death, the Shatterer of Worlds." He might equally have quoted Shelley:

> The race
> Of man, flies far in dread; his work and dwelling
> Vanish, like smoke before the tempest's stream,
> And their place is not known.   (*Mont Blanc*, 117–20)

Shelley, however, goes on in *Mont Blanc* to affirm the strength and the ability of the "human mind's imaginings" (143) to impose upon this indifferent power which dwells apart, "remote, serene and inaccessible" (97), a purely human meaning. The poet, he suggests, can grant to the inherent silence and even indifference of the universe a human voice, epitomized by the voice of the poet. "Thou hast a voice, great Mountain," he writes,

> to repeal
> Large codes of fraud and woe; not understood
> By all, but which the wise, and great, and good
> Interpret, or make felt, or deeply feel.   (80–3)

Under the inspired influence of Malcolm Ross, A.S.P. Woodhouse, Northrop Frye, Arthur Barker, and Marshall McLuhan, among others, I learned to listen to that voice, and through their various interpretations of it I became persuaded that poets were in their own particular ways, not understood by all, what Shelley called "the unacknowledged legislators of the World" (*Defence*, p. 508). More than that, first at the University of Manitoba working on Milton with Malcolm Ross and then at the University of Toronto discovering Milton fully alive in the major Romantics, I was helped by these Canadian scholars to understand the role of what Northrop Frye has called the educated imagination in the shaping and preserving of a human culture out of what had appeared during the war years to show every sign of imminent collapse. I became, in short, acutely conscious of the role of the Canadian intellectual in making the creative action of the human imagination understood and available to a world that could be, and in this country too often was, oppressively indifferent to it. That oppressive indifference – the absence of mental fight – tended to reduce to overcompensation the acclaimed heroism of physical fight. Arming himself for mental fight, Milton admits to his Muse that he is "Not sedulous by

Nature to indite / Warrs, hitherto the onely Argument / Heroic deem'd."
Precisely in that admission resided Milton's new epic ground, a ground
which the Toronto of Woodhouse and Frye, like the Manitoba of Malcolm
Ross, had continued on Canadian soil to plough, sow, harvest, and reap.
My own indebtedness to them, as to Barker and McLuhan, is such that
without them I would not be here today.

I do not personally hesitate to say the honours program in English at the
University of Toronto as I experienced it was perhaps as important a
program in the liberal or liberating arts as existed anywhere in the English-
speaking world, and one of the things that most drew me to Western
was the degree to which it shared and finally developed the telos of
Toronto. Toronto profoundly influenced and deepened my conviction of
the truth of Shelley's assertion that "we have more moral, political and
historical wisdom, than we know how to reduce into practice," that "we
have more scientific and oeconomical knowledge than can be accommo-
dated to the just distribution of the produce which it multiplies." "The
poetry in these systems of thought," he continues, "is concealed by the
accumulation of facts and calculating processes. There is no want of
knowledge respecting what is wisest and best in morals, government,
and political oeconomy, or at least, what is wiser and better than what men
now practise and endure. But we let 'I *dare not* wait upon *I would*, like the
poor cat i' the adage.' We want the creative faculty to imagine that which
we know," he goes on in one of his most justly famous passages, "we want
the generous impulse to act that which we imagine; we want the poetry of
life: our calculations have outrun conception; we have eaten more than we
can digest" (*Defence*, p. 502). As a result, he concludes, "the cultivation of
those sciences which have enlarged the limits of the empire of man over the
external world has, for want of the poetical faculty, proportionally cir-
cumscribed those of the internal world; and man, having enslaved the
elements, remains himself a slave" (*Defence*, pp. 502–3).

The Romantics, as I understand them, sought by means of the poetical
faculty to enlarge the circumference of the internal world by bringing it into
what Wordsworth called a "correspondence" with our greatly enlarged
understanding of the external world. Neither Blake nor Shelley was, of
course, comfortable with Wordsworth's notion of correspondence. "You
shall not bring me down to believe such fitting & fitted I know better &
Please your Lordship," Blake wrote in the margin of the 107 lines of
The Recluse quoted in Wordsworth's Preface to *The Excursion*.[4]

Since the 1960s, the critical enlargement of the circumference of the
internal world as the object of literary theory and practice has, however,
undergone such a swerve that it caused many of my generation to reel, to
resist, and only gradually, if at all, to come to terms with it. Beginning, I
suggest, with Nietzsche, Shelley's notion of feigning has joined forces

with the science of semiotics and linguistic theory, with structuralism and poststructuralism. Feigning, it is argued, is built into the very nature of language in which the signifier becomes a complex system of deferrals because it lacks a signified, what has been called a metaphysics of presence.

Though in no sense obtrusive, the honours and graduate programs in English at Toronto which I entered at the graduate level in 1948 affirmed a metaphysics of presence. It had, I sensed, what may be called a spiritual base which in a multitude of ways bound the life of the imagination to what Coleridge called "the eternal act of creation in the infinite I AM" (*Biographia*, 1:304). Many of us who chose literature chose it not as a substitute for theology but as a more secular, world-engaging form of it. Frye's archetypal criticism then powerfully entrenching itself at Toronto (against, of course, some opposition) is perhaps the most obvious and powerful example of this connection between literature and theology, an example wittily affirmed by Frye's characterization of himself as an underground agent of the United Church.

I recall very vividly the struggle I had, writing my thesis on Shelley under the supervision of Woodhouse and Frye in the 1950s and later revising it into a book, in turning from his *Defence of Poetry*, which in its view of the imagination served as a ground for my argument, to his last poems, particularly *Adonais* and *The Triumph of Life*. Believing that Shelley's reading of Dante's journey to the throne of the Supreme Cause prevented him from following in his footsteps in any religiously literal sense, the anagogical being for him a supreme fiction and Dante's poems notes toward it, I did not know initially what to do with what I called his apparent metaphysical defence of suicide. An ascent to suicide – or suicide as a metaphor of ascent ("Die, / If thou wouldst be with that which thou dost seek!" [*Adonais*, 464–5]) – appeared less a feigning of Dante's ascent than a demonic parody of it. In some larger, more literal sense, I did not know what to make of Shelley's drowning beyond disposing of it as an accident. I was uncomfortable with calling *Adonais* a dress rehearsal for suicide, though that is indeed what I did call it. I was, in short, haunted by the corpse of Shelley as Shelley was haunted by the corpse of his Visionary in *Alastor*, the corpse of Keats in *Adonais*, and the corpse of Rousseau in *The Triumph of Life*: by, that is, that "colossal Skeleton." I was haunted by what appeared to be something approaching a recantation of the life of the imagination as that life was celebrated in his *Defence*. I was haunted by what appeared to be happening to the radical liberal tradition to which Shelley belonged. I was haunted, if you like, by the number of corpses lying about in the Romantic canon.

It was much later that I discovered Paul de Man, who epitomized the swerve in critical theory which broke with the humanist tradition in which I was reared, a tradition based upon the authority of the Word in the biblical sense of engaging in the logocentric operations of language the authority of a Providential Will. In "Shelley Disfigured" de Man articulates what I had merely suggested and as a humanist rather backed away from. The corpse in *The Triumph of Life*, de Man suggests, is Shelley's own; the text's "decisive textual articulation" as a fragment resides in "the actual death and subsequent disfiguration of Shelley's body, burned after his boat capsized and he drowned off the coast of Lerici." "This defaced body," de Man argues, "is present in the margin of the last manuscript page and has become an inseparable part of the poem." "In Shelley's absence," he concludes, "the task of thus reinscribing the disfiguration now devolves entirely on the reader. The final test of reading, in *The Triumph of Life*, depends on how one reads the textuality of this event, how one disposes of Shelley's body." De Man makes clear how he reads "the textuality of this event": all poetry, he suggests, becomes finally a futile attempt to reinscribe a disfigured body of language because figuration itself is a form of disfiguration which places insurmountable obstacles in the way of cognition. *The Triumph of Life* as a mutilated text thus becomes what de Man calls the model which "exposes the wound of a fracture that lies hidden in all texts." It is, he writes, "more rather than less typical than texts that have not been thus truncated."[5]

In retrospect I realize that in my book on Shelley my real concern was how to dispose of Shelley's body. "What Adonais is, why fear we to become?" Shelley asks (*Adonais*, 459). But what is Adonais? Wasserman's answer, the most complete that we have, would not for me suffice because, as I argued in a review of his monumental study, he constructed from Shelley's prose a metaphysical system which the poetry would not finally support.[6] I suggested that Shelley, by feigning a Dantean ascent to what he calls "the abode where the Eternal are" (*Adonais*, 495), knew he was feigning, that what was being progressively revealed to him was a "void circumference"(*Adonais*, 420) or "intense inane" (*Prometheus Unbound*, 3.204) wearing a metaphorical disguise. The pen was the "spirit's knife" striking "invulnerable nothings" (*Adonais*, 347, 348). New figures are as "false" as they are "fragile."

So long as I isolated Shelley's poetry within its own prescribed aesthetic, I was prepared to deal with what I considered his proto-Nietzschean rejection of metaphysics in favour of metaphor. More than that, I was prepared to deal with the apparent psychic exhaustion arising from the Romantic burden of the ceaseless invention of new, "before unapprehended," relations, an exhaustion arising from usurping the role of Creator traditionally assigned to God. I was prepared to deal with a view of the imagination that went beyond imitation to creation, the mind of the poet usurping rather than merely repeating the divine act of God.

In de Man's insistence that Shelley's *The Triumph of Life* as a disfigured body serves as a model of all poetry, I sensed that within the perspective of deconstruction the life of culture in our time was perpetuating the

Nietzschean project of its annihilation. I was confronting in de Man's reading of Shelley's final fragment and the larger critical theory it subsumes – a disfigured text as the model of all literary texts – what appeared to be an elaborate staging of Wagner's *Götterdämmerung*. I thought I saw at work upon the body of Western literature the operations of a mind-set which I had earlier identified with the Nazi threat to the humanist tradition to which as a student of English I was, as a graduate of Toronto, deeply committed.

This critical position, I need hardly add, is not shared by most students of de Man. Indeed, they tend to view accusations of nihilism from the humanists as a clinging to an obsolete vision of cosmic unity such as, for example, the idea of the Great Chain of Being had once provided. Following in the tradition of Nietzsche's death of God, they are far more at ease with a mutilated body of language than I as a humanist was. "Any mode of analysis ... that sees the text as an organic unity, or uses it for a totalizing purpose (as when the right or the left speaks for history)," writes Geoffrey Hartman in partial defence of de Man, "is blind, and the text itself will subvert or 'deconstruct'such closures."[7] At the same time, however, as I gradually came to terms with deconstruction as practised in multifoliate ways by Paul de Man and others, I became far more aware of the subversions of closure which call into question the kind of unity Shelley struggled in vain to impose upon his texts. It taught me to look more closely at the "blindness" of Shelley's "insight" and the various ways in which that "blindness," despite his obvious logocentric intentions, his feigning of a Dantean ascent, created the kind of fissures or disfigurations that gradually made the text by virtue of disfiguration far more humanly meaningful than any appeal to divine inspiration would permit. I became, that is, far more aware of the way in which a literary text subverts its own apparent intentions to construct a human drama that is far more intrinsically interesting than its preconceived design. I became more sensitive to the poem as what Shelley calls "a feeble shadow of the original conception of the poet" (*Defence*, p. 504). Precisely as "a feeble shadow of the original conception," Shelley, I slowly concluded, was affirming the kind of disfigurement which de Man among others was exploring with a kind of uncanny precision which has never ceased to make me feel rather ill at ease.

Shelley's apocalyptic vision – his idealized vision of a radical imaginative recreation of the world that put an end to large codes of fraud and woe – contained within it a wished-for annihilation of the past, an annihilation which de Man, interpreting Nietzsche, identifies with modernity. The devastation described in *The Triumph of Life*, Keats's blessed awakening from the nightmare of life – what Shelley called "the contagion of the world's slow stain" (*Adonais*, 356) – find their counterpart in the cancellation in *Prometheus Unbound* of three thousand years of human history under the arbitrary rule of Jupiter, the patriarchal oppressor of humankind whom Shelley identifies with the Christian God begetting an only begotten Son to render his tyranny eternal. Jupiter, however, is not overthrown by Prometheus; he is simply forgotten. He is, in Shelley's words, "no more remembered" (*Prometheus Unbound*, 3.169). Annihilation is treated by Shelley's "Champion" with an indifference matched only by his "Oppressor" (133). And here again de Man as a post-Nietzschean helped me better to grasp the implications for modernity of Shelley's dark subtext.

In "Literary History and Literary Modernity," de Man as a post-Nietzschean argues the proposition, so radically opposed by Matthew Arnold, who feared its consequences, that "moments of genuine humanity ... are moments at which all anteriority vanishes, annihilated by the power of an absolute forgetting." "Although such a radical rejection of history may be illusory or unfair to the achievements of the past," he continues, "it nevertheless remains justified as necessary to the fulfillment of our human destiny and as the condition for action." This condition as it becomes what de Man calls "Nietzsche's ruthless forgetting, the blindness with which he throws himself into an action lightened of all previous experience," captures, he argues, "the authentic spirit of modernity." "Modernity," he explains, "exists in the form of a desire to wipe out whatever came earlier, in the hope of reaching at last a point that could be called a true present, a point of origin that marks a new departure."[8]

Reading de Man, I have at the end of my academic career been forced to look rather more closely at the apocalyptic vision with which that career rather more innocently or idealistically began. I have been forced to question the very notion of apocalypse – or at least the religious, moral, and political uses to which, in our time, it has been put. I have been forced to look again and yet again at Shelley's vision to see if, rather than seeking to fulfil, it more accurately undermined the humanist tradition to which I had chosen to remain bound. I have been forced to look again at Plato's ironic treatment of the divine madness of the poets in, for example, *Ion*, as well as at the Republic that would reject it. Partly with Arnold's *Culture and Anarchy* in mind, I have come to view with new misgivings Shelley's notion of himself as a "hierophant" even as, I believe, Shelley himself came to view it. I have, in short, been led to look more closely at Shelley's inherent fear of the consequences of didactic poetry ("Didactic poetry is my abhorrence," he wrote in his Preface to *Prometheus Unbound*, 135).

I end my formal academic career, in short, wondering again how to dispose of Shelley's body, even as I wonder how all of us now living are to dispose of our endangered planet of which Shelley's body may serve as a metaphor. We cannot, I suggest, reinscribe its disfiguration in the manner of the nine-year-old Wordsworth as Wordsworth describes him in

The Prelude. Seeing a drowned man rise "bolt upright" from the water as "a spectre shape / Of terror," the nine-year-old Wordsworth "hallowed the sad spectacle / With decoration of ideal grace" drawn from "the shining streams / Of faery land, the forests of romance."[9] Shelley, I suggest, does much the same thing when he finally disposes of Prometheus's three thousand years of wakeful anguish by sending him off with Asia to inhabit henceforth an enchanted cave "like human babes in their brief innocence" (3.33).

Reading de Man reading Shelley, I find myself now turning back to the *Prometheus Bound* of Aeschylus, which was the immediate source of Shelley's lyrical drama. I turn back in part to question the wisdom of Shelley's Preface, in which he admits what he calls his aversion to "a catastrophe so feeble as that of reconciling the Champion with the Oppressor of mankind" (133). I am no longer certain of the validity of his characterization of Oppressor and Champion. I seriously question the wisdom of an apocalyptic unbinding. Indeed, if I were now to start afresh I might consider, as a possible title for a second book on Shelley, *Prometheus Bound: The Case for Jupiter.*

As a starting point I would turn to Rousseau's invitation to Shelley in *The Triumph of Life* to turn from Olympian spectator to human actor and re-engage the human condition which had driven him to the negative inflation of suicidal despair. Nowhere is that negative inflation more evident than in his apparent withdrawal from all but the "sacred few" who, in Shelley's words,

> could not tame
> Their spirits to the Conqueror, but as soon
> As they had touched the world with living flame
>
> Fled back like eagles to their native noon.   (128–31)

The pendulum swings between negative and positive inflation. The alternation of suicide and eagle flight (what today we might diagnose as manic depression) becomes during the last year of Shelley's brief life – he died at twenty-nine – the psychic arena in which a new poetic action is beginning to take shape. Calling upon himself in *Adonais* to "dart [his] spirit's light / Beyond all world's, until its spacious might / Satiate the void circumference" (418–20), he also warns himself to "clasp with [his] panting soul the pendulous Earth," to "keep [his] heart light lest it make [him] sink / When hope has kindled hope, and lured [him] to the brink" (417, 422–3). That soul, clasping the "pendulous Earth," neither letting go nor holding on too tightly, is perhaps the Shelley who is struggling with the radical ambivalence that is the mark of human freedom. As a living poet rather than a Romantic corpse, he both confronts and engages in himself, as in Rousseau, that corpse which in this century sits all too "bolt upright" in its "spectre shape / Of terror."

Surely, however, if this review of some forty-odd years of reading and teaching Shelley suggests anything, it suggests that, like all great poetry, Shelley's poetry is and remains molten. It will not stand still. It will not settle into some final fixed form. In these years of reading and teaching, as I confessed to my more than patient classes to which I owe so much, I have never taught the same Shelley poem twice in exactly the same way. After forty years his poems still appear to me new. I still come upon them as one taken by surprise.

I conclude therefore with Shelley's own astute remark about poetry at its best – a remark that kept me going and still keeps me going:

All high poetry is infinite; it is as the first acorn, which contained all oaks potentially. Veil after veil may be undrawn and the inmost naked beauty of the meaning never exposed. A great Poem is a fountain for ever overflowing with the waters of wisdom and delight; and after one person and one age has exhausted all its divine effluence which their peculiar relations enable them to share, another and yet another succeeds, and new relations are ever developed, the source of an unforeseen and an unconceived delight.   (*Defence*, p. 500)

I can never sufficiently express my gratitude to the University of Western Ontario and the Department of English for the freedom it has granted me to enjoy without interruption this teaching career of "unforeseen and unconceived delight."

Notes

CHAPTER ONE

1 All my quotations from Byron's poetry follow the text of Jerome McGann's edition, *The Complete Poetical Works* (Oxford: Clarendon 1980–86), so far in five volumes; henceforth identified as *Works*. References to *Childe Harold's Pilgrimage* and *Don Juan* will cite canto and stanza.

2 *Works*, 2:301.

3 One also thinks of Byron's note to his stanzas on Marathon: "'Siste, Viator – heroa calcas!' was the epitaph on the famous Count Merci; – what then must be our feelings when standing on the tumulus of the two hundred (Greeks) who fell on Marathon?" See *Works*, 2:198.

4 *The Romantic Movement in English Poetry* (London: Constable 1909), 250.

5 *Poetic Form and Romanticism* (New York: Oxford University Press 1986), 151–7.

6 The most obvious analogy is with the Incantation in *Manfred*, where the line between Manfred as cursed one and Byron as curser of an extratextual Lady Byron is impossible to draw, especially in the last two stanzas.

7 *Byron's Letters and Journals*, vol. 6, ed. Leslie A. Marchand (London: John Murray 1976), 21.

8 *Lord Byron: Christian Virtues* (London: Routledge and Kegan Paul 1952), 258.

9 *Shelley's Prose*, ed. D.L. Clark (Albuquerque: University of New Mexico Press 1954), 258.

10 *Letters and Journals*, 4:81.

11 For example: Jerome McGann, *Fiery Dust* (Chicago: University of Chicago Press 1968), 36–40; Michael Cooke, *Acts of Inclusion* (New Haven: Yale University Press 1979), 235–7; Curran, 156. Cooke relates Byron's coming to

terms with St Peter's, not to Pope's figurative Alpine journey (as I go on to do), but to Wordsworth's actual one.

12 *Some Letters* (Rotterdam: Abraham Acker 1687), 199.

13 *Travels through France and Italy* in *Works*, vol. 11 (New York: Constable 1900), 335.

14 *The Spectator*, vol. 3, ed. Donald F. Bond (Oxford: Oxford University Press 1965), 555–6.

15 *Works*, vol. 2, ed. Richard Hurd (London: Cadell and Davies 1811), 69.

16 I quote from an English translation of Byron's time: *Corinna*, vol. 1 (London: Samuel Tipper 1807), 151–2.

17 Smollett, 335.

18 John Moore, *Works*, vol. 2 (Edinburgh 1820), 169.

19 Moore, 170–1.

20 One element notably missing, of course, is any comparison with the Pantheon (briefly presented a few stanzas earlier).

21 *The Poems of Alexander Pope*, ed John Butt (London: Methuen 1963), 151–2. It is even possible, although I wouldn't press the point, to see behind Byron not only Pope but also Milton, whose Pandemonium, inspired by St Peter's (as Arthur Barker once reminded me in this Byronic connection), has its dimensions altered by those shrinking and expanding devils.

22 *The Poetical Works*, vol. 4, ed. E. de Selincourt and Helen Darbishire (Oxford: Oxford University Press 1947), 72.

23 Antony Brett-James, *The Hundred Days* (London: Macmillan 1964), 61, 58; T. Siborne, ed., *Waterloo Letters* (London: Cassell and Co. 1891, photographic reprint 1983), 348; Edward Cotton, *A Voice from Waterloo* (Printed for the Proprietor, Mont St Jean, 6th ed., revised and enlarged 1862), 26; Elizabeth Longford, *Wellington: The Years of the Sword* (New York: Harper and Row 1969), 457; David Chandler, *Waterloo: The Hundred Days* (London: Osprey Publishing 1980), 163.

24 *The Miscellaneous Prose Works*, vol. 5 (Edinburgh: Robert Cadell 1843), 73, 102, 151–2.

25 Brett-James, 157.

26 *The Dynasts* (London: Macmillan 1919), 6.6.518.

27 *Poetical Works* (London: Longmans, Green 1876), 737.

28 Chandler, 172, 149; J.F.C. Fuller, *The Decisive Battles of the Western World* (London: Eyre and Spottiswoode 1955), 2:532.

29 Siborne, 234; Edmund Wheatley, *The Wheatley Diary*, ed. Christopher Hibbert (London: Longmans, Green 1964), 67.

30 Byron is, of course, using "grass" in its comprehensive sense (still common in his time) as applying to all pastoral or cereal crops.

31 *An Autobiography* (London: Constable 1922), 122.

32 *Works*, 2:302.

33 *Gustavus Vasa. The Heroes of Waterloo* (New York: Garland Publishing 1977), 14.

34 Leslie A. Marchand, *Byron: A Biography* (New York: Alfred A. Knopf 1953), 2:533.

35 *Complete Works*, vol. 15, ed. P.P. Howe (London: Dent 1931), 267.

36 *Poetical Works*, 737. "Our guide was very much displeased at the name which the battle had obtained in England. 'Why call it the battle of Waterloo?' he said, ... 'call it Mont St. Jean, call it *La Belle Alliance*, call it Hougoumont, call it La Haye Sainte, call it Papelot, ... anything but Waterloo.'"

37 *Byron's Letters and Journals*, 8:21–2.

38 Brett-James, 40, 41; General Cavalie Mercer, *Journal of the Waterloo Campaign* (London: Peter Davies 1927), 132.

39 *The Dynasts*, 6.2.454.

40 Beatrice Madan, ed., *Spencer and Waterloo: Letters* (London: Literary Services and Production 1970), 179.

41 *Waterloo* (London: B.T. Batsford 1960), 53. Naylor uses the plural "battles" because he includes Blucher's Ligny along with Quatre Bras. The most famous Victorian account of Waterloo, Thackeray's in *Vanity Fair*, whatever else it may owe to Byron's myth, makes a careful historical differentiation between Quatre Bras and Waterloo.

42 Naylor, 150.

43 *Shelley: A Critical Reading* (Baltimore: Johns Hopkins University Press 1971), 169.

44 Southey, 733; Sir Walter Scott, *The Poetical Works*, ed. J. Logie Robertson (London: Oxford University Press 1921), 621.

45 *Works*, 2:302–3.

46 In his note on these lines (*Works*, 2:303), McGann writes, "Seems to recall Henry v's speech on St. Crispin's day" in Shakespeare's play. One might add that the recollection is ironic. Henry's encouragement before a battle is strikingly transformed into Byron's consolation after one. Agincourt's surviving soldiers will remember "what feats [they] did that day"; Waterloo's dead ones will just be remembered by the future as "warring on that day."

47 *Works*, 2:303.

48 *Edinburgh Review* 27:54 (1816): 295.

CHAPTER TWO

1 *The Prelude*, ed. Ernest de Selincourt, 2nd ed. rev. Helen Darbishire (Oxford: Clarendon 1959). All further references to *The Prelude* are to this edition, and will be included parenthetically in the text.

2 *The Prose Works of William Wordsworth*, ed. W.J.B. Owen and Jane Worthington Smyser (Oxford: Clarendon 1974), 3:35. All further references to

Wordsworth's prose are to this edition, and will be included parenthetically in the text.

3   *Wordsworth Circle* 10 (1979): 3–16; 14 (1983): 213–24.

4   *Wordsworth Circle* 8 (1977): 291–315; 14 (1983): 213–24.

5   *Wordsworth Circle* 14 (1983): 221.

6   *The Letters of William and Dorothy Wordsworth: The Middle Years*, ed. Ernest de Selincourt, 2nd ed. rev. Mary Moorman (Oxford: Clarendon 1967–82), pt. 1:148. Further references to Wordsworth's letters will be identified as *MY* or *EY* (*Early Years*, 2nd ed. rev. Chester L. Shaver) parenthetically in the text.

7   Samuel Taylor Coleridge, *Biographia Literaria*, ed. James Engell and W. Jackson Bate (Princeton: Princeton University Press 1983), 1:304.

8   *The Poetical Works of William Wordsworth*, ed. Ernest de Selincourt, rev. Helen Darbishire (Oxford: Clarendon 1952–63), 3:25–6. Further references to Wordsworth's poetry are to this edition, and will be abbreviated as *PW* parenthetically in the text.

9   *The Journals of Dorothy Wordsworth*, ed. Ernest de Selincourt (London: Macmillan 1941), 1:131–2.

10 See *Wordsworth Circle* 10 (1979): 3–16.

11 Jonathan Wordsworth, *William Wordsworth: The Borders of Vision* (Oxford: Clarendon 1982), *passim*.

12 *Wordsworth Circle* 11 (1980): 2–9.

CHAPTER THREE

1   I am grateful to the Dove Cottage Trust, Yale University Library, and the Huntington Library for permission to quote from unpublished manuscripts in their possession. Helpful advice has come from Stephen Gill, Lincoln College, Oxford, and Mark L. Reed, University of North Carolina, Chapel Hill. My research for this essay has been supported by a grant from the National Endowment for the Humanities, an independent federal agency of the United States.

2   See *"Poems, in Two Volumes" and Other Poems, 1800–1807 by William Wordsworth*, ed. Jared Curtis (Ithaca: Cornell University Press 1983), 528–30 (hereafter cited as *Poems, 1800–1807*). Wordsworth's manner while composing was so described by a local man, as recorded by H.D. Rawnsley in his "Reminiscences of Wordsworth among the Peasantry of Westmoreland," in *Wordsworthiana: A Selection of Papers Read to the Wordsworth Society*, ed. William Knight (London: Macmillan 1889), 90–1. In the Fenwick note, dictated in 1843, to *To the Same [Lycoris]*, Wordsworth quoted one of his "cottage-neighbours" saying, after the poet had been away from home for some time, "Well there he is, we are glad to hear him *booing* about again"; that is, walking up and down in his "out of doors" study while composing

verses (*Shorter Poems, 1807–1820, by William Wordsworth*, ed. Carl H. Ketcham [Ithaca and London: Cornell University Press 1989], 546).

3   Edward Quillinan noted in his diary for Thursday, 4 August 1836, that he "Walked with Mr. W   Poems *tinkered*" (Quillinan's diary is in the Wordsworth Library; the entry is quoted by Paul F. Betz in *"Benjamin the Waggoner" by William Wordsworth* [Ithaca: Cornell University Press, 1981], 28). And Mary Wordsworth wrote to Isabella Fenwick on 10 May 1842 that "He [Wordsworth] has done the verses for *the Poet* – which are, or [at least] will be, satisfactory when W. has 'tinkered' them" (*The Letters of Mary Wordsworth, 1800–1855* [Oxford: Clarendon 1958], 250). Arnold confirmed this family usage in his letter to Jemima Quillinan quoted below.

4   ALS to Mark Pattison (1813–84), Saturday [1879], London. Beinecke Rare Book and Manuscript Library, Tinker 112. The date is not given but must be in July 1879, when Arnold's Preface had appeared in *Macmillan's Magazine* but had not yet been set in type for *Poems*.

5   *A Bibliographical Catalogue of Macmillan and Co.'s Publications from 1843 to 1889* (London: Macmillan 1891), 370; William E. Buckler, ed., *Matthew Arnold's Books: Toward a Publishing Diary* (Geneva: Librairie E. Droz 1958), 132–46 (hereafter cited as *Arnold's Books*); T.B. Smart, "The Bibliography of Matthew Arnold," in *The Works of Matthew Arnold, Edition de Luxe* (London: Macmillan 1903–4), 15:343–99; George H. Healey, *The Cornell Wordsworth Collection* (Ithaca: Cornell University Press 1957), items 226, 230, 312; R.H. Super, ed., *English Literature and Politics*, vol. 9 in *Complete Prose Works of Matthew Arnold* (Ann Arbor: University of Michigan Press 1973), 339 (hereafter cited as *Prose*, 9); and Jared Curtis, "The Simon Fraser University Wordsworth Collection," electronic data file, Special Collections, Simon Fraser University Library.

6   Interest in "early" Wordsworth was sufficient to encourage Frederick Warne and Company to publish a reprint of the 1827 *Poetical Works* in 1872 as one of the "Chandos Classics" (Healey, item 216). For Johnston's edition see Jared Curtis, "The Making of a Reputation: John Carter's Corrections to the Proofs of Wordsworth's *Poetical Works* (1857)," *Texte* 7 (1988): 75 n 32.

7   One such edition was produced by Moxon in 1869, *Poetical Works: The Only Complete Popular Edition*. But there were several others between 1857, the end of Wordsworth's copyright, and 1879.

8   *The Poetical Works. The Only Complete Cheap Edition* (London: Edward Moxon and Co. [1871]).

9   For Arnold's Preface I cite the 1879 "Large Paper Edition" published by Macmillan on 20 September; Preface, xi, xxv. Further references are to this edition and will be included parenthetically in the text.

10 Lane Cooper, "Matthew Arnold's Essay on Wordsworth," in his *Evolution and Repentance* (Ithaca: Cornell University Press 1935), 8; the essay first appeared in *Bookman* 79 (1929):478–84. John Dover Wilson, in the Cambridge Leslie

Stephen Lecture, "Leslie Stephen and Matthew Arnold as Critics of
Wordsworth," in 1939, took Arnold to task for using his Preface and selection
to put down the "Cambridge Wordsworthians" (first published by
Cambridge University Press in 1939 and republished by Haskell House
Publishers, New York, in 1972).

11 "Wordsworth, Arnold, and Professor Lane Cooper," *Dalhousie Review* 10
(1930):57–66. William A. Jamison, in *Arnold and the Romantics* (Folcroft, Pa.:
Folcroft Press 1969; first publ. 1958), 50–3, defended Arnold as editor by
repeating Arnold's own justifications for selecting "early" texts and for his
omissions, and concluded that "within Arnold's lifetime his volume was
accepted as sufficient evidence of Wordsworth's genius" (53).

12 R.H. Super gives a succinct and helpful account of Arnold's undertaking of
the Wordsworth volume for Macmillan, a brief description of its characteris-
tics and mention of its reception; see *Prose*, 9:336–40.

13 Like Arnold, both were Balliol College men. Benjamin Jowett's translations of
and commentaries on the works of Plato and Thomas Hill Green's major
critique of English empiricism in his introduction to his edition of the works
of David Hume were widely known and justly famous.

14 Arnold to Mark Pattison, Saturday, [April, 1879]. See note 4.

15 Arnold to Macmillan, 19 April 1879, in *Arnold's Books*, 137; ALS to Lady
Richardson, 10 September 1879, Ambleside, Beinecke Rare Book and
Manuscript Library (Tinker 114).

16 20 January 1880, Arnold Letters, Wordsworth Library. William Wordsworth,
Jr, one of the executors of Wordsworth's estate, dealt closely with the
publishers of his father's poems for more than thirty years; he died in 1883.

17 Matthew Arnold to Miss Arnold, 14 April 1879, *Letters of Matthew Arnold,
1848–1888*, col. and arr. by George W.E. Russell (New York and London:
Macmillan 1895), 2:181 (hereafter cited as *Letters*). "Fan" is Frances Bunsen
Trevenen Whatley Arnold (1833–1923).

18 S.O.A. Ullmann, "A 'New' Version of Arnold's Essay on Wordsworth," *Notes
and Queries* 200 (1955): 543–4.

19 On 16 February 1879, at the very time Arnold was turning his attention to his
edition of Wordsworth, he wrote to Macmillan that he would make "few
corrections" to his own *Selected Poems* (Macmillan Archive, Add. MS. 54978,
British Library). The third edition of Arnold's *Selected Poems* appeared in
January 1880, a few months after the Wordsworth volume was published.

20 Noting the error to Frederick Locker, Arnold added, "This is the sort of thing
which hurries the sensitive into suicide" (24 September 1879; Huntington
Library autograph letter, HM24009). Arnold noted the same error to Lady
Richardson (see the letter cited in note 15, above). An error stemming from
Arnold's choice of copy-text was pointed out by Macmillan in the sonnet
called *The Trossachs* (Wordsworth's *Trosachs*). Wordsworth printed "Guest"

for "quest" in 1835, correcting the misprint in an erratum to the volume and incorporating the correction in subsequent editions. Arnold dropped the poem from later editions of *Poems of Wordsworth*.

21 In a letter of 19 April 1879 (*Arnold's Books*, p. 137), Arnold refers to the 1858 edition (London: Moxon 1857; rpt. 1858), a reissue of the one prepared by John Carter for the trustees of Wordsworth's estate; at the head of each poem Carter included the appropriate note (called "explanatory headings" by Arnold) from the biographical and critical notes dictated by Wordsworth to Isabella Fenwick in 1843. For an account of this edition see pp. 60–81 of my article, cited in note 6 above.

22 Arnold to Frederick Locker, 24 September 1879 (Huntington Library autograph letter, HM24009); the corrected spine read only "POEMS | OF | WORDSWORTH" with the publisher's name at the foot. In the same letter Arnold seconded Locker's displeasure with the way the vignette of Wordsworth, based on Haydon's portrait, was printed on the title page: "I quite agree with you about the name at the foot of the vignette; I saw it with horror. I was not consulted about it, and should certainly not have allowed it to stand; but I told them to put the dates, I confess, and then they added the [engraver's] name also. The dates of his birth and death I always like to have in my mind while I am reading a poet, and I thought these might be so much *effaced* by the manner in which they were attached to the vignette that they could not do harm." The vignette was altered in later printings to moderate the intrusiveness of the engraver's name.

23 Though technically speaking this edition was used only to correct the type set from a later edition, Arnold himself prepared printer's copy by consulting it.

24 He toiled over the "list" of contents for the volume, sending the first version of the list to Macmillan early in March and adding to it on the 25th. This list was used by the printer to ascertain the size of the collection. But Arnold was not satisfied with it and asked to have it returned. He sent back a corrected list on 16 April, which was relayed to the printer, and tendered further additions and deletions on the 19th. He retrieved the list yet again on 3 May for further revision, returning this latest version before 22 May when he reported to Macmillan the news from the Edinburgh printer that "the Wordsworth is in full print" (*Arnold's Books*, 134–8).

25 Wordsworth offered to act on Arnold's behalf to effect the purchase of the Fox How "estate" from Mr Simpson, the owner (*The Letters of William and Dorothy Wordsworth: The Later Years, 1821–1850*, ed. Ernest de Selincourt, 2nd ed. rev., arranged, and ed. Alan G. Hill (Oxford: Clarendon 1978, 1979, 1982, 1988), pt 2: 555). See also Robert Woof, *Matthew Arnold: A Centennial Exhibition*, preliminary catalogue of the exhibition in The Wordsworth Museum (Grasmere, 22 July 1988–15 January 1989) (Kendal: Titus Wilson [1988]), p. [1].

26 In the Rydal Mount Guest Book, now in the Wordsworth Library, Mary Wordsworth recorded "Dr Arnold" of Rugby in 1831 and from 1832 to 1841 noted "Dr & Mrs Arnold & family" (on one occasion, "Dr & Mrs Arnold & chicks") seven times. In 1845 she recorded "The Arnolds" from "Oxford," perhaps Matthew and his brother Tom.

27 Coleridge thought the first two books of *The Excursion* should be published separately under the title *Deserted Cottage*: "They would have formed, what indeed they are, one of the most beautiful poems in the language." George Routledge and Company published such a volume, so titled, in 1859. Coleridge's remark appeared in *Specimens of the Table Talk of the Late Samuel Taylor Coleridge* (2 vols., London: John Murray 1835), 2:69. The fashion among editors, if it can be called that, of renaming Wordsworth's poems, seems to have begun with Joseph Hine in 1831, when he published, with Wordsworth's approval, *Selections from the Poems of William Wordsworth, Esq.: Chiefly for the Use of Schools and Young Persons* (London: Moxon 1831). *The Embowering Rose*, for example, is Hines's title for *In the Grounds of Coleorton, The Seat of Sir George Beaumont, Bart.*

28 In a letter to Sir John (afterwards Lord) Coleridge, 30 July 1873, *Letters of Alexander Macmillan*, ed. George A. Macmillan (privately printed, Glasgow 1908), 271–2.

29 In her Grasmere journal for 1802, when the poem was being composed, Dorothy Wordsworth referred to it several times as "The Leech-gatherer" and the earliest manuscript copies of the poem, one in Sara Hutchinson's hand, one in Mary Wordsworth's and one in Coleridge's, are so titled (see *Poems, 1800–1807*, 123, 317.

30 Super reports that this *Margaret* was included at the request of Macmillan (*Prose*, 9:337). *Margaret* differs from earlier printings of excerpts from *The Excursion* as *The Deserted Cottage* in focusing entirely on Margaret by omitting the Pedlar's biography and later wanderings. Thus it comes very close to the earliest version of *The Ruined Cottage* which Wordsworth completed in 1798–99 (see *The Ruined Cottage and "The Pedlar" by William Wordsworth*, ed. James Butler [Ithaca: Cornell University Press 1979]).

31 Matthew Arnold, *Poetical Works*, ed. C.B. Tinker and H.F. Lowry (London: Oxford University Press 1969 [1950]), 210. Arnold's conscious play on Wordsworth's poem in his own *Dover Beach* has been noted by U.C. Knoepflmacher in his excellent essay, "Dover Revisited; The Wordsworthian Matrix in the Poetry of Matthew Arnold," *Victorian Poetry* 1 (1963): 17–26. He notes as well Arnold's "inversion" of Wordsworth's sonnet, *Dover Beach, September, 1802* ("Inland, within a hollow Vale, I stood"), turning the older poet's belief into scepticism. Knoepflmacher seems to believe, however, that Arnold's work as editor of Wordsworth was a "revision of entire lines and phrases" to satisfy "the cultural responsibility of preserving Wordsworth as

an emotional fount for his age" (26). This claim, as we shall see, does not hold up.

32 Most "selections" published after 1857 and before Arnold's volume created a reduced version of Wordsworth's *Poetical Works* by using his "Classes" and selecting from their contents. But Francis Taylor Palgrave in his *A Selection from the Works of William Wordsworth*, in the series Moxon's Miniature Poets (London: Moxon 1865), made his selection on undisclosed principles of his own and included four of the "Lucy" poems in sequence, omitting "Strange fits of passion." Hugh Sykes Davies traces the history of the arrangement and consequent interpretation of the "Lucy" poems in "Another New Poem by Wordsworth" (*Essays in Criticism* 15 [1965]: 136–61); he notes Palgrave's and Arnold's initial groupings and several others which followed, but it was Arnold who made the set "complete" in 1879 by adding the fifth.

33 See the notes to these poems in *"Lyrical Ballads," and Other Poems, 1797–1800*, ed. James A. Butler and Karen Green (Ithaca: Cornell University Press 1992).

34 Wordsworth to S.T. Coleridge, 5 May 1809, Ketcham, *Shorter Poems, 1807–1820*, 20–1. See also *The Letters of William and Dorothy Wordsworth: The Middle Years*, pt. 1, 1806–1811, ed. Ernest de Selincourt, 2nd ed. rev. Mary Moorman (Oxford: Clarendon 1969), 334–5.

35 For the dating of the manuscript list see Ketcham, *Shorter Poems, 1807–1820*, 26–7; for the lists themselves see 608–12 and 623–4 in his appendix 2, "Wordsworth's Arrangements and Classification of His Poems, 1807–1820: Manuscript Lists and Contents of Editions."

36 Knoepflmacher, in the article cited above, also mentions briefly Arnold's dependence on Wordsworth's "use of his 'Lucy'" for the conception of his own "Marguerite" poems (25). For Arnold's arrangements of the "Marguerite" poems see Smart's bibliography, *Works*, 12:345–51.

37 Beyond lifting first lines to title status, that is.

38 Hugh Sykes Davies, in the article cited above, showed how subsequent editors and critics rearranged the poems to achieve different narrative effects (149–151), but their common object was to tell a story.

39 See *A Map of Misreading* (New York: Oxford University Press 1975).

CHAPTER FOUR

1 *The Letters of John Keats*, ed. Hyder E. Rollins (Cambridge: Harvard University Press 1958), 2:378; hereafter cited in the text as *Letters*.

2 Lowell, *John Keats* (Boston: Houghton Mifflin 1925), 1:358, 498; Trilling, Introduction to *The Selected Letters of John Keats* (New York: Farrar, Straus and Young 1951), 5; Ward, *John Keats: The Making of a Poet* (New York: Viking Press 1963), 40. Douglas Bush, in his *John Keats* (New York: Macmillan 1966), follows Trilling's lead in seeing Keats (66) as "a poet of tragic vision."

3 *The Uses of Division: Unity and Disharmony in Literature* (London: Chatto and
   Windus 1976), 147. Christopher Ricks advanced the view that "Keats is one of
   the few erotic poets who come at embarrassment ... from the wish to pass
   directly through ... the hotly disconcerting" in *Keats and Embarrassment*
   (Oxford: Clarendon 1974), 68. More recently, John Barnard's *John Keats*
   (Cambridge: Cambridge University Press 1987), 21, reminds us how "visions
   of poetry insistently transform themselves into dreams of sexuality" in Keats.
4 *John Keats* (Cambridge: Harvard University Press 1963), 192.
5 John Keats, *Complete Poems*, ed. Jack Stillinger (Cambridge: Harvard
   University Press 1982), 39–40; all subsequent citations of Keats's poetry will
   be drawn from this edition.
6 Curiously, Bate and de Man agree on the fundamental literariness of Keats:
   Bate observes that Keats was "the most purely 'literary' of the great nine-
   teenth-century poets" (*John Keats*, 28) and Paul de Man, in his Introduction to
   John Keats: Selected Poetry (New York: New American Library 1966), xi, warns
   us that "in reading Keats, we are reading the work of a man whose experi-
   ence is mainly literary."
7 "Keats's Depressive Poetry," *Psychoanalytic Review* 58 (1971): 395. Wolf Z.
   Hirst, in *John Keats* (Boston: Twayne 1981), 31, remarks on "Keats's fondness
   for expressions of ingestion and surfeit"; Ricks (181) adds another dimension
   when he says that "eating was a natural metaphor not only for love but also
   for reading" in Keats.
8 As quoted in C.L. Finney, *The Evolution of Keats's Poetry* (New York: Russell
   and Russell 1963), 1:339.
9 Earl R. Wasserman, in *The Finer Tone: Keats's Major Poems* (Baltimore: Johns
   Hopkins University Press 1967), 101, states the idealist position on Keats
   succinctly: "In Keats' mind dreams are synonymous with imagination, for
   both are powers whereby man may penetrate into heaven's bourne, where
   the intensities of mortal life are repeated in a finer tone and divested of their
   mutability." The most extreme version of this approach is pursued by James
   Land Jones, who in *Adam's Dream: Mythic Consciousness in Keats and Yeats*
   (Athens: University of Georgia Press 1975), attributes to Keats a concept of
   the imagination Jones (205) calls "mythic apprehension ... in which being is
   revealed, the solidarity of all life affirmed, and death denied."
10 See Nina Auerbach, *The Woman and the Demon: The Life of a Victorian Myth*
   (Cambridge: Harvard University Press 1982), 138–9. Auerbach also notes (35)
   that although "Victorian womanhood is most delectable as a victim" this
   victim could be transformed by the literary imagination into a figure of
   disturbing power.
11 *John Keats* (Boston: Little, Brown 1968), 359. Gittings believes (324) that
   Keats's relationship with Fanny was coloured by "a jealous and vindictive
   neurosis, against which he fought with all the healthier side of his being."
12 *John Keats: Selected Poems and Letters*, ed. Douglas Bush (Boston: Houghton
   Mifflin 1959), 351n.

13 Walter H. Evert, in *Aesthetic and Myth in the Poetry of Keats* (Princeton: Princeton University Press 1965), 268, makes this connection in developing what he calls (269) Keats's "demonic view of the poetic imagination."

14 See Jacques Derrida, *Of Grammatology*, trans. Gayatri Chakravorty Spivak (Baltimore: Johns Hopkins University Press 1976), 18; the phrase quoted is probably Derrida's most evocative description of the problematics of the sign. Derrida, in his *Spurs: Nietzsche's Styles*, trans. Barbara Harlow (Chicago: University of Chicago Press 1979), 97, 109, introduces the concept of "phallogocentrism" in his discussion of the "process of propriation" in language; Margaret Homans, in her important analysis of "phallogocentrism" in *Women Writers and Poetic Identity* (Princeton: Princeton University Press 1980), 34–7, sees in Derrida's inquiry into the "cultural commonplace" of linguistic appropriation "a useful locus for the connection between language and sexual difference." On the role of the trace in the economy of presence and absence, see Derrida's comments in *Positions*, trans. Alan Bass (Chicago: University of Chicago Press 1981), 26.

15 Though the published version of the poem differs somewhat from the original found in *Letters*, 2:95–6, I accept the opinion of virtually all the commentators that the first version is superior; the changes introduced would not affect my analysis in any case. Stillinger, in his edition of the *Complete Poems* (270–1), prints only the original version. The ablest close reading of the poem is performed by Charles I. Patterson in his *The Daemonic in the Poetry of John Keats* (Urbana: University of Illinois Press 1970), 125–50. Stuart Sperry argues (240) that "'La Belle Dame' is most of all about the essence of poetry itself" in his discussion of the poem in *Keats the Poet* (Princeton: Princeton University Press 1973), 231–41.

16 Francis Utley, in "The Infernos of Lucretius and Keats's *La Belle Dame sans Merci*," *ELH* 25(1958): 121, uses the quoted phrase; Evert (*Aesthetic and Myth*, 245) also believes that the knight falls victim to "cruelly delusive enchantment by a demon." Charles Patterson, who argues convincingly that "there is nothing intrinsically evil" about the lady, nevertheless sees her as "a supramortal female," a neutral and blameless daemon, in *The Daemonic in Keats*, 127–8. Sperry connects the lady with Morgan la Fay and calls her a "fairy enchantress," in *Keats the Poet*, 234. Even Wasserman, who reads the poem as the knight's quest for a spiritual ideal, says in *The Finer Tone* that, from one point of view, "the fairy lady is a Circe," while from the other she is the ideal itself (83). A third possibility is never canvassed.

CHAPTER FIVE

1 The first section of this essay is an abbreviated version of chapter 7 of my book *The Supplement of Reading: Figures of Understanding in Romantic Theory and Practice* (Ithaca: Cornell University Press 1990), 197–220. The chapter deals with issues of canonicity and intertextuality in Blake's corpus.

2   William Blake, *The Complete Poetry and Prose of William Blake*, ed. David V. Erdman, with commentary by Harold Bloom (rev. ed. Berkeley: University of California Press 1982). In citations in the text the abbreviation "E" is followed first by the page number; the numbers following the semicolon indicate the plates and/or lines.

3   *The Gnostic Gospels* (New York: Vintage 1981), 137.

4   Although some of these formal strategies are present in the later works, their effect is quite different. See *The Supplement of Reading*, 204.

5   See, for instance, Susan Fox, *Poetic Form in Blake's Milton* (Princeton: Princeton University Press 1976), 9.

6   "Cubism," in Robert L. Herbert, ed., *Modern Artists on Art: Ten Unabridged Essays* (Englewood Cliffs: Prentice-Hall 1964), 13.

7   *S/Z*, trans. Richard Miller (New York: Hill and Wang 1974), 3–4.

8   "Theses on the Transition from the Aesthetics of Literary Works to a Theory of Aesthetic Experience," in *Interpretation of Narrative*, ed. Mario J. Valdés and Owen J. Miller (Toronto: University of Toronto Press 1978), 138.

9   I use the term "state" as Blake himself used it. But the term is also used in the graphic arts to denote a particular "state" of an engraving, and so it is worth noting that Blake sold his plates in earlier states, thus allowing our philosophical and bibliographical uses of the term to coincide.

10 See for instance Harold Bloom, *Blake's Apocalypse: A Study in Poetic Argument* (1963; rpt. Ithaca: Cornell University Press 1970), 52–62. An exception to this reading is W.J.T. Mitchell, *Blake's Composite Art: A Study of the Illuminated Poetry* (Princeton: Princeton University Press 1980), 78–106.

11 David Erdman, *Blake: Prophet against Empire* (1954; rev. ed. Garden City, NY: Doubleday 1969), 131n.; Nancy Bogen, *The Book of Thel: A Facsimile and Critical Text* (Providence: Brown University Press 1971), 3.

12 In *Visions* (iii:7–8) Oothoon is a cloud rent by Bromion's thunders, and in *Europe* the shadowy female is associated with clouds (1:12). My point is not that clouds are female, but that Blake does not always make them male.

13 For instance, in *Europe* Oothoon's openness is positively contrasted with Enitharmon's secrecy (E66; 14:21–2).

14 *Symbol and Truth in Blake's Myth* (Princeton: Princeton University Press 1980), 197–8.

15 Since it is Oothoon who plucks the marigold (and thus "deflowers" it), it is not entirely clear that she is raped according to prevailing legal definitions of the term, though it is clear enough that Blake perceives what Bromion does as a rape, and most critics have accordingly treated it as such. Leslie Tannenbaum, however, is an example of someone who takes the legal interpretation, thus opening the whole issue of "openness": *Biblical Tradition in Blake's Prophecies* (Princeton: Princeton University Press 1982), 188.

16 In this copy the sun is rising, whereas in others it is setting, and in yet others the spaces left for sun and sky are coloured blue-black so as to efface the sun entirely.

17 "Blake, Trauma, and the Female," *New Literary History* 15 (1984): 475–90.
18 *The Dehumanisation of Art and Other Writings on Art and Culture* (New York: Doubleday 1956), 31.
19 See Erdman, *Blake: Prophet against Empire*, 213–17.
20 *Biblical Tradition in Blake's Prophecies*, 99.

CHAPTER SIX

1   Mary Jacobus, "Apostrophe and Lyric Voice in *The Prelude*," in *Lyric Poetry: Beyond New Criticism*, ed. Chaviva Hosek and Patricia Parker (Ithaca: Cornell University Press 1985), 171. Jonathan Culler, *The Pursuit of Signs: Semiotics, Literature, Deconstruction* (Ithaca: Cornell University Press 1981), 135, 137. (Culler's essay originally appeared in *Diacritics* 7 [Winter 1977]: 59–69.) Further references to *Pursuit* will be included parenthetically in the text. Many critics have used this essay. Jacobus, for example, explicitly echoing Culler, writes: "Apostrophe, as Jonathan Culler has observed, is an embarrassment" (171). Barbara Johnson, in *A World of Difference* (Baltimore: Johns Hopkins University Press 1987), also cites Culler's argument: "Jonathan Culler indeed sees apostrophe as an embarrassingly explicit emblem of procedures inherent, but usually better hidden, in lyric poetry as such" (185). And Patricia Parker also turns to Culler on this point: "The vocative, or apostrophe, remarks Jonathan Culler in the course of a well-known essay on the subject ... is also frequently a subject of embarrassment" (*Literary Fat Ladies: Rhetoric, Gender, Property* [London: Methuen 1987], 30).
2   Jonathan Culler, "Changes in the Study of the Lyric," in Hosek and Parker (note 1, above), 39, 50.
3   Jonathan Culler, "Reading Lyric," in *The Lesson of Paul de Man*, Yale French Studies 69 (1985):99. Further references will be included parenthetically in the text. For additional examples of critics who have referred to Culler on apostrophe, see especially Cynthia Chase (*Decomposing Figures: Rhetorical Readings in the Romantic Tradition* [Baltimore: Johns Hopkins University Press 1986], 68), who reiterates Culler's argument approvingly; and L.M. Findlay ("Culler and Byron on Apostrophe and Lyric Time," *Studies in Romanticism* 24 [1985]: 336–40), who challenges Culler on his analysis of temporality in apostrophe.
4   Jacques Derrida, *Of Grammatology*, trans. Gayatri Chakravorty Spivak (Baltimore: Johns Hopkins University Press 1974), 3–26.
5   The earliest use of the word "apostrophe" is in Philodemus, first century BC; it was not until much later that the word became used in its technical rhetorical sense. See James A. Arieti and John M. Crossett, trans., *Longinus. On the Sublime.* Texts and Studies in Religion, vol. 21 (New York: Edward Mellen 1985), 101. For sixteenth- through eighteenth-century commentary on apostrophe see Richard Sherry, *A Treatise of Schemes and Tropes* (1550), intro. Herbert W. Hildebrandt (Gainesville: Scholars' Facsimiles and Reprints 1961);

Henry Peacham, *The Garden of Eloquence* (London 1593); Dudley Fenner, *The Artes of Logike and Rhetorike* (n.p. 1584); Abraham Fraunce, *The Arcadian Rhetoric* (1588; Menston: Scolar Press 1969); George Puttenham, *The Arte of English Poesie* (London 1589); Angel Day, *A Declaration of al such Tropes, Figures or Schemes. The English Secretary* (London 1599); John Hoskins, *Directions for Speech and Style* (1599), ed. Hoyt H. Hudson (Princeton: Princeton University Press 1935); Thomas Blount, *The Academy of Eloquence* (1654; Menston: Scolar Press, 1971); John Smith [of Montague Close], *The Mysterie of Rhetorique unvail'd* (London 1657); Hugh Blair, *Lectures on Rhetoric and Belles Lettres* (1783), ed. Harold F. Harding, foreword David Potter, 2 vols. (Carbondale: Southern Illinois University Press 1965).

6 Roman Jakobson, *Language in Literature*, ed. Krystyna Pomorska and Stephen Rudy (Cambridge: Harvard University Press 1987), 67–8.

7 See Erich Auerbach, "Dante's Addresses to the Reader," *Romance Philology* 7 (1953–54):270. I am indebted for this reference to Paul H. Fry's citation of Auerbach in *The Poet's Calling in the English Ode* (New Haven: Yale University Press 1980), 298n6.

8 Quintilian, *Institutio Oratoria*, trans. H.E. Butler, 4 vols. (London: Heinemann 1921).

9 [Cicero], *Ad C. Herennium (Rhetorica ad Herennium)*, trans. Harry Caplan (London: Heinemann 1954).

10 This inaccurate translation has caused other commentators to fail to distinguish the two terms. See, for example, Annabel M. Patterson, *Hermogenes and the Renaissance: Seven Ideas of Style* (Princeton: Princeton University Press 1970), 128n10, where, in her discussion of the *Rhetorica ad Herennium*, she follows Caplan in equating apostrophe and exclamation.

11 Since Longinus, the prerequisite for a sublime apostrophe or prosopopoeia has been passion or elevated emotion in the speaker or writer. Without this rhetorical *sine qua non* both figures are in danger of falling from the sublime to the ridiculous. "How ridiculous," Coleridge is reported as saying, "would it seem in a state of comparative insensibility to employ a figure used only by a person under the highest emotion, such as the impersonation of an abstract being, and an apostrophe to it" (Samuel Taylor Coleridge, *Shakespearean Criticism*, ed. Thomas Middleton Raynor [London: Constable 1930], 2:103). Wordsworth, who is frequently thought of as dismissing prosopopoeia altogether in his Preface to *Lyrical Ballads*, makes an important yet traditional qualification: personifications, he writes, "are, indeed, a figure of speech occasionally prompted by passion, and I have made use of them as such" (*The Prose Works of William Wordsworth*, ed. W.J.B. Owen and Jane Worthington Smyser [Oxford: Clarendon 1974], 1:131). Hence it goes without saying that Culler's deliberately corny apostrophe in "Apostrophe" (*Pursuit*, 135) fails precisely because it lacks this one prerequisite. The point is that no figure is inherently embarrassing; only bad figures are so.

12 Fry (note 7, above) writes: "Apostrophe, the blanket form of *invocatio*, is defined in all the Rhetorics as a turning aside to address some absent hearer. ... The poet speaks these asides to a pro tem audience and then re-turns to the audience that is understood to be listening, as it were, under contract" (11). My only amendment to this definition is that the hearer does not need to be absent, as my examples from Quintilian, Sherry, and Hoskins make clear.

13 Compare Abraham Fraunce, in *The Arcadian Rhetoric* (1588): "*Apostrophe* turning away, is when the speach is turned to some such person to whom it was not first prepared, sometimes the turning is to men ... sometimes from men, to Gods ... sometimes to a dumb and senseless creature" (cap. 30). Puttenham, in his *Arte of English Poesie* (1589), has an entry on "Apostrophe, or the turne tale," in which we "either speake or exclaime at some other person or thing" (198–9). "The Greekes," he says, "call such figure (as we do) the turnway or turnetale" (199).

14 Other examples could be added, though some later rhetoricians simply repeat without acknowledgment these basic definitions. Thomas Blount, for example, in *The Academy of Eloquence* (1654), takes his definition from John Hoskins's *Directions for Speech and Style* (1599), as does John Smith in *The Mysterie of Rhetorique unvail'd* (1657).

15 Thomas Gibbons, *Rhetoric; Or a View of Its Principal Tropes and Figures* (1767; Menston: Scolar Press 1969), 213.

16 See John Holmes, *The Art of Rhetoric Made Easy; Or, The Elements of Oratory* (London 1766); John Walker, *A Rhetorical Grammar* (Boston: Cummings and Hilliard 1822); and Blair (note 5, above). See also John Stirling, *A System of Rhetoric* (1733; Menston: Scolar Press 1968); the anonymous *Rhetoric; or the Principles of Oratory Delineated*, attributed to Rollins (London 1736), 23–7; Alexander Jamieson, *A Grammar of Rhetoric* (New Haven: A.H. Maltby 1826), 174, 162; Henry N. Day, *Elements of the Art of Rhetoric* (Hudson: W. Skinner 1850), 277.

17 See Sister Miriam Joseph, *Shakespeare's Use of the Arts of Language* (New York: Columbia University Press 1947), 246–7, 390; Fry (note 7, above), 11; Patterson (note 10, above), 64, 107, 126–8; Paul de Man, *The Resistance to Theory*, foreword Wlad Godzich (Minneapolis: University of Minnesota Press 1986), 27–53 (further references will be included parenthetically in the text); and Michael Riffaterre, "Prosopopeia," in *The Lesson of Paul de Man, Yale French Studies* 69 (1985):107–23. Numerous contemporary handbooks also define apostrophe. Both the *Princeton Encyclopedia of Poetry and Poetics* (ed. Alex Preminger [Princeton: Princeton University Press 1974]) and C. Hugh Holman's *A Handbook to Literature* (4th ed. Indianapolis: Bobbs-Merrill 1983), to take only two well-known examples, give essentially correct definitions of the figure, though they both err in their choice of texts meant to illustrate apostrophe, on grounds that I shall demonstrate later. See note 23 below.

18 Jacques Derrida, *The Post Card: From Socrates to Freud and Beyond*, trans. Alan

Bass (Chicago: University of Chicago Press 1987), 4.

19 Compare Puttenham, who gives the following definition of "Ecphonesis or the Outcry": "The figure of exclamation, I call him [the outcrie] because it utters our minde by all such words as do shew any extreme passion, whether it be by way of exclamation or crying out, admiration or wondering, imprecation or cursing, obtestation or taking God and the world to witnes, or any such like as declare an impotent affection" (177).

20 Thomas Wilson, *Wilson's Arte of Rhetorique* (1560), ed. G.H. Mair (Oxford: Clarendon 1919), 205.

21 *The Prelude*, 1.1. Unless otherwise noted, all references to *The Prelude* are to the 1850 version in William Wordsworth, *The Prelude: 1799, 1805, 1850*, ed. Jonathan Wordsworth, M.H. Abrams, and Stephen Gill (New York: Norton 1979).

22 Paul de Man, *Blindness and Insight: Essays in the Rhetoric of Contemporary Criticism,* 2nd ed., intro. Wlad Godzich (Minneapolis: University of Minnesota Press 1983), 208.

23 This is the point where the *Princeton Encyclopedia* and Holman's *Handbook* err. They both offer as an example of apostrophe the first line of Wordsworth's sonnet "London, 1802": "Milton! thou shouldst be living at this hour. ... "

24 See de Man's note explaining how all "poem[s] of address" (*Resistance*, 48) could be entitled *Prosopopoeia* – "As they in fact often are, though preferably by the more euphonic and noble term 'ode' or 'Ode to X'" (*Resistance*, 53n22). It should be added that for de Man, X here refers to an inanimate object.

25 There exists a genre or mode of "address" as such: Wordsworth's *Address to My Infant Daughter Dora*, *Address to Kilchurn Castle*, and *Address from the Spirit of Cockermouth Castle* are examples. Similarly, Wordsworth's more than three dozen poems entitled *To X* (for example, *To a Butterfly*, *To Joanna*, *To the Daisy*, *To a Skylark*, *To H.C.*) all announce themselves as instances of this mode. One could add the genres of the verse epistle, conversation poem, hymn, sonnet dedicatory, and so on, to this category. Hence I differ with Fry's terminology in his discussion of the apostrophe called "To 'H.C.'" (157). By definition, no poem called *To X* can be an apostrophe; apostrophe is a figure, not a genre.

26 George N. Shuster, *The English Ode from Milton to Keats* (New York: Columbia University Press 1940).

27 Compare Chase, who closely paraphrases Culler here: "Critics as various as George Shuster (in *The English Ode from Milton to Keats*) and Michael Riffaterre (in *La Production du texte*) have tended to dismiss apostrophe as being insignificant because it is simply conventional" (68).

28 But in Wordsworth, it should be added, the ear usually implies a voice to follow, often in alien, surprising, or usurping ways, as the Boy of Winander episode demonstrates.

29 How are we to account for the persistence of this error in Culler and those who follow him? Here we can only speculate. It may not be enough to say

that the problem begins with Culler's incorrect definition of apostrophe, and that therefore everything that stems from this misunderstanding is wrong, for what Culler has to say about the temporality of apostrophe is useful. Nor is Culler the first person to make the mistake, as a glance at any of a number of handbooks will show. A better way might be to begin with the effect and work back to the cause – that is, to begin with the notion of embarrassment and then attempt to figure out why apostrophe, of all figures, might be the source of such ticklishness or discomfiture. But here too we reach a dead end, for nowhere does Culler explain exactly why apostrophes are necessarily embarrassing; as I suggest, some are, and some aren't. I suspect the real motive for misreading has to do with a larger misunderstanding of Romanticism – perhaps the unexamined tendency to see it in terms of Mill's opposition between rhetoric or eloquence as public discourse ("heard"), and poetry as private and subjective ("overheard") soliloquy (see John Stuart Mill, *Essays on Poetry*, ed. F. Parvin Sharpless [Columbia: University of South Carolina Press 1976], 12). If, as Shelley said, the poet "is a nightingale, who sits in darkness and sings to cheer its own solitude with sweet sounds," then it is possible that a reader might misunderstand this to imply that the poet-nightingale has no need of rhetoric, no artfulness in its unpremeditated song. What could be sillier than a diversion of address when you're just talking to yourself? But this surely by-now outdated view of Romantic lyricism neglects what Shelley goes on to say in the same sentence: the poet may be a nightingale, but "his auditors are as men entranced by the melody of an unseen musician, who feel that they are moved and softened, yet know not whence or why" (Percy Bysshe Shelley, *Shelley's Poetry and Prose*, ed. Donald H. Reiman and Sharon B. Powers [New York: Norton 1977], 486). As Shelley well knew, a word like "entranced," from Longinus on, has clear associations with rhetoric and the power of persuasion: this bird is convincing. Or to turn the tables, in anticipation of my reading of Wordsworth's "There Was a Boy," the poet is an owl, whose auditors are moved and then "removed," as Peacham would say, through an aversion of voice. Much work, obviously, still needs to be done to dispel lingering fallacies about Romantic or lyric voice; we need, I think, to revise our understanding of Romanticism from the perspective of the history of rhetoric. Quite apart from social history or politics, the unwritten history of Romanticism lies in the history of its words. The present essay is one chapter in this unwritten history.

30 As I have described it, apostrophe may be thought of as a movement of language analogous to the Saussurean notion of "difference" – that is, the play or shuttling of terms within a closed language system. Every signifier evokes or recalls every other signifier in the system, so that the linguistic sign is constituted as an effect or function of this periphrasis. For Derrida, language attempts to cover up this effect of difference through a vocabulary of presence (see *Writing and Difference*, trans. Alan Bass [Chicago: University

of Chicago Press 1978], 279–80); linguistic identity thus is seen not as a
function of movement, a turning or troping of signs, but as a stable self-
presence. The concept may be applied to our case. If the question of apostro-
phe is not one of voice as such, but of the movement or translation of voice
from one addressee to another, then it is possible to see why apostrophe, as
the very figure of difference – intersubjective, intertextual, intervocative –
might be mistaken for address, the shuttling mistaken for presence.
Apostrophe, however, is a carrier of voice, not voice itself. Regarding the
concept of voice in Wordsworth, see especially Geoffrey Hartman's essays
"Words, Wish, Worth" and "Timely Utterance" for the connection of voice
and divine fiat (in *The Unremarkable Wordsworth*, foreword Donald G.
Marshall [Minneapolis: University of Minnesota Press 1987], 90–119 and
152–62); "Blessing the Torrent" for the relation of voice to the domestication
of the sublime (*Unremarkable*, 75–89); and "The Use and Abuse of Structural
Analysis" for voice in a ghostly or intermediary mode (*Unremarkable*, 129–51).
31 In 1800 Wordsworth added the following note to *Tintern Abbey* in *Lyrical
Ballads*: "I have not ventured to call this Poem an Ode; but it was written with
a hope that in the transitions, and the impassioned music of the versification,
would be found the principal requisites of that species of composition" (see
R.L. Brett and A.R. Jones, eds., *"Lyrical Ballads": Wordsworth and Coleridge*
[London: Methuen 1963], 296). I am suggesting rhetorical grounds for
considering this poem as an ode. Fry interprets Wordsworth's statement in a
contrary, but persuasive, way: "'Tintern Abbey,' Wordsworth's greatest
lyric," he writes, "is nothing like an ode" (179). Fry's echo of Shakespeare's
sonnet ("My mistress' eyes are nothing like the sun") confirms the logic of
what follows: "It is most probable that Wordsworth thought 'Tintern Abbey'
too good to be called an ode" (179). However, see also Lee M. Johnson, who
argues that *Tintern Abbey* is "a blank verse Pindaric ode designed as a double
golden section" (*Wordsworth's Metaphysical Verse: Geometry, Nature, and Form*
[Toronto: University of Toronto Press 1982], 19).
32 John Milton, *Complete Poems and Major Prose*, ed. Merritt Y. Hughes (New
York: Odyssey 1957), 124. All references to Milton's poetry are to this edition.
33 M.H. Abrams, "Structure and Style in the Greater Romantic Lyric," in
Romanticism and Consciousness, ed. Harold Bloom (New York: Norton 1970),
201–29.
34 See Geoffrey Hartman's comments on what he sees as the eloquent "break"
after "There Was a Boy" in *The Fate of Reading* (Chicago: University of
Chicago Press 1975), 183, 289, 341 n. 10.
35 The bibliography of modern commentary on the Boy of Winander is long
and varied. Here are some selected sources. For the definitive reading of the
episode in relation to the theme of self-consciousness, see Geoffrey H.
Hartman, *Wordsworth's Poetry 1787–1814* (New Haven: Yale University Press
1964), 19–22; see also his discussions in *Criticism in the Wilderness: The Study of*

Literature Today (New Haven: Yale University Press 1980), 222–5, and *The Fate of Reading*, 182–3, 286–92. Other valuable recent studies include Heather Glen, *Vision and Disenchantment: Blake's "Songs" and Wordsworth's "Lyrical Ballads"* (Cambridge: Cambridge University Press 1983), 264–71, and Morris Dickstein, "Coleridge, Wordsworth, and the 'Conversation Poems,'" *Centennial Review* 16 (1972): 379–82 (for parallels with Coleridge's *The Nightingale*); Robert Rehder, *Wordsworth and the Beginnings of Modern Poetry* (London: Croom Helm 1981), 81–9, A.H. Gomme, "Some Wordsworthian Transparencies," *Modern Language Review* 68 (1973): 509–12, and Frank McConnell, *The Confessional Imagination: A Reading of Wordsworth's "Prelude"* (Baltimore: Johns Hopkins University Press 1974), 166 (on syntax); Leslie Brisman, *Milton's Poetry of Choice and Its Romantic Heirs* (Ithaca: Cornell University Press 1973), 262–5 and *Romantic Origins* (Ithaca: Cornell University Press 1978), 337–61, 373 (on "voice"); D.G. Gillham, "Wordsworth's Hidden Figures of Speech," in *Generous Converse: English Essays in Memory of Edward Davis*, ed. Brian Green (Cape Town: Oxford University Press 1980), 82–3, William Shullenberger, "'Something' in Wordsworth," in *Ineffability: Naming the Unnamable from Dante to Beckett*, ed. Peter S. Hawkins and Anne Howland Schotter (New York: AMS 1984), 115–7, A.W. Phinney, "Wordsworth's Winander Boy and Romantic Theories of Language," *Wordsworth Circle* 18 (1987): 67–70, and Mary Jacobus, "The Art of Managing Books: Romantic Prose and the Writing of the Past," *Romanticism and Language*, ed. Arden Reed (Ithaca: Cornell University Press 1984), 215–8 (on language); Helen Regueiro, *The Limits of Imagination: Wordsworth, Yeats, and Stevens* (Ithaca: Cornell University Press 1976), 54–7, 88, 107 (on incompleteness of self); Stephen J. Spector, "Wordsworth's Mirror Imagery and the Picturesque Tradition," *ELH* 44 (1977): 86–8, 103–4 (on mirror imagery); Thomas R. Frosch, "Wordsworth and the Matrix of Romance: *The Prelude*, Book v," *CUNY English Forum*, vol. 1, ed. Saul N. Brody and Harold Schechter (New York: AMS 1985), 185–6, 192, Lionel Morton, "Books and Drowned Men: Unconscious Mourning in Book v of *The Prelude*," *English Studies in Canada* 8 (1982): 23, 29–32, Richard J. Onorato, *The Character of the Poet: Wordsworth in "The Prelude"* (Princeton: Princeton University Press 1971), 193–7, and Susan J. Wolfson, "The Illusion of Mastery: Wordsworth's Revisions of 'The Drowned Man of Esthwaite,' 1799, 1805, 1850," *PMLA* 99 (1984): 923–5 (for psychoanalytic approach); Tilottama Rajan, "Romanticism and the Death of Lyric Consciousness," in Hosek and Parker (note 1, above), 198–200 (on intertextualization); William H. Galperin, "Authority and Deconstruction in Book v of *The Prelude*," *Studies in English Literature* 26 (1986): 624–5, Karl R. Johnson, *The Written Spirit: Thematic and Rhetorical Structure in Wordsworth's "The Prelude"* (Salzburg: Institut fur Englische Sprache und Literatur 1978), 197–204, Joel Morkan, "Structure and Meaning in *The Prelude*, Book v," *PMLA* 87 (1972): 253, Kenneth R. Johnston, *Wordsworth and "The Recluse"* (New

Haven: Yale University Press 1984), 141–3 (on education); Frances Ferguson, *Wordsworth: Language as Counter-Spirit* (New Haven: Yale University Press 1977), 77, 167–70, 242–9 (on episode as "reading"); Andrzej Warminski, "Missed Crossing: Wordsworth's Apocalypses," *MLN* 99 (1984): 991–6, Jonathan Arac, *Critical Genealogies: Historical Situations for Postmodern Literary Studies* (New York: Columbia University Press 1987), 63–4, and Cynthia Chase, *Decomposing Figures*, 13–31 (on interpretation). See also Michael Ragussis, *The Subterfuge of Art: Language and the Romantic Tradition* (Baltimore: Johns Hopkins University Press 1978), 30; David Ferry, *The Limits of Mortality: An Essay on Wordsworth's Major Poems* (Middletown: Wesleyan University Press 1959), 87–9; Ernest Bernhardt-Kabisch, "The Stone and the Shell: Wordsworth, Cataclysm, and the Myth of Glaucus," *Studies in Romanticism* 23 (1984): 490; J. Robert Barth, "The Poet, Death, and Immortality: The Unity of *The Prelude*, Book V," *Wordsworth Circle* 10 (1979): 71–2; F.W. Bateson, *Wordsworth: A Re-Interpretation* (2nd ed. London: Longmans 1956), 21, 25, 28–30; Steven Lukits, "Wordsworth Unawares: The Boy of Winander, the Poet, and the Mariner," *Wordsworth Circle* 19 (1988): 156–60; Evelyn Shakir, "Books, Death, and Immortality: A Study of Book V of *The Prelude*," *Studies in Romanticism* 8 (1969): 163; C.C. Clarke, *Romantic Paradox: An Essay on the Poetry of Wordsworth* (Westport: Greenwood Press 1962), 6–8; John F. Danby, *The Simple Wordsworth: Studies in the Poems 1797–1807* (London: Routledge 1960), 111–14; Roger N. Murray, *Wordsworth's Style: Figures and Themes in the "Lyrical Ballads" of 1800* (Lincoln: University of Nebraska Press 1967), 107–9; Aldous Huxley, *Texts and Pretexts: An Anthology with Commentaries* (London: Chatto and Windus 1932), 57–8, 155–6; David Ellis, *Wordsworth, Freud, and the Spots of Time: Interpretation in "The Prelude"* (Cambridge: Cambridge University Press 1985), 114–20; Herbert Lindenberger, *On Wordsworth's "Prelude"* (Princeton: Princeton University Press 1963), 41–3; John Jones, *The Egotistical Sublime: A History of Wordsworth's Imagination* (London: Chatto and Windus 1954), 91–3; J. R. Watson, *Wordsworth's Vital Soul: The Sacred and the Profane in Wordsworth's Poetry* (London: Macmillan 1982), 147–9.

36 Compare David P. Haney, who cites this passage to trace the development of Nature in book 1 of *The Prelude* "from a *ministering* force ... to a *witnessing* agent" (59) and ultimately to a narrator who recounts "what the poet cannot" ("The Emergence of the Autobiographical Figure in *The Prelude*, Book I," *Studies in Romanticism* 20 [1981]: 60).

37 The turning to Nature in "There Was a Boy" could stand as a textbook example of Quintilian's fourth class of metaphor, in which animate things are substituted for inanimate things (*Institutio*, 8.6.9–11). But this metaphorical substitution, one immediately recognizes, is also a prosopopoeia. Quintilian elaborates: "Above all, effects of extraordinary sublimity are produced when the theme is exalted by a bold and almost hazardous metaphor and inanimate objects are given life and action" (8.6.11). His example demonstrates

how metaphor, apostrophe, and prosopopoeia at times (especially in sublime writing occasioned by passion) may be interimplicated.

38 *The Poetical Works of William Wordsworth*, ed. Ernest de Selincourt, rev. Helen Darbishire, 5 vols. (Oxford: Clarendon 1952–63), 1: 264. This text is more than pseudo-Miltonic pastiche, for it shows the sixteen-year-old Wordsworth experimenting with several poetic conventions at once: the tradition of pastoral elegy, the translation of Wales into the Lake District, and the invocation of Druid lore. Even the simple trimeter of "Nor in Winander's stream" seems unarguably derived from the style of *Lycidas*.

39 There is a strong creative power in the ambiguity of the antecedent of "they speak." Who speaks? The "they" obviously can be read as referring to "The Poets" three lines earlier, but following so closely upon the catalogue of hills and streams and rocks, the simple clause "they speak" can also be read as personifying these "senseless" objects, thus validating Wordsworth's claim that the poetic invocation is not "idly" done.

40 A related shift of pronouns is also found in the Boy of Winander fragment in MS. JJ.: the turn from the third-person "he" and "his," referring to the Boy, to the speaking "I" and "my" at line 12 and thereafter complicates the issue of original authorial intent, since by the time the poem appears in *Lyrical Ballads* (1800) the pronouns have been changed back to third person. It is not, as is often claimed, simply a question of Wordsworth's switching from first- to third-person discourse; the text *originally* (that is, in MS. JJ.) is divided over the identity of the Boy. See Norton *Prelude*, 492.

41 I have written elsewhere about the intersection of voice and the master trope of epitaph in Wordsworth; see my *Monumental Writing: Aspects of Rhetoric in Wordsworth's Poetry* (Lincoln: University of Nebraska Press 1988).

42 Thomas De Quincey, *Recollections of the Lakes and the Lake Poets*, ed. David Wright (Harmondsworth: Penguin 1970), 160.

43 See, for example, Brisman, *Romantic Origins*, 373: "The boy of Winander episode commences with a shaky image of the power of communion"; Barth: "deep communion between the boy and the natural world" (71); Rajan: "communion with nature" (198); Shakir: "intimate and unconscious communion" (163); Gillham: profound "communion" (82); Ferry: "perfect and equal exchange" between the boy and nature (89). A minority view, held by Hartman (*Wordsworth's Poetry*, 22), McConnell (166), and Warminski (992–6), emphasizes instead confrontation and asymmetry in the episode. See note 35, above, for full citations of these sources.

44 All references to Shakespeare's writings are to *The Complete Works*, ed. Alfred Harbage (Baltimore: Penguin 1969).

45 I have not forgotten that Wordsworth originally describes the vocal interchange as "a wild scene / Of mirth and jocund din" (Norton *Prelude*, 492). But this "play" has its serious side, in the way that the skating episode in *The Prelude*, book 1 has its own "alien sound / Of melancholy" (1.443–4) that cuts

across the "rapture" (1.430) of the child. One might pursue further parallels between the Boy of Winander episode and the skating scene in terms of the interplay of voice and echo.

46 Francis Jeffrey, Review of *Poems* by George Crabbe, *Edinburgh Review* 12 (1808): 135.

47 There is a prosopopoeia within prosopopoeia here, in the conferring of "voice" on Nature. Wordsworth turns to apostrophize/personify the cliffs and islands and then recounts the story of the Boy of Winander. Within that story the animating power of voice again is used to personify Nature through the "mimic hootings." Though no apostrophe is explicit with the Boy, there is nevertheless a strange "diversion" of discourse when the owls stop answering and "the voice / Of mountain torrents" responds instead. The effect is as if the speaker had turned from his "proper" listener to an invoked listener "unawares" (5.385). As such, the narrative *in* the Boy of Winander passage may be read as a repetition-with-a-difference of the narrative *of* the Boy of Winander episode.

48 Robert Frost, *Complete Poems of Robert Frost* (London: Jonathan Cape 1951), 368.

49 See Derrida, *Writing*, for "the call of the supplement" (211). Any approach to a deconstruction of the Boy of Winander's "speech act" must be chastened by Derrida's reminder that "it is not enough to recall that one always writes for someone; and the oppositions sender-receiver, code-message, etc., remain extremely coarse instruments. We would search the 'public' in vain for the first reader: i. e., the first author of a work" (*Writing*, 227). What it means to be the "first" sender or "first" receiver is precisely what the Boy of Winander episode puts in question.

50 Paul de Man, *The Rhetoric of Romanticism* (New York: Columbia University Press 1984), 78.

51 Thomas Gray, *The Complete Poems of Thomas Gray*, ed. H.W. Starr and J.R. Hendrickson (Oxford: Clarendon 1966), 41.

52 See the extended apostrophe to the sister (*Prelude*, 14.232–75), in which she is praised for "teach[ing] the little birds to build their nests / And warble in [the] chambers" of the poet's rock-like soul (14.255–6). Compare the "daylong voice" of the Eve-figure in Frost's poem *Never Again Would Birds' Song Be the Same* (*Complete Poems*, 369):

> Admittedly an eloquence so soft
> Could only have had an influence on birds
> When call or laughter carried it aloft.
> Be that as may be, she was in their song.
> Moreover her voice upon their voices crossed
> Had now persisted in the woods so long

That probably it never would be lost.
Never again would birds' song be the same.
And to do that to birds was why she came.

CHAPTER SEVEN

Research for this paper was initiated with the generous assistance of the Social Sciences and Humanities Research Council of Canada, the Department of English, Yale University, and the Yale Center for British Art.

1 Between them, Martin Butlin and Christopher Heppner confirm that none of the copies of *Pity* is inscribed with a title. See, respectively, "Blake's 'God Judging Adam' Rediscovered," in *The Visionary Hand: Essays for the Study of William Blake's Art and Aesthetics*, ed. Robert N. Essick (Los Angeles: Hennessey and Ingalls 1973), 309; and "Reading Blake's Designs: *Pity* and *Hecate*," *Bulletin of Research in the Humanities* 84 (Autumn 1981): 339.

2 *Macbeth*, 1.8, in *The Plays of William Shakespeare*, ed. Samuel Johnson (London 1765), 6:398–9.

3 For example, W. Moelwyn Merchant notes, not entirely correctly, that "the formal relation of *Pity* to the Shakespeare text is quite different [from that of *Hecate*] and indeed unique in Blake's work." See "Blake's Shakespeare," *Apollo* n.s. 79 (April 1964): 322. Martin Butlin argues more expansively that "'Pity' ... is one of the most inspired of all 'literal' illustrations of a text in the history of art." See "The Evolution of Blake's Large Color Prints of 1795," in *William Blake: Essays for S. Foster Damon*, ed. Alvin Rosenfeld (Providence: Brown University Press 1969), 109. I might add here that, despite these enthusiastic claims, little sustained work has been done on *Pity*, the notable exception being a persuasive and ground-breaking essay by Christopher Heppner (note 1, above). Heppner argues that Blake "constructs" out of Shakespeare's similes an "implicit or virtual second-level text in the form of a dramatized episode implying a supportive narrative" and that this "episode is presented visually in a manner that implies an interpretation and valuation of both the dramatized situation and of the original text" (Heppner, 353).

4 I borrow this phrase from a dense passage in *Jerusalem* (E242;83:47) in which Blake unsettles the conventional metaphysical identification of interiorities with epochal truth and exteriorities with derivation and error. For Blake, the "Surface" world of changefulness is made "real" at the moment that the notion of a "deep" world of changeless truth has been declared false or Urizenic. *Pity*'s implicit valuation of the text's linguistic surface to the disadvantage of its referential depth seems analogous. See my "'The Innocence of Becoming Restored': Blake, Nietzsche, and the Disclosure of Difference," *Studies in Romanticism* 29 (1990): 91–113. All Blake quotations are from *The Complete Poetry and Prose of William Blake*, ed. David V. Erdman

(Berkeley and Los Angeles: University of California Press 1982), abbreviated as E. Citations generally note page numbers in Erdman, followed by plate (or page) numbers and line numbers in Blake. The following abbreviations will be used in citing Blake: *Jerusalem*, J; *Milton*, M; *A Descriptive Catalogue*, DC.

5 *Allegories of Reading: Figural Language in Rousseau, Nietzsche, Rilke, and Proust* (New Haven: Yale University Press 1979), 201.

6 See W.J.T. Mitchell, *Blake's Composite Art: A Study of the Illuminated Poetry* (Princeton: Princeton University Press 1978), 14.

7 John Boydell, Preface, *Collection of Prints, From Pictures Painted for ... the Dramatic Works of Shakespeare by the Artists of Great Britain* (London 1793; facs. rpt. New York: Benjamin Blom 1968). Boydell's remarks are cited by Ronald Paulson in *Book and Painting: Shakespeare, Milton, and the Bible: Literary Texts and the Emergence of English Painting* (Knoxville: University of Tennessee Press 1982), 27. Paulson's chapter on "Shakespearean Painting" discusses the impact of Shakespeare on English art during the late eighteenth century. On the same issue see Winnifred Friedman, *Boydell's Shakespeare Gallery* (Ph.D. diss., Harvard University 1974; facs. rpt., New York: Garland 1976), and A.D. Nuttall, *A New Mimesis: Shakespeare and the Representation of Reality* (London: Methuen 1983), 66–71.

8 For a reproduction of the illumination of Psalm 44 see E.T. DeWald, *The Illustrations of the Utrecht Psalter* (Princeton: Princeton University Press 1934), plate 40. Several art historians have noted cases of literalism in medieval illuminations, though none, so far as I know, point to the revival of this technique in Blake. See Meyer Schapiro, *Words and Pictures: On the Literal and the Symbolic in the Illustration of a Text* (The Hague: Mouton 1973), 13–15; and Otto Pächt, *Book Illumination in the Middle Ages*, trans. H. Miller (London: Oxford University Press 1986), 167–70.

9 *Appreciations*, in *The Works of Walter Pater* (London: Macmillan 1901), 5:20.

10 Freud argues that "the whole domain of verbal wit is put at the disposal of the dream-work." Chief among the modes of representation adopted by dreams is what he calls "verbal disguise," in which the dream-work exploits the literal sense of a phrase or word in order to express a figurative meaning; the dream, for example, represents a person of high-standing literally standing high. "[N]euroses ... no less than dreams," Freud concludes, "make unashamed use of the advantages thus offered by words for purposes of condensation and disguise." See *The Interpretation of Dreams*, in *The Standard Edition of the Complete Works of Sigmund Freud*, trans. and ed. James Strachey (London: Hogarth Press 1953), 5:340–1. Walter Benjamin's theorizing about the nature and limits of translation raises similar issues, to which I want to return. For now let me note that for Benjamin the unintelligibility of Hölderlin's literalist translations of Sophocles discloses an important fact about language; as Paul de Man describes it, this literalism demonstrates

how "the letter can disrupt the ostensible stable meaning of a sentence and introduce in it a slippage by means of which that meaning disappears, evanesces, and by means of which all control over that meaning is lost." See Benjamin's "The Task of the Translator," *Illuminations,* trans. H. Zohn (New York: Schocken Books 1969), 69–82. Paul de Man's remarks come from "'Conclusions' on Walter Benjamin's 'The Task of the Translator,'" ed. William D. Jewett, *Yale French Studies* 69 (1985): 41.

11 Pater discusses Giotto's frescoes at Padua in *Greek Studies,* in *The Works of Walter Pater,* 7:99. Ruskin mentions the same figures in *Fors Clavigera,* vols. 27–9 in *The Works of John Ruskin,* ed. E.T. Cook and A. Wedderburn (London: George Allen 1903–12), 27:130, and in *Giotto and His Works in Padua,* in *Works,* 24:118. Giotto's work is cited in Proust's *Remembrance of Things Past,* vol. 1, trans. C.K.S. Moncrieff (London: Chatto and Windus 1949), 164–7. J. Hillis Miller draws attention to the similarity between all three writers on the same subject in "Walter Pater: A Partial Portrait," *Daedalus* 105 (Winter 1976): 104–13.

12 Pater, *Greek Studies,* in *The Works of Walter Pater,* 7:98.

13 Linnell is cited in *Blake Records,* ed. G.E. Bentley, Jr (Oxford: Clarendon 1969), 402.

14 Blake's transcription and commentary reads in part:
>   And Young & Old come forth to play
>   On a Sunshine Holiday.
> In this design is Introduced
>   Mountains on whose barren breast
>   The Labring Clouds do often rest
> Mountains Clouds Rivers Trees appear Humanized on the Sunshine Holiday (E683).

15 See Milton Klonsky, *Blake's Dante: The Complete Illustrations to the "Divine Comedy"* (New York: Harmony Books 1980), esp. 34 and 84.

16 *As if an Angel Dropped Down from the Clouds* was one of the sixteen "Poetical & Historical Inventions" included in Blake's exhibition of his work in May 1809.

17 (New York: Harcourt, Brace and World 1947), 29.

18 *The Resistance to Theory* (Minneapolis: University of Minnesota Press 1986), 24.

19 As Grover Smith observes, "for almost three centuries scholars have taken turns confessing bafflement at the babe striding the blast." See "The Naked New-Born Babe in *Macbeth*: Some Iconographical Evidence," *Renaissance Papers* (1964): 24.

20 *Shakespeare's Plays,* ed. John Bell (London 1774; facs. rpt. London: Cornmarket Press 1969), 1:18. Another editor adds: "Of this soliloquy the meaning is not very clear; I have never found readers of Shakespeare agreeing about it."

21 *Macbeth,* in *A New Variorum Edition of Shakespeare* (Philadelphia: Lippincott

1873), 2:72–3.

22 *An Approach to Shakespeare* (Garden City: Doubleday 1956), 162 and 164.

23 *The Well-Wrought Urn*, 22 and 31.

24 *Irony and Authority in Romantic Poetry* (Totowa, NJ: Rowman and Littlefield 1979), 141.

25 *The Supplement of Reading: Figures of Understanding in Romantic Theory and Practice* (Ithaca: Cornell University Press 1990), 282.

26 The fact that Blake's design borrows from iconographic contexts that have nothing to do with *Macbeth* further complicates matters. The attitude of the cherub in the print's upper background, for example, is "taken almost literally from an engraving after Raphael's design of *God Appearing to Isaac.*" (I cite Anthony Blunt, *The Art of William Blake* [New York: Columbia University Press 1959], 36, and plate 32d.) Similarly, the new-born babe cites *Macbeth* but refers in its posture to leaping figures associated with what Janet Warner calls "creative desire and the essential energies of nature" found elsewhere in Blake's pictorial work. (See *Blake and the Language of Art* [Kingston and Montreal: McGill-Queen's University Press 1984], 127.) That paintings allude to other paintings is, of course, a given in art history; what bears emphasizing here, however, is that despite the illustration's conspicuous focus on the letter of Shakespeare's text there is, strictly speaking, nothing literal about its literal expression. *Pity*'s allusiveness demonstrates in the pictorial field what is already strongly evident in the text from *Macbeth*: the reiteration of concepts in figures, like that of words in images, is also their reproduction, their point of exposure to significant displacement and self-difference. *Reading* Shakespeare's similes but *seeing* Raphael's images when he paints his heavenly cherubim, Blake underlines how illustration is never simply the repetition of language in pictures, but a complex construction suspended between two worlds, at once the representation of a verbal pre-text *and* the site of various iconographic inscriptions which exceed and precede its illustrative function.

27 *Complete Works*, 5:339 and 4:312.

28 *Complete Works*, 4:312 and 5:339.

29 *Complete Works*, 5:340.

30 *Complete Works*, 4:312.

31 George Puttenham calls catachresis "the Figure of abuse" in *The Arte of English Poesie*, ed. G.D. Willcock and A. Walker (1589; facs. rpt. Kent: Kent University Press 1970), 180.

32 Personification is characterized this way by Paul de Man in "Lyrical Voice in Contemporary Theory: Riffaterre and Jauss," in *Lyric Poetry: Beyond New Criticism*, ed. Chaviva Hosek and Patricia Parker (Ithaca: Cornell University Press 1985), and in "Autobiography as De-facement," in *The Rhetoric of Romanticism* (New York: Columbia University Press 1984).

33 See, for example, Anne K. Mellor, *Blake's Human Form Divine* (Berkeley and Los Angeles: University of California Press 1974), 162–3; and Martin Butlin, *The Paintings and Drawings of William Blake* (New Haven: Yale University Press 1981), "Text" 157.

34 For example, Martin Butlin argues that the design refers us to "the divisive effects of Pity and Procreation," whereas Morton Paley suggests that *"Pity* introduces another gleam of grace into the nightmare world of the colour prints." See, respectively, *William Blake: A Complete Catalogue of the Works in the Tate Gallery* (London: Tate Gallery Publication 1971), 38; and *William Blake* (Oxford: Phaidon 1978), 38.

35 Mark Twain, *Life on the Mississippi* (New York 1906), 332. Twain is cited by W.J.T. Mitchell in *Iconology: Image, Text, Ideology* (Chicago: University of Chicago Press 1986), 40–2. Christopher Heppner notes that the print might just as easily have been labelled *"Heaven's Cherubin, The Sightless Couriers of the Air,* or *The Naked Babe"* (Heppner, 339).

36 *William Blake*, 38.

37 I borrow this phrase from Paul de Man, who notes, in the context of a discussion of Wordsworth's *Essays upon Epitaphs*, that "the language of metaphor, of prosopopeia and of tropes" is "the solar language of cognition that makes the unknown accessible to the mind and to the senses." See *The Rhetoric of Romanticism*, 80.

38 For a discussion of the phenomenality of language see especially Jonathan Culler, "Reading Lyric," *Yale French Studies* 69 (1985): 105–6, and Rodolphe Gasché, "In-difference to Philosophy: de Man on Kant, Hegel, and Nietzsche," in *Reading de Man Reading*, ed. Lindsay Waters and Wlad Godzich (Minneapolis: University of Minnesota Press 1989), 262–88.

39 *Easy Pieces* (New York: Columbia University Press 1985), 142. Hartman's term "switching" no doubt echoes Freud's notion of "switch-words" or "nodal points," the "verbal bridges" whose capacity for multiple meanings can be construed as the very condition of dream-work and psychoanalysis. See Freud, *Complete Works*, 5:340, 341.

40 *The Sister Arts: The Tradition of Literary Pictorialism in English Poetry from Dryden to Gray* (Chicago: University of Chicago Press 1958), 149 and 150.

41 "Blake and the Sister Arts Tradition," in *Blake's Visionary Forms Dramatic*, ed. David Erdman and John Grant (Princeton: Princeton University Press 1970), 85.

42 *Blake's Composite Art*, 23.

43 *Blake's Illustrations to the Poems of Gray* (Princeton: Princeton University Press 1971), 45.

44 *Blake's Illustrations to the Poems of Gray*, 27.

45 Ed. James T. Boulton (Notre Dame: Notre Dame University Press 1968), 64. Emphasis mine.

46 *Personification and the Sublime: Milton to Coleridge* (Cambridge: Harvard University Press 1985), 9.

47 John Payne Collier, *Seven Lectures on Shakespeare and Milton by the Late S.T. Coleridge* (London 1856), 66. Steven Knapp cites this passage from Collier's transcription of Coleridge's remarks in *Personification and the Sublime*, 9. Blake's *Satan, Sin and Death: Satan Comes to the Gates of Hell* can be found in *The Paintings and Drawings of William Blake*, plate 633. In *The Romantics on Milton: Formal Essays and Critical Asides* (Cleveland: Press of Case Western Reserve University 1970) Joseph Anthony Wittreich, Jr argues that Blake's design is "the only exception to Coleridge's observation" (286n77) on the failure of painters to respect Milton's verbal obscurity. But as Steven Knapp responds, "in Blake's versions Death is transparent but nevertheless distinctly outlined, in accordance with ... [the artist's] well-known aesthetic" (148n4).

48 *Macbeth*, 100.

49 "The grandest efforts of poetry are where the imagination is called forth not to produce a distinct form," Coleridge says in a lecture on Shakespeare, "but a strong working of the mind ... the result being what the poet wishes to impress, namely, the substitution of a sublime feeling of the unimaginable for a mere image." This lecture is cited and discussed by Steven Knapp, *Personification and the Sublime*, 7–10.

50 *The Complete Works*, ed. P.P. Howe (London: Dent 1930), 4:248.

51 "Exchanging Visions: Reading *A Midsummer Night's Dream*," *ELH* 49 (1982): 546.

52 "Walter Pater: A Partial Portrait," 111.

53 See Jean Hagstrum, *The Sister Arts*, 141–50.

54 "The Inherent Values of Eighteenth-Century Personification," *PMLA* 65 (1950): 450.

55 Wasserman, 452. Wasserman cites Fordyce's *Principals of Taste, or the Elements of Beauty* (2nd ed. Edinburgh 1786).

56 "The Metaphorical Process as Cognition, Imagination, and Feeling," in *On Metaphor*, ed. Sheldon Sacks (Chicago: University of Chicago Press 1979), 143.

57 Here I recall Alan Bass's remarks, after Derrida: "[T]he difference between the *e* and *a* of *difference/différance* can neither be seen nor heard. It is not a sensible – that is, relating to the senses – difference. But, [Derrida] ... goes on to explain, neither is this an intelligible difference, for the very names by which we conceive of objective intelligibility are already in complicity with sensibility." See *Margins of Philosophy*, trans. Alan Bass (Chicago: University of Chicago Press 1982), 5n3.

58 "Missed Crossing: Wordsworth's Apocalypses," *Modern Language Notes* 99 (1984): 986.

59 I cite Cathy Caruth, "Past Recognition: Narrative Origins in Wordsworth and Freud," *Modern Language Notes* 100 (1985): 944–5.

60 See "The Task of the Translator," *Illuminations*, 81–2. For a discussion of de Man's work on the threat which "reine Sprache" poses for reading, see my "Monstrous Reading: *The Martyrology* after de Man," *Studies in Canadian Literature* 15, no. 1 (1990): 1–32.
61 *Blake's Composite Art*, 18.
62 Henry Fuseli, *Analytical Review*, June 1788. Emphasis mine. Fuseli is cited by David Bindman, *Blake as an Artist* (Oxford: Phaidon 1977), 106. Bindman also argues that Fuseli's intermittent interest in depicting "not only the salient episodes [of *Paradise Lost*], but striking similes may ... have helped to increase the freedom with which Blake treated poetic passages" like the one illustrated in *Pity.*
63 Leonardo da Vinci, *Treatise on Painting*, trans. A. Philip McMahon (Princeton: Princeton University Press 1956), 1:18. Leonardo's phrase is cited and discussed by both Wendy Steiner, *The Colors of Rhetoric: Problems in the Relation between Modern Literature and Painting* (Chicago: University of Chicago Press 1982), 6, and W.J.T. Mitchell, *Iconology: Image, Text, Ideology*, 116.
64 *Illuminations*, 80.
65 So Deborah Esch describes Benjamin's conception of translation. See "A Defence of Rhetoric/The Triumph of Reading," in *Reading de Man Reading*, 75.
66 *Blindness and Insight: Essays in the Rhetoric of Contemporary Criticism* (Minneapolis: University of Minnesota Press 1983), 164.
67 *Image Music Text*, ed. and trans. Stephen Heath (New York: Hill and Wang 1977), 147.
68 *The Complete Works*, 4:312.

AFTERWORD

1 *Shelley's Poetry and Prose*, ed. Donald H. Reiman and Sharon B. Powers (New York: Norton 1977), 497. Further references to Shelley's poetry and prose will be included parenthetically, with page numbers for prose and line numbers for poetry.
2 C.E. Pulos, *The Deep Truth: A Study of Shelley's Scepticism* (Lincoln: University of Nebraska Press 1954).
3 See Samuel Taylor Coleridge, *Biographia Literaria*, ed. James Engell and W. Jackson Bate (Princeton: Princeton University Press 1983), 1:304. Further references will be included parenthetically.
4 William Blake, *The Poetry and Prose of William Blake*, ed. David V. Erdman. Commentary by Harold Bloom (New York: Doubleday 1965), 656. For Wordsworth's Prospectus to *The Recluse*, see William Wordsworth, *Poems*, ed. John O. Hayden (Harmondsworth: Penguin 1977), 2:37–40.
5 Paul de Man, "Shelley Disfigured," *Deconstruction and Criticism*, by Harold

Bloom et al. (New York: Seabury Press 1979), 66–7.

6   Earl R. Wasserman, *Shelley: A Critical Reading* (Baltimore: Johns Hopkins University Press 1971). My review appeared in *Keats-Shelley Journal* 21–2 (1972–73): 244–52.

7   Geoffrey H. Hartman, "Blindness and Insight: Paul de Man, Fascism, and Deconstruction," *New Republic*, 7 March 1988, 29.

8   Paul de Man, *Blindness and Insight: Essays in the Rhetoric of Contemporary Criticism* 2nd ed., intro. Wlad Godzich (Minneapolis: University of Minnesota Press 1983), 147–8.

9   William Wordsworth, *The Prelude: 1799, 1805, 1850*, ed. Jonathan Wordsworth, M.H. Abrams, and Stephen Gill (New York: Norton 1979), 5.448–59.

Selected Bibliography of Ross G. Woodman

COMPILED BY J. DOUGLAS KNEALE

LITERARY CRITICISM

"Shelley's Changing Attitude to Plato." *Journal of the History of Ideas* 31 (1960): 497–510.

"An Approach to the Study of Literature." *The Bulletin* 40 (January 1960): 23–4.

"Literature and Belief." *English Exchange* 3 (Spring 1961): 3–12.

"Shelley's Prometheus." *Alphabet* 2 (September 1962): 25–9.

"Literature and Life." *Queen's Quarterly* 67 (1962): 621–32.

The Apocalyptic Vision in the Poetry of Shelley. Toronto: University of Toronto Press 1964.

James Reaney. Canadian Writers Series, no. 12. Toronto: McClelland and Stewart 1972.

"Satan in the 'Vale of Soul-Making': A Survey from Blake to Ginsberg." *Humanities Association Review* 25 (1974): 108–22.

"Imagination as the Theme of *The Prelude*." *English Studies in Canada* 1 (1975): 406–18.

"Adonais." In *Shelley's Poetry and Prose*. Norton Critical Edition. Ed. Donald H. Reiman and Sharon B. Powers. New York: Norton 1977. 659–75.

"The Death and Resurrection of Milton According to the Gospel of Blake." *English Studies in Canada* 3 (1977): 416–32.

"Freud and Jung: The Parting of the Ways." *Queen's Quarterly* 85 (1978): 93–108.

"Shelley's Urania." *Studies in Romanticism* 17 (1978): 61–75.

"Shelley's Urania and Her Romantic Descendants." *University of Toronto Quarterly* 48 (1979): 189–209.

"Child and Patriot: Shifting Perspectives in *The Prelude*." *Wordsworth Circle* 11 (1980): 83–92.

"Shaman, Poet and Failed Initiate: Reflections on Romanticism and Jungian Psychology." *Studies in Romanticism* 19 (1980): 51–82.

"Literature and the Unconscious: Coleridge and Jung." *Journal of Analytical Psychology* 20 (1980): 364–75.

"The Androgyne in *Prometheus Unbound*." *Studies in Romanticism* 20 (1981): 225–47.

"Shelley's 'Void Circumference': The Aesthetics of Nihilism." *English Studies in Canada* 9 (1983): 272–93.

"Milton's Satan in Wordsworth's 'Vale of Soul-Making.'" *Studies in Romanticism* 23 (1984): 3–30.

"Nietzsche's Madness as Soul-Making: A View contra Jung's." *Spring: An Annual of Archetypal Psychology and Jungian Thought*. Ed. James Hillman. Dallas: Spring Publications 1986. 101–18.

"Wordsworth's Crazed Bedouin: *The Prelude* and the Fate of Madness." *Studies in Romanticism* 27 (1988): 3–29.

"Nietzsche, Blake, Keats, and Shelley: The Making of a Metaphorical Body." *Studies in Romanticism* 29 (1990): 115–49.

"'The Mind in Creation': Life as Metaphor." In *Approaches to Teaching Shelley's Poetry*. Ed. Spencer Hall. New York: Modern Language Association 1990. 32–5.

"The Idiot Boy as Healer." *Romanticism and Children's Literature in Nineteenth-Century England*. Ed. James Holt McGavran, Jr. Athens: University of Georgia Press 1991. 72–95.

"Metaphor and Allegory in *Prometheus Unbound*." *The New Shelley: Later Twentieth-Century Views*. Ed. G. Kim Blank. New York: St Martin's Press 1991. 166–83.

"Blake as Milton's Pastoral Counsellor." *Journal of Pastoral Counselling* 26 (Spring/Summer 1991): 29–45.

Commentary on "Honest to Babylon," *Journal of Pastoral Counselling* 26 (Spring/Summer 1991): 92–5.

PUBLICATIONS ON ART AND FILM

Jack Chambers. Toronto: Coach House Press 1965.

"The New Regionalism." *artscanada* 24 (August/September 1967): 5-page insert.

"Artists as Filmmakers." *artscanada* 118/119 (June 1968): 35.

"Canada Trust Exhibition." *artscanada* 122/123 (October/November 1968): 42.

"The Canada Council Collection." *artscanada* 132/133 (June 1969): 27–8.

"Notes by a Private Collector." *artscanada* 132/133 (June 1969): 34–5.

"London: Regional Liberation Front." *Globe and Mail*, 13 December 1969, 27.

"The Realism of John Chambers." *Art International* 14, no. 9 (November 1970): 37–41.

"Ron Martin at the 20/20 Gallery, London." *artscanada* 148/149 (October/November 1970): 81.

"Three Easy Pieces." *Film* no. 62 (Summer 1971): 28.

"Gino Lorcini." *University of Western Ontario Alumni Gazette* 48 (February 1972): 8.

"Two Artists: One Environment." *Business Quarterly* 37 (1972): 5+.

"Making the Real Appear." *Business Quarterly* 37 (1972): 5+.

"Eskimo Art in the White Man's Market." *Business Quarterly* 37 (1972): 5+.

"Jack Chambers: Canada's Finest Painter." *Business Quarterly* 37 (1972): 72–6.

"The Art Crisis." *Business Quarterly* 38 (1973): 79–80.

"The Lover as a Landscape." *Business Quarterly* 38 (1973): 90–1.

"National Gallery Exhibit Invites Criticism but It Is 'Best Ever.'" *Business Quarterly* 38 (1973): 9+.

"The Defeating of the Curse." *Business Quarterly* 38 (1973): 93+.

"Letters and Notes." *artscanada* 188/189 (Spring 1974): 91–2.

"The Artist as Prophet." *Business Quarterly* 39 (1974): 15–17.

"Curnoe's New Drawings: Homage to Van Donagen." *artscanada* 204/205 (April/May 1976): 68–9.

"London Painting Now." *artscanada* 204/205 (April/May 1976): 75–6.

"Alex Katz." *artscanada* 208/209 (October/November 1976): 71–2.

"Clark McDougall." Catalogue Essay. Vancouver: Vancouver Art Gallery 1977. Revised and reprinted in *Capilano Review* 33 (1984): 47–64.

"Jack Chambers as Film-Maker." *Chambers: The Last Decade.* London, Ontario: London Regional Art Gallery 1980.

"Spring Hurlbut." Catalogue Essay. London, Ontario: London Regional Art Gallery 1984.

"Hurrell's Crawford." Afterword in *Legends: Joan Crawford.* Intro. Anna Raeburn. Series ed. John Kobal. Boston: Little, Brown and Co. 1986. N.p.

"A Celebration of the Human Spirit: Five Canadian Artists." Catalogue Essay. London, Ontario: McIntosh Gallery, University of Western Ontario 1988.

REVIEWS

The Valley of Vision: Blake as Prophet and Revolutionary, by P.F. Fisher. *Alphabet* 5 (1962): 80–3.

"Six Volumes of Canadian Poetry." *Alphabet* 13 (1967): 73–4.

Shelley's "Prometheus Unbound": A Critical Reading, by Earl R. Wasserman. *Dalhousie Review* 46 (1966): 259–60.

"Tiriel": Facsimile and Commentary, by G.E. Bentley, Jr. *University of Toronto Quarterly* 37 (1968): 415–17.

A Study of English Romanticism, by Northrop Frye. *University of Toronto Quarterly* 38 (1969): 371–3.

Shelley: A Critical Reading, by Earl Wasserman. *Keats-Shelley Journal* 21–2 (1972–73): 244–52.

"Building Jerusalem Here." Rev. of *The Arts in Canada: The Last Fifty Years*, ed. W.J. Keith and B.-Z Shek. *Canadian Poetry* 7 (1980): 96–8.

"From the Belly of the Whale: Frye's 'Personal Encounter.'" Rev. of Northrop Frye, *The Great Code: The Bible and Literature*; and Northrop Frye, *Divisions on a Ground*, ed. James Polk. *Canadian Poetry* 10 (1982): 124–31.

"Behind the Bay Window: Gerald Parker's *The Eagle and the Lion*." *Canadian Review of American Studies* 18 (1987): 495–7.

PAPERS READ

"Demonic Vision in the Poetry of Shelley." Humanities Association, University of Western Ontario, London 1957.

"Shelley as Critic." Modern Language Association Convention, New York 1958.

"Literature and Life." Humanities Association, Queen's University, Kingston 1961.

"Literary Modes in *The Prelude*." University of Michigan Lecture Series, Ann Arbor 1966.

"The Pedlar in *The Prelude*." Humanities Association, Sir George Williams University, Montreal 1966.

"The London (Ont.) Art Scene." Fanshawe College Symposium on the Arts 1969.

"Abstract Expressionism." London Art Gallery Association Lecture Series 1969.

"The Romantics as Critics of Wordsworth." A series of papers on Hazlitt, Wordsworth, and Keats, University of Western Ontario, London 1969–70.

"The London, England Art Scene." London Art Gallery Association Lecture Series 1971.

"Imagination as the Theme of *The Prelude*." Association of Canadian University Teachers of English, Toronto, May 1974.

"Jung and Freud: The Parting of the Ways." Dean's Lecture Series, University of Western Ontario, Autumn 1974. Also presented to The Harvey Club, London, Winter 1975.

"Blake and Milton: A Preliminary Sketch." University of Western Ontario Department of English Colloquium Series, February 1976. Also read at Queen's University Faculty of Arts Lecture Series, February 1976, and Association of Canadian University Teachers of English, Laval University, May 1976.

"The Canadian Landscape." Read at the invitation of the Department of External Affairs in conjunction with exhibition of Canadian landscape painting, De Cordova Art Gallery, Newton, Mass. 1977.

"Shaman, Poet and Failed Initiate: Coleridge and Jung." Society of Analytical Psychologists, London, England, February 1978. Also presented to the Analytical Psychology Society of Ontario, Toronto, October 1978.

"Coleridge and Jung." Conference on Creativity, Miami University, Oxford, Ohio, April 1979.

"William Blake." Metropolitan United Church, London, Ontario, September 1979.

"Literature and Landscape." London Regional Art Gallery Lecture Series, October 1979.

"Blake's Body." University of Western Ontario Department of English Colloquium Series, October 1981.

"The Hermaphrodite in Shelley's *Alastor*." Modern Language Association Convention 1984.

"Coleridge's Theory of the Imagination." Queen's University Lecture Series, November 1984.

"Coleridge and Shelley: Who Is the Poet, Where Is the Text?" University of Western Ontario Department of English Colloquium Series 1985.

"The Cultural Crisis in London, Ontario." Annual Meeting of the London Regional Art Gallery Board, December 1985.

"The Roots of Creativity." Tartan Lecture Series, 3M, London, Ontario, May 1986.

"Keats Reading Keats: *The Fall of Hyperion*." Modern Language Association Convention, New York, December 1986.

Contributors

DAVID L. CLARK is assistant professor of English at McMaster University. He has published articles on Blake, Nietzsche, and de Man in *Studies in Romanticism, Studies in Canadian Literature,* and other journals. In addition to guest-editing an issue of *Recherches sémiotiques/Semiotic Inquiry* entitled "Language, History, and the 'Romance of Fact'" (Spring 1992), he is currently coediting two volumes: with Tilottama Rajan, *Intersections: Nineteenth-Century Philosophy and Contemporary Theory* (SUNY Press); and with Donald Goellnicht, *New Romanticisms: Recent Developments in Theory and Critical Practice* (University of Toronto Press).

JARED CURTIS is professor of English at Simon Fraser University. He is the author of *Wordsworth's Experiments with Tradition* (Ithaca: Cornell University Press 1971), and the editor of *"Poems, in Two Volumes," and Other Poems, 1800–1807 by William Wordsworth* (Ithaca: Cornell University Press 1983). He is currently editing *Late Poems, 1820–1850 by William Wordsworth,* and coediting, with Carol Landon, *Early Poems, 1785–1797 by William Wordsworth,* for the Cornell Wordsworth Series.

J. DOUGLAS KNEALE is associate professor of English at the University of Western Ontario. He is the author of *Monumental Writing: Aspects of Rhetoric in Wordsworth's Poetry* (Lincoln: University of Nebraska Press 1988), and other essays on Romanticism. He is currently working on a book on the history of rhetoric in the English Romantic poets.

W.J.B. OWEN is professor of English (Emeritus) at McMaster University. He is the author of *Wordsworth as Critic* (Toronto: University of Toronto Press 1969), and the editor of several volumes, including *Wordsworth and Coleridge: Lyrical Ballads, 1798* (Oxford: Oxford University Press 1967), *The Prose Works of William Wordsworth* (with Jane Worthington Smyser), 3 vols. (Oxford: Clarendon 1974), and *The Fourteen-Book Prelude* (Ithaca: Cornell University Press 1985).

TILOTTAMA RAJAN is professor in the Department of English and the Centre for the Study of Theory and Criticism at the University of Western Ontario. She is the author of *Dark Interpreter: The Discourse of Romanticism* (Ithaca: Cornell University Press 1980) and *The Supplement of Reading: Figures of Understanding in Romantic Theory and Practice* (Ithaca: Cornell University Press 1990). She is currently working on a book on *Deconstruction before and after Post-Structuralism*.

RONALD TETREAULT is professor of English at Dalhousie University. He is the author of *The Poetry of Life: Shelley and Literary Form* (Toronto: University of Toronto Press 1987) and other articles on the English Romantics. He is currently working on a book on Keats and masculinity.

MILTON WILSON is professor of English (Emeritus) at Trinity College, University of Toronto. He is the author of *Shelley's Later Poetry: A Study of His Prophetic Imagination* (New York: Columbia University Press 1959) and *E.J. Pratt* (Toronto: McClelland and Stewart 1969), and the editor of two anthologies of Canadian literature. Some of his recent work has been concerned with the literary relations of natural philosophy in the Restoration-to-Regency period.